Republicanism

Republicanism

An Introduction

Rachel Hammersley

polity

First published in 2020 by Polity Press

Polity Press
65 Bridge Street
Cambridge CB2 1UR, UK

Polity Press
101 Station Landing
Suite 300
Medford, MA 02155, USA

ISBN-13: 978-1-5095-1341-3
ISBN-13: 978-1-5095-1342-0 (pb)

A catalogue record for this book is available from the British Library.

Library of Congress Cataloging-in-Publication Data
Names: Hammersley, Rachel, 1974- author.
Title: Republicanism : an introduction / Rachel Hammersley.
Description: Cambridge, UK ; Medford, MA : Polity, 2020. | Includes bibliographical references and index. | Summary: "The best single-volume introduction to the political theory and history of republicanism ever written"-- Provided by publisher.
Identifiers: LCCN 2020006722 (print) | LCCN 2020006723 (ebook) | ISBN 9781509513413 (hardback) | ISBN 9781509513420 (paperback) | ISBN 9781509513451 (epub)
Subjects: LCSH: Republicanism--History.
Classification: LCC JC421 .H25 2020 (print) | LCC JC421 (ebook) | DDC 321.8/6--dc23
LC record available at https://lccn.loc.gov/2020006722
LC ebook record available at https://lccn.loc.gov/2020006723

Typeset in 10.5 on 12pt Sabon
by Fakenham Prepress Solutions, Fakenham, Norfolk NR21 8NL
Printed and bound in Great Britain by CPI Group (UK) Ltd, Croydon

For further information on Polity, visit our website: politybooks.com

Contents

Acknowledgements

This book is the fruit of many years of studying, writing, and teaching intellectual history. It is dedicated to the teachers, colleagues, and students who have helped to shape and clarify my thinking over many years. The importance of discussing ideas and of having one's assumptions, prejudices, and opinions challenged and subjected to close examination cannot be underestimated. This has been the core of scholarship for millennia and it is imperative that it remains so in the future. It is also crucial that the fruits of such debate are not reserved to a closed scholarly world but are made available to, and thus are able to benefit, new generations and wider publics. This book is an attempt to do just that.

Several people have read and commented on this volume in advance of publication. I am grateful, for their insightful comments, to Richard Whatmore, Katie East, and Martyn Hammersley, as well as to the three anonymous reviewers for Polity Press. The spirit of scholarly engagement in which they approached the task was exemplary and I hope that the revisions undertaken in the light of their comments are testimony to the benefits to be gained from subjecting one's ideas to the scrutiny of others. It goes without saying that any errors that remain are my responsibility rather than theirs.

I am grateful to the Fitzwilliam Museum in Cambridge for permission to include an image of a Halfpenny token produced by Thomas Spence. The image of Jacques-Louis David's drawing 'Brutus and the Lictors' has been reproduced here thanks to the Getty's Open Content Program. I am grateful to the Getty Center for making the image freely available for this purpose.

I also owe a heavy debt of gratitude to the staff at Polity, and especially to George Owers and Julia Davies, for commissioning the volume and seeing it through to publication, and to Manuela Tecusan for her excellent copy-editing. George has gone well beyond what would normally be expected of an editor, acting as an informed and attentive fourth reader and engaging in constructive dialogue with me through the whole process. I feel very fortunate to have had the opportunity to work with him and his team. Finally, thanks go once again to Thomas, Anna, and John, who, along with my parents, Joan and Martyn, have encouraged and supported me throughout the process of producing this book.

For my teachers, colleagues, and students past and present

Introduction: What Is Republicanism?

Introduction

Republicanism is a term with multiple, complex, and contested meanings. While Ireland, the United States, and France are all currently ruled by republican regimes, the term is used in very different ways and has distinct connotations in each place. It is therefore crucial that we begin by thinking about its meaning and engaging with some of the complexity surrounding it before we embark on a more detailed exploration of its history.

At the most basic level, republicanism is linked to a notion of self-government. For a political community, this means not being ruled by another state. The establishment of republican city-states in Italy during the Renaissance signalled the refusal of their citizens to be ruled as vassals of the Holy Roman Empire. The Dutch republic emerged after the Dutch Revolt against Spanish rule. And the republic of the United States of America was established after the thirteen colonies declared independence from Britain.

Self-government applies not just to the state but also to its citizens. It means that individuals are subject only to laws to which they have consented, rather than being ruled by another's will. It is for this reason that, in common speech, republics – ruled as they are by and for their citizens – tend to be distinguished from monarchies. In the modern world, of course, most states are ruled by and for their citizens via a system of representation. In this context republics are distinguished from monarchies on account of whether the head of state is elected for a limited term of office or inherits the role for life.

The distinction between republics and monarchies is equally problematic when viewed historically. Take the following passage from the fragmentary work *De republica* by Marcus Tullius Cicero, the famous Roman statesman, philosopher, and political writer: 'a commonwealth [republic] (that is the concern of the people) then truly exists when its affairs are conducted well and justly, whether by a single king, or by a few aristocrats, or by the people as a whole.'[1] For Cicero, then, republican government was simply good government, and republics and monarchies were not necessarily mutually exclusive.[2] The eighteenth-century Genevan-born political theorist Jean-Jacques Rousseau expressed something very similar in a famous passage from his *Social Contract*:

> I therefore give the name 'Republic' to every State that is governed by laws, no matter what the form of administration may be: for only in such a case does the public interest govern, and the *res publica* rank as a *reality*. Every legitimate government is republican.

In the accompanying footnote he continued:

> I understand by this word, not merely an aristocracy or democracy, but generally any government directed by the general will, which is the law. To be legitimate, the government must be, not one with the Sovereign, but its minister. In such a case even a monarchy is a republic.[3]

While deliberately playing on the apparent contradiction inherent within this final statement, Rousseau's account indicates that the key to understanding this apparent paradox lies in the precise meaning of the term 'republic', which comes via etymology.

Defining the Republic

Government in the Public Interest

'Republic' comes from the Latin *res publica*, which means 'common thing' (*res*) or 'the common good'. On this account, a government or a state is deemed to be republican not because it adopts a particular form, but rather depending on its purpose or object. Republican government, on this reading, is a system in which the public good takes precedence over the private interests of those in positions of power. This idea harks back to Aristotle's typology of government, although of course Aristotle wrote in Greek, so his lexic was different (he was talking about *politeia* rather than *res publica*, which is in fact the Latin translation of the Greek concept).[4] Aristotle argued that there were two fundamental criteria by which governments might be distinguished from one another. The first was the proportion of the population involved in ruling (the ruler could be one, a few, or the many); the second was whether the government was ultimately good or bad. Good forms of government were those in which the governing was conducted in the common interest and according to justice, while the perverted or bad forms operated in the interests of the ruler(s) alone.[5] When combined, the two criteria produced six distinct types of government, as illustrated in Table 0.1 here:

	Good Government (in the interest of the ruled)	Bad Government (in the interest of rulers)
One	Monarchy	Tyranny
Few	Aristocracy	Oligarchy
Many	Polity	Democracy

Table 0.1   Aristotle's typology of government

If you set out the matter this way, it is easy to see how Aristotle's sense of good constitutional forms underpinned Cicero's later account of republican government.

Republic and Commonwealth

Just as the terms 'republic' and 'republicanism' are multivalent, so they are not the only ones used to describe the underlying idea; various associated or overlapping terms are also used. The main equivalent, in an anglophone context, is 'commonwealth'. In a strict sense 'commonwealth' is simply the anglicised version of the Latin *res publica*. 'Common' and *publicus* render effectively the same notion and, in this context at least, 'thing' (*res*) and 'wealth' or 'weal', are also nearly equivalent. While 'commonwealth' in English has generally been seen as a more benign term, not necessarily having the anti-monarchical connotations of 'republic', it has been used just as flexibly. 'Commonwealth and Free State' was the name given to the regime established in England after the execution of Charles I in 1649. In the aftermath of the regicide, England was ruled for just over ten years without a king or queen. Yet Elizabeth I's reign during the previous century was also characterised as a commonwealth; and, later, self-confessed 'Commonwealthmen' were keen to distance their position from anti-monarchism.[6]

The Ciceronian understanding of republican government as simply good government continued to be influential well into the eighteenth century, as the quotation from Rousseau makes clear. Yet from the fifteenth century on it was challenged by the emergence of a new way of thinking about republican government – one that paved the way for the modern dichotomy between republics and monarchies.

Republican Exclusivism

It was during the Italian Renaissance that this new understanding first emerged. James Hankins has labelled it 'republican exclusivism' since it presented republican government as the only legitimate form, on account of its being grounded in the will of the people.[8] Advocates of this position rejected all forms of non-elective monarchy and all hereditary political privileges. While this new conception was popularised and spread beyond Italy during the sixteenth century, not least in the works of Niccolò Machiavelli, it was in the course of the English Revolution of the mid-seventeenth century that the idea began to find practical expression. When the English executed their king, transforming the regime by severing it from its traditional monarchical form, several thinkers emphatically insisted that freedom could be preserved only by proscribing monarchy. Marchamont Nedham argued that all kings were in effect tyrants. Speaking of English people (many of whom were proving reluctant to accept the new regime), he insisted: 'Had they but once tasted the sweets of peace and liberty both together, they would soon be of the opinion of Herodotus and Demosthenes that there is no difference between king and tyrant and become as zealous as the ancient Romans were in defence of their freedom.'[9] Similarly, a decade later, John Milton asserted: 'I doubt not but all ingenuous and knowing men will easily agree with me, that a free Commonwealth without single person or house of lords, is by far the best government, if it can be had.'[10] This new understanding of the nature of republican government by no means obscured the earlier Ciceronian conception completely. The restoration of monarchy in 1660 made the expression of republican exclusivism treasonous in England. Consequently, in the late seventeenth and early eighteenth centuries the Ciceronian notion of a republic compatible with monarchy returned to the fore, particularly in the aftermath of the Glorious Revolution of 1688–9.

Equally unsurprising is the fact that exclusivist republicanism found a new momentum in the context of the revolutions of the late eighteenth century. Yet, while the age of revolution gave it the edge over the earlier Ciceronian conception, the precise definition of a republic was subtly transformed in the process. Among exclusivist republicans of the Italian Renaissance and English Revolution it was accepted that a key difference between a republic and a monarchy was that the former meant the rule of the many, in contrast to the latter, which meant the rule of one. Initially it was assumed that this should apply to executive as well as to legislative power. Consequently the seventeenth- and eighteenth-century revolutions saw various attempts to institute conciliar executives such as the Rump Parliament and Council of State in England and the Directory and Consulate in France. In the end, however, revolutionary states tended to revert to a single executive ruler – a Lord Protector or a president, for instance – and focused instead on containing that person's powers and restricting the term of office.

By the twentieth century most republics incorporated a role for a single person at the apex of the system. At the same time, European monarchies had largely shifted away from their earlier absolutist mode towards more constitutional forms, incorporating an increasingly influential role for representative bodies such as parliaments or estates. As a result, monarchies and republics were no longer distinguished by whether they embodied the rule of the one or that of the many; the distinction between them was grounded instead in questions about how 'the one' was selected, what his or her role was to be, how long (s)he would hold power for, and what limits were placed on the exercise of that power. Ultimately the contrast was often reduced to one between states in which the single-person component of the government was embodied in a hereditary monarch who ruled from his or her accession until death and states where the same component was provided by an elected head of state who ruled for a limited period of time. The narrowing of the gap between the two was also compounded by the fact that during the nineteenth and twentieth centuries the political role of the monarch in many European monarchies declined, reducing the office to little more than a ceremonial head of state.

The Dynamism of Republicanism

Not only did the meaning of the term 'republic' change in response to circumstances, but the concept was also adapted and developed in the light of both theory and practice. It is worth outlining some of the more significant changes here before exploring in greater detail, in subsequent chapters, how republican ideas were used and adapted at different points in time.

Mixed Government

One tendency, which became particularly influential in the Renaissance and early modern periods (though it had its origins in the ancient world), was the association of republics with mixed government. This concept is usually traced back to the Greek second-century BCE historian and thinker Polybius. He was a constitutionalist who saw the form of government as a defining factor in determining how a state fared: 'Now in all political situations we must understand that the principal factor which makes for success or failure is the form of a state's constitution: it is from this source, as if from a fountainhead, that all designs and plans of action not only originate but reach their fulfilment.'[11]

Responding to Aristotle's analysis, which noted the tendency of the good forms of government to degenerate into their corrupt counterparts, Polybius argued that by combining elements of monarchical, aristocratic, and popular rule within a single system it would be possible to preserve the benefits of each of the distinct forms without incurring their disadvantages, and that this would help to secure a more stable form of government. Since Polybius's time mixed forms have proved particularly popular with republican authors, from Cicero down to the American revolutionary John Adams, though there have also been some, including Thomas Paine and Maximilian Robespierre, who have argued against mixed government – and especially against dividing sovereignty.

Sovereignty and Government

The whole question of sovereignty and its relationship to government is another key development that has affected the modern understanding of republicanism. The distinction between sovereignty and government was first articulated by the theorist of absolutism Jean Bodin in his *Six Books of the Commonwealth* of 1576. Bodin insisted that the errors of Aristotle and other thinkers with regard to forms of government arose directly from their failure to recognise this crucial distinction:

> To judge of an estate [state], the question is not to know who have the magistracies or offices: but only who they bee which have the soveraigntie and power to place and displace the magistrats and

officers, and to give lawes unto every man. And these absurdities, and other also much greater than they, ensue hereof, in that *Aristotle* hath mistaken the manner and forme of the government of a Commonweale, for the sovereign state thereof.[12]

This distinction was fundamental to Rousseau's understanding of republican government just discussed earlier (and see note 3). Following Bodin, Rousseau assumed a clear distinction between sovereignty (the making of the laws) and government (the administration of those laws). Hence he could envisage the possibility of a system that was republican (in the sense that the laws were made by the body of citizens) but was governed by a monarch who would administer those laws on behalf of the citizen body.

The concept of republicanism was transformed not only as a result of these theoretical developments, but also in response to the new political circumstances in which the ideas were discussed and to which they were applied. Key developments included the rise of Christianity, the establishment of republican regimes in states that were far larger – both in terms of area and population – than those of the ancient world, and debates over the legitimacy of slavery and the rise of the working class.

Republicanism and Religion

The citizens of the ancient city-states of Greece and Rome tended to practice polytheistic religions that were often closely tied to, and supportive of, the state and its government. The form of religion supposedly introduced into Rome by Romulus's successor as king, Numa Pompilius (fl. c. 700 BCE), was generally believed to have had a positive impact on the establishment of republican government in Rome and to have encouraged and supported public-spirited behaviour in Roman citizens.[13]

The rise of Christianity broke this bond between politics and religion, and by the late medieval and early modern period there were concerns about there being irreconcilable tensions between the good citizen and the good Christian. The importance of *otium* ('leisure'), the free time for contemplative life that was indicative of pious religious belief, was contrasted with the importance of *negotium* ('non-leisure', 'busy time'), the main ingredient of the active political life that made a good citizen. Moreover, the expectation was that a good Christian would always prioritise the afterlife over this life. In the case of Catholics, the oath of allegiance to a foreign ruler – the pope – was believed to undermine their commitment to their own state. Some republicans, including Machiavelli and Rousseau, attacked Christianity also on account of the threat it posed to republican government. Partly as a result of this, the religious dimension of republicanism was long neglected in the historiography. Yet recently the work of Jonathan Scott, Justin Champion, and Eric Nelson (among others) has highlighted the crucial religious dimension of early modern English republican thought, while scholars such as Mark Goldie and Ronald Beiner have presented the notion of civil religion as one of the solutions adopted by republican thinkers (though not exclusively by them) to the problem of reconciling religion and politics.[14]

Small States versus Large States

In general, republics flourished in small city-states. This was true in the ancient world, and the republican regimes of the early modern period either were centred on a single city (such as Venice or Genoa) or adopted a federal system linking several towns or cities together (as in the United Provinces and Switzerland). Therefore thinkers pondered over the question of whether a republic could be made to flourish in a large nation-state of the kind that dominated Europe by the early modern period – and, if so, how. Some simply insisted that republics could flourish only in small states. But others believed that representative government made it possible to conceive of large state republics. According to the seventeenth-century English political theorist James Harrington, the utility of representation had already been proved; all that was required was for it to be applied to a commonwealth: 'And why should that be impossible or impracticable unto a representative of the people in a commonwealth, which was so facile and practicable to a representative of the people under monarchy?'[15]

It was the American Revolution, however, that brought this innovation to the heart of republican government. John Adams was well aware of the significant differences of scale between traditional republics and the new United States – and of the implications of this aspect of things for the form of government: 'The United States are large and populous nations, in comparison of the Grecian commonwealths, or even the Swiss cantons; and are growing every day more disproportionate, and therefore less capable of being held together by simple governments.'[16] Yet he believed, just like Harrington, that making the popular assembly a representative body made it possible to create a large-state republic. To support his claim, he quoted a passage from Montesquieu's *The Spirit of the Laws*:

As, in a free state, every man who is supposed a free agent, ought to be his own governor; so the legislative power should reside in the whole body of the people. But since this is impossible in large states, and in small ones is subject to many inconveniences; it is fit the people should execute by their representatives what they cannot execute by themselves.[17]

Moreover, Adams went on to highlight a further advantage of representative government: 'The great advantage of representatives is their being capable of discussing affairs; for this the people collectively are extremely unfit, which is one of the greatest inconveniences of a democracy.'[18] This idea was developed further by Adams's fellow countrymen James Madison, Alexander Hamilton, and John Jay, who wrote under the pseudonym Publius in *The Federalist Papers*. That work offered a definitive statement of the idea of representation not merely as a necessary evil, but as a positive good. It also associated republican government directly with representative government and contrasted it with democracy.[19] There was, however, no definitive republican position on these issues. Where Publius (and Paine) firmly associated republican government with representative government, Rousseau insisted that sovereignty could not be represented and that in a republic the laws had to be ratified by people directly, in person.[20]

Slavery and Labour

Ancient republicanism, as well as being established in small city-states, was grounded in the institution of slavery. The exercise of citizenship in antiquity depended on the existence of a large number of non-citizens (many of them slaves but also women, servants, resident aliens (metics in classical Athens), etc.): these carried out basic work so that the citizens could devote their attention to political and military matters. As will be explored in greater detail in Chapter 9, during the modern period the relationship between republicanism and slavery came to be contested: by the time of the American Revolution there were people who argued that the institution of slavery was incompatible with the commitments to liberty and equality that lay at the heart of a republican government.

It was not just slavery that presented problems for republicanism in the nineteenth century. While in one sense the introduction of representative government made things easier by obviating the need for citizens to devote their lives to politics, the development of a separate political elite was at odds with the fundamental idea of republican government as self-government. It also raised questions about who should be eligible to stand for office – and, indeed, to vote for representatives.

These tensions were only heightened by the emergence of a large working-class population often concentrated in huge numbers in cities and towns. The ways in which republicanism was adapted to deal with these changes will be explored in Chapter 9. It will be demonstrated that, despite its reputation as an elitist and aristocratic discourse, republicanism could be adapted to further the cause of the working classes and to support their claims to civil equality – and even to having a political voice.

Republican Concepts

Frustrated by the difficulties inherent in constitutional approaches, some scholars have argued that republicanism is best understood not as a particular set of constitutional provisions, but rather as a phenomenon defined by the values that republican authors celebrated and sought to protect. In particular, two key concepts have emerged as central to republican thinking: liberty and virtue.

Liberty

Liberty is by no means a simple, uniform, or straightforward concept. The philosopher Isaiah Berlin famously drew a distinction between what he called 'positive' and 'negative' liberty.[21] According to him, negative liberty was simply the state of not being 'prevented by another person from doing what I want' and could be contrasted with coercion, understood as 'the deliberate interference of other human beings within the area in which I wish to act'. Positive liberty designated a kind of self-realisation, as expressed for example in the notion of being free to become fully human, such notions being defined by some ideal whose validity was taken to be absolute.[22] On this account, liberalism would tend to be associated with negative liberty and republicanism with positive liberty; for republicans often take self-government to be a defining feature of the good life.

Quentin Skinner, however, has challenged the simple dualism of Berlin's conception, arguing that there are in fact two distinct negative concepts of liberty and that republican thinkers have tended to favour one of those negative forms rather than the positive conception.[23] The best understood version of negative liberty (and the one Berlin primarily intended) is a liberal understanding whereby liberty is marked by the absence of physical interference. For Thomas Hobbes, a leading exponent of this understanding, '*A FREE-MAN, is he, that in those things which by his strength and wit he is able to do, is not hindred to doe what he has a will to*'.[24] By contrast, the other kind of negative liberty – which Skinner initially labelled 'republican liberty' but later clarified as 'neo-Roman liberty' on account of its origins in the Roman legal distinction between the freeman and the slave – required not just the absence of physical interference, but freedom from dependence on the will of anyone else. Moreover, this insistence on the capacity for self-government also suggested a close connection between the freedom of the individual and that of the state. If a state is to be free, then the laws governing it must be enacted with the consent of its citizens.[25] Algernon Sidney expressed it neatly: 'As liberty consists only in being subject to no man's will, and nothing denotes a slave but dependence on the will of another; if there be no other law in a kingdom than the will of a prince, there is no such thing as liberty.'[26] According to Skinner, this understanding of liberty is evident during the Renaissance and rose to prominence during the English Revolution. It was used to attack the ruling oligarchy in the eighteenth century and to defend the American Revolution, before it was effectively eclipsed by the liberal conception in the nineteenth century.[27]

Virtue

The concept of virtue, like that of liberty, has long been associated with republican government, and its precise meaning is equally elusive. Ancient thinkers placed great emphasis on virtue as a value crucial to good government. However, their conception of it was plural rather than singular. In the Hellenistic and Roman period, Cicero, for example, stressed the cardinal virtues of prudence, temperance, fortitude, and justice. The rise of Christianity further complicated the picture, not least through the addition of the three theological virtues – faith, hope, and charity – to the list.

The simplest way of describing republican virtue is to say that it involved putting the public good, or the interests of the state, above one's own private interests. While this idea could be traced back well beyond Cicero, it was articulated particularly clearly by Montesquieu in the mid-eighteenth century. Montesquieu described virtue in a republic as 'love of the homeland' and insisted that it was not a moral or Christian virtue, but a '*political* virtue'.[28] Often this notion of virtue was associated with the rule of reason and with being able to control one's passions. Of course, these ideas were not exclusive to republicans. Frederick the Great of Prussia, for example, offered this assessment of good princely rule: 'He is only the first servant of the state, who is obliged to act with probity and prudence; and to remain as totally disinterested as if he were each moment liable to render an account of his administrations to his fellow citizens.'[29]

Just as respect for virtue was acknowledged by individuals who could not easily be deemed republicans, so those to whom that label could be applied did not necessarily agree on the means by which rule in the public interest should be implemented. Republicans could be divided into those who believed that securing republican government meant choosing virtuous rulers and educating citizens to make them virtuous too, and those who insisted that relying on virtuous people alone was not enough. The former placed great emphasis on methods such as education, military training, religious practices, and civil ceremonies as means of inculcating devotion to the state and commitment to the public good, among rulers and citizens alike. The latter argued that all individuals are potentially fallible and that even good people tend to become corrupted when holding power, particularly for long periods of time. Thus they emphasised the need for alternative measures that could secure the appearance of virtue (though not necessarily genuine virtue) or curb the worst effects of self-interested behaviour. This issue lay at the heart of debates among English republicans in the late 1650s concerning whether good laws or good men were essential to successful republican rule.[30]

Different solutions were proposed even by those who were sceptical of the possibility of cultivating and sustaining, among the population (or even just among rulers), sufficient virtue to satisfy the requirements of republican rule. While Harrington placed his faith in good laws, insisting that the rule of a legislator should be to 'give us good orders, and they will make us good men',[31] others insisted that only passion could counter passion. Gabriel Bonnet de Mably, the French philosopher and author, spoke about how certain passions could be channelled towards encouraging virtuous behaviour:

> I could give you a thousand other examples, my dear pupil, and all of them would prove that the passions that are the most ardent ... the most impetuous ... and the most impatient ... are tamed and even become great virtues in a government that is well enough constituted to contain them within just bounds, or rather to direct them by the love of glory, of the *patrie* and of liberty to the greatest good of the *patrie*.[32]

Here Mably is advocating the idea of countervailing passions – of using an individual's desire for glory to propel that individual into curbing baser passions such as greed, idleness, or cowardice; and this amounts to using self-interest to encourage virtuous behaviour on behalf of the public good.

While virtue was, then, a concept to which most republican writers at least paid lip service, there were important differences among them regarding which particular virtues should be valued, how virtuous behaviour could best be implemented, and even whether genuine virtue was possible in the case of flawed human beings.

Conclusion

Evidently not just 'republic' and 'republicanism' but also 'commonwealth', 'liberty', and 'virtue' are complex, contested, and multivalent terms. Given that the corresponding concepts have been around for more than two thousand years of human history – and have been engaged with and employed by a variety of individuals in a host of different settings – this should hardly surprise us. Yet it is equally clear that the constitutional models and values that have been explored here all have some part to play in the story. Rather than constituting a fixed and consensual tradition, republicanism is more akin to a living language that contains in it distinct varieties and is subject to adaptation and development over time. It can therefore be best understood, as I have argued elsewhere, via Ludwig Wittgenstein's notion of family resemblances.[33] By adopting this approach to the definition of republicanism, we make it possible to think of each variant or form as sharing some features with others, yet we do not require them all to share in a single set of core, defining features.

The present book has this conception at its centre. Its aim is not to identify a single, 'true' understanding of republicanism, but rather to explore the history of the concept in all its complexity. This will involve engaging with the debates among republican thinkers, with the different understandings of key republican concepts that they generated, and with the development of those concepts over time. In this respect the methodology adopted here owes much to the Cambridge School approach to the history of political thought. This approach, which is particularly associated with figures like John Pocock and Quentin Skinner, emphasises a wide range of thinkers and explores the debates in which they engaged, placing their ideas firmly in the political and intellectual contexts that generated them.

Chapter 1 explores the theoretical and practical ideas from antiquity that fed into later accounts of republican government. Chapter 2 turns to Renaissance Italy and the revival of ancient political ideas.

In this context complex theories of republican government were developed to solve the practical political problems facing the Italian city-states. Chapters 3 and 4 consider the development of those ideas in places such as the United Provinces, Geneva, and England during the early modern period. The new stimuli offered by these different contexts – and the challenges they posed – brought developments such as the application of republican government not just to city-states but to federations, and even nation-states. Chapters 5 to 8 take the story into the eighteenth century. With the collapse of the English republic and trouble in both the United Provinces and Geneva, the prospects for republican government did not look strong in 1700. Yet discussion of republican ideas intensified, and by the end of the century new 'modern' republics had been established after revolutions in the United States of America and France. Those revolutions have often been viewed as marking the high point of republican thought; after them decline set in, as republicanism was eclipsed by the new ideologies of liberalism, conservatism, and socialism. Still, as Chapter 9 demonstrates, republican ideas continued to prove influential into the nineteenth century, were adopted by new groups of people, and adapted to new ends. The book ends with a brief consideration of the fate of republicanism in the twentieth and twenty-first centuries that looks both at historiographical developments and at the influence that a deeper understanding of the history of republican ideas has exerted on political theory.

Examining the history of republican ideas over the longue durée reveals certain general trends. In particular, we can see here the gradual acceptance of the exclusivist understanding of republican government that first emerged during the Renaissance and gradually took root in the seventeenth and eighteenth centuries. There is also a definite shift away from seeing republican government as suited only for small city-states and towards its adoption in a much broader variety of contexts, including in states that rule over vast and diverse areas and populations. Thirdly, while both narrow, aristocratic, or elitist and broad, democratic, or popular conceptions of republican government have been in play at least since the Renaissance, there has been a shift in favour of the latter over time. By taking a long view and examining when and how these changes came about, we will not only gain a better understanding of the history of republicanism but also be better placed to assess the merits and relevance of what it offers in politics today.

1

Republican Ideas in the Ancient World

Introduction

The ancient world provided the foundations for many modern political concepts, and republicanism is no exception. The idea of government for the public good was articulated, forms of participatory government were developed, and various republican institutions experimented with during the Roman republic just as they had been in earlier centuries in Greek city-states such as Athens or Sparta. These provided models that would inspire and guide future republicans. The ancient world also nurtured a number of political theorists and historians whose contributions to the language and ideology of republicanism were salient. Although Plato and Aristotle would not have regarded themselves as republicans, the typologies of government they developed had a profound impact on later republican thought; and so, too, did Plato's detailed exploration of the concept of justice and Aristotle's notion of the human being as a political animal. Similarly, Polybius's theory of mixed government, Cicero's definition of what constitutes civic virtue, the accounts of Roman history by Livy, Sallust, and Tacitus, and the definition of liberty in ancient Roman law all contributed towards the development of a republican political culture.

The various components of what became known as the republican tradition were worked out during this period. Vital components were the crucial concepts of liberty as the antithesis of slavery and of virtue as involving the subordination of one's own personal or familial interests to the public good; the favouring of *negotium*, conceived of as active political engagement, over the *otium* of contemplative life; and the model of the mixed constitution as a means of preserving the advantages of good forms of government in the face of the constant danger of degeneration. Yet tensions and conflicting views were already evident. Ancient theorists disagreed over whether consensus and harmony were essential to the life and health of the republic, as Cicero argued, or whether, as Sallust claimed, antagonism was necessary to a flourishing state. Debates about the relative importance of constitutional structures versus virtuous citizens also emerged at this time. Moreover, the line between democracy and republicanism, and between republics and monarchies, remained fluid.

This chapter will lay out the ancient foundations of later republican thought by examining, one by one, the main systems of government in the ancient world that influenced the republican form (it does not matter here whether they were actually described at the time as republics or not), by considering the contributions to republican thought made by leading ancient political thinkers and historians, and by exploring the points on which they agreed and the issues of contention between them. Ultimately the chapter will argue that, even at its origin, republicanism was already a multifarious and contested concept.

Ancient Republican Models

Sparta

The Spartan constitution was said to have been established by the quasi-mythical lawgiver Lycurgus around the ninth century BCE, when he was acting as regent for his infant nephew.[1] The constitution applied not just to Sparta itself but also to the surrounding area – Laconia in the Peloponnese. Owing to Sparta's historical success, particularly in war, as well as to its remarkable stability and longevity, both Sparta and Lycurgus have come to exercise a significant influence on European thought.[2] Already in the second century BCE Polybius was able to comment: 'for securing unity among the citizens, for safeguarding the Laconian territory, and for preserving the liberty of Sparta inviolate, the legislation and provisions of Lycurgus were so excellent that I am forced to regard his wisdom as something superhuman.'[3] This sense that Lycurgus was almost divine was no doubt due to his alleged method of proceeding as much as to the wisdom behind the constitution attributed to him. Plutarch describes how, once Lycurgus was sure that his government was firmly settled, he sought to render it unalterable and immortal.[4]

To achieve this, he gathered the citizens together, explaining to them that he was going to Delphi to consult the oracle of Apollo about the constitution, and made them swear to observe his laws without any alteration until his return. Having received a positive response from the oracle, he immediately dispatched this news back to Sparta. Then, in order to ensure that his citizens would be forever bound by their oath, he committed suicide – which meant that he could never return.

At a more practical level, Sparta's success owed much to the mixed and balanced system that Lycurgus had supposedly introduced. As Polybius explains, Lycurgus was aware of the tendency of unmixed constitutions to degenerate

> and accordingly combined together all the excellences and distinctive features of the best constitutions, that no part should become unduly predominant, and be perverted into its kindred vice; and that, each power being checked by the others, no one part should turn the scale or decisively out-balance the others; but that, by being accurately adjusted and in exact equilibrium, the whole might remain long stead like a ship sailing close to the wind.[5]

The Spartan constitution thus comprised elements of monarchy, aristocracy, and democracy. Its distinctive double kingship (which preceded Lycurgus's reforms) was supposed to ensure peace between two distinct and often hostile houses. To this end the kings were granted equal powers, though by the fourth century they were little more than hereditary commanders-in-chief with mainly ceremonial and religious functions.[6] The aristocratic element rested in the Gerousia, a senate or council of elders consisting of twenty-eight men over the age of sixty and elected for life. This body had both a legislative and a judicial function, working with the kings to initiate legislation and acting as the highest court of justice. The Spartan assembly comprised all the male citizens who fulfilled a basic property qualification. It met to elect officials, to decide on war and peace, and to accept or reject any legislation proposed by the kings and the Gerousia. Although ostensibly the democratic element of the constitution, in the fifth century this assembly had only a few thousand members; and this fact (together with the superiority of the Gerousia) contributed to the perception of Sparta as an aristocracy or oligarchy. A century later, during the reign of Theopompus, the institution of the ephorate was established: five ephors acted as guardians of the constitution.

Lacedaemonia was also renowned for the simple, pared-back, and disciplined nature of the citizens' lives – characteristics also reflected in the modern use of the adjective 'spartan'. Lycurgus was heralded not just for instituting the mixed constitution, but also for establishing an egalitarian division of land and for banning the possession and use of gold and silver within the territory. There was a strong communal ethos: men and youths took their meals (*sussitia*) together, in public; children were taken away from their parents from the age of seven and given military training from the age of twelve. Since the land was cultivated by helots, who were public or state-owned slaves, the citizens could focus on their military and political duties.

Sparta's militarism was particularly important, not least as a source of discipline and as a means of cultivating a strong public spirit. Polybius acknowledged that the moral discipline of the Spartan system contributed to its success: 'when both these virtues, courage and high morality, are combined in one soul or in one state, vice will not readily spring from such a soil, nor will such men easily be overcome by their enemies'.[7] He did note, however, that the emphasis was on maintaining the safety of the territory and the freedom of the state rather than on acquiring additional territory. Consequently, when Lacedaemonians (i.e. Spartans) strove to become the dominant power in Greece, they jeopardised their own freedom. Nevertheless, the Spartan emphasis on freedom, the rule of law, and the state's powers to shape and educate the population led to Sparta's being a considerable source of influence for later republican thinkers.

Athens

Although the ancient city-state of Athens tends to be associated with democracy rather than republicanism, many republican concepts and institutions were put into practice there. The Athenian model sparked responses from leading philosophers of the time, not least Plato and Aristotle. Moreover, in later years a small but not insignificant number of republican thinkers – including James Harrington in seventeenth-century England and Camille Desmoulins in eighteenth-century France – looked back to the Athenian model and drew directly on it.

The system of democratic government in Athens was gradually introduced over a period of just over a century, which starts traditionally in 594 BCE – the year of Solon's archontate:[8] it is the poet and legislator Solon, in his capacity as *archōn*, who is seen as the initiator of democratic change. His reforms were designed as a means of quelling conflict between the masses and the nobility. They were mainly economic – such as the famous *seisachteia*, the cancellation of debts, or the introduction of a clearer distinction between slaves and non-slaves – and political reforms – for example widening the eligibility for office, placing the emphasis on wealth rather than birth, establishing a council (*boulē*) of 400 Athenian citizens to develop legislative proposals, and probably also creating some kind of popular assembly (*ekklēsia*). In addition, magistrates were made more accountable, the law court providing the means for the populace to appeal against magistrates' decisions. These reforms shifted the focus away from the household or family and towards the *polis*. Further reforms were introduced at the other end of the same century, in 508 BCE, again in response to conflict, by Cleisthenes – a statesman and legislator who had served as *archōn*. Cleisthenes reorganised the council, now composed of 500 members and made to represent the whole region, including the rural parts of Attica. Each tribe would send fifty representatives to sit in the council. These men would be chosen by lot and would serve for a year. An individual could serve no more than twice during his lifetime, thereby ensuring that a large number of members of the male citizen body would have the opportunity to participate in the council at some point. Cleisthenes also defined more clearly the composition and role of the popular assembly. Further reforms were added in 487 and 461 BCE. These increased the powers of the council, assembly, and popular courts at the expense of more exclusive bodies.

By such means, popular government was firmly established in Athens roughly between 461 and 322 BCE (a period conventionally limited by the two key events of Pericles's coming to power and Athens's defeat and loss of independence in the Lamian War). Several key features characterised this period and sowed the seeds for later ideas. One is the fundamental contrast between slavery and freedom. Citizens were living in a world above slaves and completely apart from them; yet the existence of slaves was crucial, given that the work they and Athenian women undertook gave male citizens the leisure time to participate in politics.

Another key element was a shift in the balance of power from the elite to the masses. Having carefully analysed the meaning of the prefix *dēmo-* in compounds that occur in pre-democratic Greek sources, Daniela Cammack has challenged the conventional view that the description *dēmos* applied to the entire citizen body.[9] Rather, as she demonstrates, the term originally referred to the assembly, or the common people acting as a collective political agent (as distinct from the orators, who constituted the political elite). The shift to *dēmokratia*, then, marked not so much rule by all as a reversal in the balance of power between the leaders and the masses. Moreover, the power and influence of popular bodies increased over time, as a more general use of lots and the regular rotation of office ensured that power was spread as broadly as possible.

One of the most treasured rights of Athenian citizens was free speech within the assembly. As a result of the exercise of this right, Athenian democracy has traditionally been seen as deliberative. Cammack challenges this assumption.[10] Rather than public deliberation, she argues, Athenian politics relied on judgement by the *dēmos*, the audience functioning as a decision-maker and voting after it received advice from others.[11] Thus in ancient Athens listening, judging, and voting were actually more important than speaking. The courts were crucial, too, since it was through them that mechanisms such as scrutiny, audit, and impeachment could be made to hold orators to account. Cammack's revisionist interpretation does not completely undermine the importance of free speech, however, since the right to speak freely was open to all. Moreover, the emphasis on judging and voting actually places the Athenian experience more closely in line with arguments made by later republican writers, from Harrington to Rousseau.

Of course, there were many restrictions and limitations, particularly with regard to who could be a citizen. Apart from being male and above the age of eighteen, citizens also had to be of free birth and both their parents had to be Athenians (a restriction famously introduced by Pericles). This meant that in practice just 10–20 per cent of the Athenian population were citizens – around 30,000 people out of a population of approximately 200,000 – a far smaller proportion than would be acceptable today. Moreover, only about one fifth of the total citizen body could actually attend the assembly at any one time. Nonetheless, the ideas of freedom, popular rule, and free speech have all been central to the subsequent history of republicanism. Moreover, Athens offered an interesting contrast to Sparta through its willingness to embrace trade and commerce even at the expense of military discipline and prowess.

Rome

Unlike the constitutions of Athens and Sparta, the Roman constitution was not the creation of a wise lawgiver.[12] Rather than being established all at once, it evolved gradually over several centuries. This dynamism, together with the nature of the sources, can make it hard to characterise the constitution with any accuracy.[13] Polybius is a key source, but his description does not always fit with other accounts of Roman practice.

According to tradition, Rome was founded as a monarchy by Romulus – its first king and a mythical figure. The shift to a republican form of government came around 509 BCE, when the last king of Rome, Lucius Tarquinius Superbus, was expelled in a popular uprising led by Lucius Junius Brutus. As in Sparta, the constitution that evolved incorporated three layers, which reflected the powers of the one, the few, and the many: the magistrates (particularly the consuls), the senate, and the people (more precisely their assemblies). The magisterial offices were shared among several people who occupied them for limited terms, so as to avoid any possible return to monarchy.[14] Military and political power was in the hands of two consuls who divided it between them for no more than a year. While dominant, they shared their power with praetors, tribunes, aediles, censors, and other minor magistrates responsible for specific jurisdictions. All these, together, oversaw the day-to-day running of the state. These magistrates undertook the main executive and administrative functions, as well as initiating legislation and acting as judges. Terms of office usually lasted one year and there was considerable scrutiny of those in positions of power. This was made easier by the fact that particular magistrates were assigned specific duties. Of special importance were the tribunes of the plebs; initially these were representatives of the greater part of the people rather than regular magistrates, but gradually they became more firmly entrenched.[15] They had the power to veto the actions of the consuls and other magistrates so as to protect the interests of the lower orders.

A much noted feature of the Roman system was the conflict between elite patricians and the plebeian masses – the *optimates* and the *populares*.[16] The former were keen to maintain and enhance their own status, while the latter sought to gain more wealth and power. The plebeians achieved some success in this endeavour over time, not least because the patricians needed them to fill the army and to support the state's ambitious military campaigns in other ways. In the eyes of many commentators, this internal conflict was fundamental to Roman liberty; but it also affected the organisation of the constitution in particular ways.[17] The senate, often seen as the locus of political power in Rome – at least until the final years of the republic – was a forum for political discussion. Its capacity was mainly advisory, but its control over finances gave it authority in practice – a practical edge.[18] The senate was able to shape and guide legislation, could debate issues presented by magistrates (even digressing, where appropriate), and had control over foreign policy as well as over public finances. Legislative authority lay ultimately with the assemblies, particularly the plebeian one, which passed bills and elected magistrates as well as performing certain judicial functions. Thus sovereignty was shared between the senate and the people, as reflected in the acronym SPQR (*senatus populusque romanus*, 'the senate and people of Rome') – the emblem of Rome's republican government that was used on official documents, coins, and buildings. The system operated by means of a series of checks and balances designed to prevent any one individual or group from dominating the political system, and Polybius comments explicitly on the ways in which the different powers were able to check one another.[19] Indeed, the Roman constitution was so mixed and balanced, Polybius suggested, 'that no one could say for certain, not even a native, whether the constitution as a whole were an aristocracy or democracy or despotism'.[20] Despite this uncertainty, the result was, in his view, a profound success: 'The result of this power of the several estates for mutual help or harm is a union sufficiently firm for all emergencies, and a constitution than which it is impossible to find a better.'[21]

Polybius even argued that Rome was superior to Sparta in one respect: not only would it secure the safety and freedom of its citizens, but it was also well suited for expansion.[22] Polybius attributed this feature, in part, to the constitution, while acknowledging that it also had much to do with the emphasis on military training and with the insistence on using citizen-soldiers rather than relying on mercenaries; but there must have been more to it, since Sparta had these features as well. The ambition of Rome's leaders, the perpetual conflict between patricians and the plebs, and the state's success in inspiring a thirst for glory among its citizens, all played a part. While the Roman state was deemed to be the product of evolution rather than that of a single mind, the military measures imposed by Romulus, the religious policies of his successor Numa, and the consequences of the expulsion of the Tarquins on the self-confidence of citizens have all been deemed important.

The Hebrew Republic

Many later republican thinkers set the Hebrew republic alongside the ancient city-states of Sparta, Athens, and Rome. The idea of Moses as a lawgiver, just like that of Lycurgus and Solon, was represented in visual form in John Toland's frontispiece to his edition of Harrington's works (Figure 1.1).

There was a source of this syncretism in the ancient world in the works of Flavius Josephus, who moved to Rome in the first century CE and presented Jewish practices in a way that would be comprehensible to his Roman audience.[23] Josephus offered a history of the Jews in the language of classical political philosophy, coining the term *theocratia*, 'government by God', to rectify the failure of Aristotle's

Figure 1.1 Frontispiece to *The Oceana and Other Works of James Harrington Esq.*, edited by John Toland (London, 1737). Author's own copy

constitutional typology to accommodate Israel's institutions. In this way he acknowledged the distinctiveness of the Hebrew commonwealth, while simultaneously setting the latter firmly alongside other ancient models.

Yet, despite its ancient origins, viewing the Hebrew republic in parallel with other ancient states was controversial. In part this was because the idea was associated with Niccolò Machiavelli and his advocacy for a 'politic religion'. Many thinkers in the early modern period did not believe that the Hebrew commonwealth could be used as a model, or that its lessons could be transplanted to other times and places. In part, Israel's exceptionalism was based on the fact that it was held to be divinely inspired, the work of God rather than of humans; but it also reflected the belief that the Hebrew commonwealth was built for the Jews alone. Just as the moral laws governing circumcision, the sabbath, and the preparation of food were applicable only to Jews, the same could be said about their distinctive constitutional structures. Moreover, even among those who were willing to see Israel as a relevant political model, many interpreted it as offering a justification for theocracy, or even monarchy, rather than as an example of republican government.

Nevertheless, in the early modern period humanist authors developed the tradition of combining Greek and Roman thought with Christian ethics and respect for Israelite political institutions. As Eric Nelson has noted, after the Reformation, Christian authors increasingly turned to the constitutional model provided in the five books of Moses.[24] In this context, the Hebrew Bible began to be seen as a political constitution and rabbinic materials as guides to the institutions and practices of the perfect republic. In 1574, in his *De politia iudaica tam civili quam ecclesiastica*, Bonaventure Cornelius Bertram described the Mosaic commonwealth as a mixed constitution, along the lines of Polybius's account of Rome.[25] In the following century, Hugo Grotius's *De republica emendanda* portrayed the Hebrew republic as representing God's constitutional preferences, and in 1617 Petrus Cunaeus offered a detailed and influential account of that system of government.[26] Cunaeus stressed the essential role of the laws within that state, declaring it 'An excellent Constitution: for seeing even the best Men are sometimes transported by passion, the Laws alone are they that always speak with all persons in one and the same impartial voice'.[27] He also placed emphasis on the equal division of land and on the regular return of lands to their original owners at the Jubilee, which he referred to as an agrarian law. In addition, he set out the division of power between the magistrates and the Great Sanhedrin – the supreme council of seventy-one wise elders – emphasising that the latter's powers extended over both temporal and spiritual affairs.[28]

Ancient Republican Theories

Plato

The diverse range of constitutional models in operation in the ancient world provided rich material for the political theorists of the time to reflect upon. One of Plato's (c. 429–347 BCE) best known works is the *Republic*, though this title is a Roman translation of the Greek *Politeia* and is slightly misleading from a modern point of view, because the form of government favoured in this work is not democratic, popular, or what we may call 'republican' government but rule by an elite, namely the philosopher-kings. The aim of the work was to explore the complex concept of justice, an idea that loomed large in later republican thought alongside several other of Plato's ideas.

In book 8 of the *Republic*, Plato (through the mouth of the regular main character in his dialogues, Socrates) distinguished five forms of government – aristocracy, timocracy, oligarchy, democracy, tyranny – and described the process by which each one degenerates into the next.[29] He also made important contributions to moral philosophy, suggesting that human beings comprise a mixture of rational and irrational elements that have to be put to their proper uses and kept in check. He drew a parallel between the human individual and the state, between the components of each and their different characters and constitutions, and thereby contributed to the later idea of a 'body politic'. Ultimately he insisted that all elements of society must work together towards the common good. As Socrates explains, 'our purpose in founding the city was not to make any one class in it surpassingly happy, but to make the city as a whole as happy as possible'.[30]

Aristotle

Plato exercised a profound influence upon his pupil Aristotle (384–321 BCE), who joined Plato's Academy at the age of seventeen. But Aristotle went on to challenge the views of his master on a number of issues, or to take them in new directions. In the *Nichomachean Ethics* he explored the question of what constitutes the good life, while in the *Politics* his focus was on the form of political community that best serves the actualisation of that life.

For Aristotle, the good life was one that enabled the realisation of virtues or the fulfilment of human potential. In book 1 of the *Politics* he stated as one of his foundational principles that 'man is a political animal'.[31] This suggested that the *polis* was crucial not just for survival, but also for self-development. Aristotle was not consistent on this. Ultimately he probably believed the active political life to be less fulfilling than the philosophical life of contemplation. Nevertheless, for most human beings political participation was essential to the pursuit of a good life – an uncomfortable observation for someone like Aristotle, who was himself excluded from Athenian citizenship on account of his Macedonian origins.

Book 3 of the *Politics* goes into more detail on the nature of citizenship, defining the citizen as someone who shares in the administration of justice and in offices. In fulfilling such roles, citizens would be expected to consider the good of the whole rather than simply their own personal interests. Aristotle acknowledged that, in order to achieve this, citizens would need to be appropriately educated, and a degree of political equality would have to be secured via public provision of land and employment and via payment for political duties. He was also clear that some – including non-Greeks, slaves, and women – were not capable of citizenship.

While Aristotle acknowledged that the precise role played by citizens will differ under different forms of government, he asserted: 'He who has the power to take part in the deliberative or judicial administrations of any state is said by us to be a citizen of that state; and, speaking generally, a state is a body of citizens sufficing for the purposes of life.'[32] This assertion followed from Aristotle's analysis of various political communities (real and ideal) in book 2 and, specifically, from his critique of Plato's proposal of holding property in common. In contrast to Plato, Aristotle insisted that citizens ought to take turns at ruling and being ruled.[33] The remainder of book 3 examines the various possible forms of government, producing the typology that was discussed in the Introduction to this book and that provided the crucial foundation for the pluralist understanding of a republic as government operating in the interests of the common good. Aristotle also emphasised the potential benefits of the rule of law, insisting that where the laws are good they should be supreme.[34]

Polybius

One problem with the forms of government that Plato and Aristotle identified is that each had the potential to degenerate into something worse. As noted in the Introduction, it was another Greek author,

Polybius (c. 208–c. 125 BCE), who offered a solution to this problem. Although Greek by birth, Polybius had been taken hostage to Rome, and his constitutional theory owed much to his observation of the Roman system. In the sixth book of his *Histories*, Polybius digresses from the historical narrative to offer an analysis of the Roman constitution that is designed to explain how that state rose to power in so short a space of time. In doing so Polybius builds on Aristotle's typology of government.

The exact labelling of the different forms varies a little from Aristotle's original (and from translation to translation), but essentially Polybius agrees that there are three good forms of government, kingship, aristocracy, and democracy (note that the last is now on the positive rather than negative side), and three corrupt forms that correspond to them, despotism, oligarchy, and ochlocracy or mob rule. Kingship is distinguished from despotism on the grounds that it is accepted voluntarily and exercised through common consent more than through fear and violence. Aristocracy can be set apart from oligarchy on the grounds of being managed by the wisest and best men. Democracy does not mean everyone is doing simply as they please; it is rather a state in which the gods are honoured, parents and the old are revered, and the laws are respected.

Each of these good forms, however, has a tendency to degenerate over time, following a cyclical process: kingship degenerates into tyranny, which is replaced by aristocracy, which gets perverted into oligarchy, which is supplanted by democracy, which turns into mob rule. Polybius's solution is to combine the three good forms into one system. 'For it is plain that we must regard as the best constitution that which partakes of all these elements.'[35] Polybius suggests that this can be demonstrated not simply by the logic of what is likely to work, but also by looking at the effects. A mixed form of government was the model that Lycurgus adopted for Sparta, which was known for its durability: '[t]he result of this combination has been that the Lacedaemonians retained their freedom for the longest period of any people with which we are acquainted'.[36] Polybius also argued that Rome was ruled on the same model, though there it was the outcome of struggles rather than abstract reasoning. Nonetheless, '[t]he result has been a constitution like that of Lycurgus, and the best of any existing in my time'.

Cicero

Marcus Tullius Cicero (106–43 BCE) drew upon various elements of earlier theories, but his ideas were also shaped by his direct observations and practical political experience in his native Roman republic. Cicero was a notorious philosopher, a key political actor, and a prolific writer whose letters and speeches provided important Latin models, but it was in his dialogue *De republica* (*On the Commonwealth*) and in his treatise *De officiis* (*On Duties*) that his ideas on the republican form of government and on the values required to establish and preserve it are most deeply explored.

De republica was one of three dialogues modelled on those of Plato that Cicero produced between 55 and 51 BCE.[37] It constituted Cicero's version of the *Republic*, setting out and comparing the various constitutional models, identifying that which was most suitable to Rome, and exploring the nature and consequences of justice and injustice. The work was canonical in antiquity and widely known until the fifth century CE, but after that point it survived only in fragmentary form. It was rediscovered in 1819 and first published in 1822, though elements of it (quotations, citations) were to be found in earlier commentaries and works.

De officiis took the form of a letter to Cicero's twenty-one-year-old son Marcus, who was studying in Athens. Its aim was to guide him on how to operate and succeed within the republican political system. It was very loosely modelled on the treatise *On Duty* by the Stoic scholar Panaetius.[38] Cicero's version was written in 44 BCE, in the context of Julius Caesar's assassination. Consequently it grappled with the justification for tyrannicide, but also with the concern that this act had not brought a return of the republic.

Cicero's decision to produce a series of Platonic dialogues in the 50s BCE reflected his broader concern to bring Greek philosophy to the attention of Roman citizens and to tailor Greek learning to the needs and values of Roman society.[39] Cicero had travelled to Rhodes in the early 70s BCE and had studied there, so he was well placed to act as a conduit for Greek ideas. The central interlocutor in *De republica*, Publius Cornelius Scipio Aemilianus Africanus, had been a friend of Polybius, though, as will be demonstrated in what follows, Cicero's engagement with Polybius's ideas was not straightforward.

It was in *De republica* that Cicero laid out his famous definition of republican government. Drawing directly on the etymology of the term and on Aristotle's typology of government, Cicero described a 'commonwealth as the property of a people' and went on to point out that 'a people is not any collection of human beings brought together in any sort of way, but an assemblage of people in large numbers associated in an agreement with respect to justice and a partnership for the common good'.[40] Consequently, his definition of a commonwealth or republic did not tie it to a particular type of regime; for him monarchy was a version of a republic rather than its antithesis:

> And so, when the control of everything is in the hands of one person, we call that one person a king and that type of commonwealth a monarchy. When it is in the control of chosen men, then a state is said to be ruled by the will of the aristocracy. And that in which everything is in the hands of the people is a 'popular' state – that is what they call it.[41]

This was paraphrased by Saint Augustine in *City of God* 2.21, a passage that made Cicero's understanding accessible to medieval and early modern thinkers. Scipio was clear that none of the simple forms of monarchy, aristocracy, and democracy was ideal, though all were tolerable. Each had its strengths and its faults, but each was likely to degenerate. For this reason Cicero, via Scipio, declared his adherence to the theory of mixed government: '[t]herefore I consider a fourth form of government the most commendable – that form which is a well-regulated mixture of the three which I mentioned at first'.[42]

Cicero not only contributed to general ideas about the form of a commonwealth, he also wrote at length about one of the fundamental republican concepts: virtue. Virtue was central to his philosophy and of particular importance to him personally, given its association with action rather than contemplation. This aspect was captured early in *De officiis*, where Cicero notes that some people tended to devote excessive time and effort to matters that are obscure, abstruse, and of little practical relevance. 'It is, however, contrary to duty to be drawn by such a devotion away from practical achievements: all the praise that belongs to virtue lies in action.'[43] The noblest use of one's virtue, he argued in *De republica*, was to apply it to the government of the state. 'For there is really no other occupation in which human virtue approaches more closely the august function of the gods than that of founding new States or preserving those already in existence.'[44] He expanded on this idea in book 1 of *De officiis*, noting that '[t]here have been many, and there still are, who have sought that kind of Tranquillity by abandoning public business and fleeing to a life of leisure'. He argues that they are no better than kings who live as they please – though the former do so for the sake of leisure and the latter for the sake of power. Both were to be contrasted with those 'who have adapted themselves to great achievements in the service of the political community' and who 'lead lives more profitable to mankind and more suited to grandeur and fame', Of course, Cicero had followed his own dictates on this matter. He could have remained at Tusculum, but chose to be tossed by the storms of public life 'rather than to live a life of complete happiness in the calm and ease of such retirement'.[45]

Cicero's emphasis on active virtue was directly associated with his definition of the commonwealth as encompassing the public good. Drawing on the statement that 'we are not born for ourselves alone' – which he found in an epistle attributed to Plato – and on the Stoic doctrine that everything produced on the earth is created for the sake of humans, Cicero insists on the importance of contributing 'to the common stock the things that benefit everyone together, and, by the exchange of dutiful services, by giving and receiving expertise and effort and means, to bind fast the fellowship of men with each other'.[46] A little later he returns to Plato, extracting from the *Republic* two crucial pieces of advice, which those in charge of public affairs ought to 'hold fast to': 'first to fix their gaze so firmly on what is beneficial to the citizens that whatever they do, they do with that in mind, forgetful of their own advantage. Secondly, let them care for the whole body of the republic rather than protect one part and neglect the rest.'[47] Though many fellowships bind humans together, 'none is more serious, and none dearer', he insisted, 'than that of each of us with the republic'. Therefore one may ask: 'What good man would hesitate to face death on her behalf, if it would do her a service?'[48]

Cicero certainly engaged with Polybius's works; and in many respects the two of them come to similar conclusions. However, Jed Atkins argues that this surface similarity hides fundamental differences in the way they approached politics, which produced two very different conceptions of mixed government.[49] On this account, Cicero remains within a Platonic–Aristotelian framework: it retains the ideal of a rational rule while accepting that the best regime is merely the most practicable one, given that human nature is unpredictable and human affairs unstable; and it aims at eliminating faction and producing civic harmony.[50] Polybius, on the other hand, was not interested in ideal conditions but rather sought to understand human affairs as they are. Human nature was a subject that could be investigated and understood rather than having to be accommodated, as Plato and Aristotle seemed to suggest.[51] It is possible to study it, Polybius believed, because humans are rationally self-interested creatures, which means that one can predict how they would behave, and therefore when constitutional decline would occur. Polybius's mixed constitution is, then, aimed at providing an appropriate balance between different powers, so that ambition would check ambition. For this reason, conflict and discord cannot be avoided within the polity but are given instead a role to play.

In the first two books of *De republica*, Cicero brings Polybius's theory to the attention of his reader, but his approach makes clear that he does so in order to critique it and to assert against it the Platonic–Aristotelian view. For Cicero, speaking as he does through Scipio, the mixed constitution was a means of incorporating the authority of the senate, the liberty of the people, and 'something outstanding and kingly' within a single constitution.[52] It was not, however, a matter of balancing these elements against one another, since Cicero believed the understanding of human nature as driven by self-interest to be too simplistic. Humans are motivated by a complex mix of reason and passions that it is not easy to predict. Moreover, Atkins points out that Cicero adopts the broader Roman understanding of *politeia*, which embraces not just the constitution or institutional structure but political culture more generally. This means that, for Cicero, education, law, custom, and religion are as important to the creation of the best regime as the constitutional framework in its narrower sense.

What we have here, then, is two distinct approaches. The first aimed at producing as rational and peaceful a state as possible and attempted to draw both on constitutional architecture and on the broader political culture to do so. The second involved accepting and embracing self-interested human nature and the conflict it produces and relying on balancing the different elements of the constitution to check and contain these forces. As we will see, both continued to exercise an influence on republican thinkers well beyond the classical era.

History Writing: Sallust, Livy, and Tacitus

Alongside the writings of ancient political theorists, works of history in the ancient world also provided material for later republicans. Ancient history writing was seen as having an explicit moral purpose in that it provided *exempla* by which both the past and the present could be judged and against which future action could be calibrated. The history of Rome was a particularly potent subject, as figures such as Sallust, Livy, and Tacitus offered accounts of different periods of Roman history, always with a view to what lessons could be learned from them in the present. Moreover, as Daniel Kapust has argued, all three authors grappled with issues central to republicanism, both then and now: '[t]he preservation of republican liberty and civic virtue, the boundaries of republican communities, the role of rhetoric in political conflict, the relationship between rhetoric, conflict, and liberty'.[53] However, they did not always come to the same conclusions. Where Sallust presented social conflict as inherent in Roman society and antagonism as something that could not be banished but had to be channelled instead towards the public good, Livy placed much greater emphasis on securing harmony and consensus.

For Sallust, the expulsion of the Tarquins from Rome raised the public spiritedness of the Roman people: 'every man began to lift his head higher and to have his talent more in readiness'.[54] These energies were good for the state, providing it with its life force, but they could easily pose a risk if they got out of hand. Initially they were kept in check by fear of Carthage; but, with the fall of that city, these internal energies and the struggles they produced posed a real threat to the republic. Indeed, Sallust goes so far as to suggest that it was the fall of Carthage that marked the beginning of Rome's corruption. One double conclusion that might be drawn from this is that fear is necessary in politics and that discursive republicanism, which allows for the expression of different views, will lead to destruction. This was the interpretation of Sallust that was offered by Thomas Hobbes, though, as Kapust shows, Sallust's actual position was more complex.[55]

Sallust argued that, in Rome, conflict had been structurally inherent long before the fall of Carthage and could not simply be removed. This was because Roman society contained within it competing views that could not be properly labelled good or bad and right or wrong but were all of value. Romulus and Numa, for example, displayed contrasting virtues and suggested different directions for Rome to take. Rome's success lay not simply in dismissing one in favour of the other but in finding a way to take both into account. Similarly, at the heart of Roman society was the clash between the people's love of freedom and the nobles' thirst for domination, which, despite causing conflict, was the founding source of republican liberty. For Sallust, then, the community was inherently antagonistic; hence conflict had been crucial to Rome's development and remained necessary in the present. The trick was to use elite conflict as an outlet for the antagonisms of political life and as a means of channelling and blending opposing elements within the political community. But, as Sallust showed in his *War with Jurgurtha* and *War with Catiline*, when the opposite happens and factional conflict results in one faction's taking all the political space for itself, that space would become private rather than public; and *res publica* would then be a *dominium*.

This aspect of Sallust's thought had a huge impact on Machiavelli, who is renowned for having moved away from the humanists' traditional Ciceronian emphasis on unity and order as the foundations of the public good and for drawing instead a close connection between liberty and conflict.[56] Yet what Machiavelli learnt from Sallust was that conflict and opposition, just by themselves, do not produce liberty; rather they need to be of the right kind, and to be channelled and limited in the right way. In place of violence and force, they must be pursued through speech in assemblies and through legal proceedings in the courts.

Interestingly, Livy, on whom Machiavelli drew directly, was less favourable to conflict and contestation and emphasised the importance of consensus and harmony within the political community. His solution, then, was to use rhetoric and goodwill as a means of building and maintaining consensus. Following Cicero, Livy placed great emphasis on the need for civic virtue, particularly among those in positions of power. Their virtue needed to be genuine rather than just a matter of appearance, and virtuous deeds needed to be observed and evaluated by the people.[57]

William Walker suggests a further way in which Sallust's position was different from that of Livy and Cicero.[58] He challenges Quentin Skinner's assumption that Sallust, along with Cicero, Livy, and Tacitus, adopted the neo-Roman understanding of liberty as freedom from interference and domination. Instead Walker shows that Sallust was more concerned about actual interference than about the potential for it, and that he sought to ensure the enjoyment of specific civil rights. He also asserts that elsewhere Sallust adopted a position closer to Aristotle's more positive conception of liberty as the fulfilment of particular ends, celebrating above all the attainment of glory and renown. Walker also suggests that, where Skinner presented, as a prerequisite for liberty, the existence of a non-monarchical constitution in which citizens elect individuals to political and judicial offices on fixed terms, Sallust himself offers a more complex account, in which liberty can be secured under monarchy and can rule in a republic, but is not guaranteed under either. For Sallust, the introduction of the tribunate, which would act on behalf of the people, was more important than the banishment of the Tarquins, and both the virtue of rulers and that of citizens were crucial to the preservation of liberty. Ultimately, Walker proposes that what we have here is a distinction between a more aristocratic attitude, represented by Cicero, and one that emphasises popular rule and is reflected in the works of Sallust.

Writing under the very different circumstances of the empire, Tacitus's historical accounts are more circumspect in their presentation of republican rule, but still convey his critique of monarchy and lament the loss of the Roman republic. The focus of the *Annals* and *Histories* is on the shift from the republic to the principate, the rise of imperial rule, and its decline into corruption and oppression. Benedetto Fontana shows how in those works Tacitus not only traces but also passes judgement on that transformation.[59]

Under the republic, on Tacitus's view, internal rule is characterised by liberty, debate, and competition for office, and the powers of magistrates are limited and clearly delineated. This is very different from external rule, where force, violence, and unlimited power prevail. Yet, with the shift to the empire, that distinction was erased. Free speech was no longer allowed in the assembly, offices were no longer decided on a competitive basis, according to merit, but were in the gift of the emperor, and force and violence invaded the public space. Competition between the senate and people had been extinguished because they no longer existed as autonomous agents. The former was now a servile instrument in the emperor's employ and governed by fear, and the latter an undifferentiated mass, motivated by appetites and controlled by violence. The struggle for power and for the glory of advancing the public good had degenerated into private struggles designed to further particular interests, and virtue either degenerated into corruption or was transformed into retreat from the world. The public space that once defined the political and social life of the state no longer existed. *Res publica* had become a *res privata* – the personal domain of the emperor.

In *Agricola* and the *Dialogue on Oratory* Tacitus uses history subtly, to present his own views. He praises and condemns past emperors, juxtaposing the good against the bad in order to show his readers how to judge rulers and how to respond to them. By criticising Domitian and Tiberius, but setting them against more recent rulers, whom he views more positively, such as Nerva and Trajan, Tacitus succeeds in navigating the difficult line between flattery and excessive criticism and avoids explicitly undermining the *principate* itself. Yet, Kapust argues, by showing that it is difficult to speak freely under imperial rule and that criticism has to be projected backwards, Tacitus is effectively recalling the republic, and the liberty it offered, in an ironic and poignant way.[60]

Conclusion

Ancient models, and the writings of ancient philosophers and historians, provided a foundation for republican ideas. The importance of liberty, virtue, the public good, and participatory government was asserted, and the means for realising them were proposed and enacted. Ancient theorists built on one another's works and were inspired and provoked by the political systems they saw around them. And yet many of the ambiguities and tensions that would affect later republican thinking are already in evidence.

It was generally agreed that a republic served the public good rather than the interests of rulers or private individuals. In theory this could be true of monarchy, aristocracy, or democracy and, following Polybius, many ancient republicans favoured a combination of all three. Yet there was also an acknowledgement that Rome had risen to greatness after the expulsion of its kings and that it declined again under the rule of Augustus and his successors. Moreover, the importance of citizen political participation was often underscored. The key distinction between citizens and slaves was firmly established in the ancient period, and was explicitly articulated in Roman law. Moreover, the participatory elements of the Spartan, Athenian, and Roman constitutions depended on the presence of substantial slave populations that would allow citizens the leisure necessary to fulfil their political duties.

In the contrasts between the different ancient forms of government we can also see the seeds of some later tensions. Should republics focus entirely on military prowess, as Sparta and Rome did, or were commerce and trade equally valuable pursuits, as the Athenian model suggested? Would engagement in trade necessarily undermine republican virtue and concern for the public good? Should a republic focus on defence and stability, as Sparta did, or was expansion crucial to republican success, as advocates of the Roman model would insist?

Ancient republicans also disagreed among themselves, on various issues. One important division was between those who followed Cicero and insisted on the importance of establishing concord and harmony within the citizen body, and those who accepted Polybius and Sallust's argument that conflict – together with the manipulation and containment of contrasting views and virtues – was essential to the existence and flourishing of republican government. Another key question was whether the active political life or the contemplative life was the best means of securing human flourishing and fulfilment. And ancient republicans were already aware of the discussion of whether virtue required self-denial and self-restraint or whether constitutional balance or the rewarding of glory and honour might be useful means of encouraging virtuous behaviour.

These topics will arise again in the chapters that follow, as the adoption and development of republican ideas by later thinkers and activists is explored. But adapting republicanism to new circumstances and using it to address problems unforeseen by its ancient progenitors also brought new solutions, ideas, and initiatives into play. It is the account of these debates, adaptations, and developments that forms the material for the rest of this book. While the ancient world provides the starting point, republican ideas all but disappeared from western political thought for over a millennium after the fall of the Roman republic. The next chapter is focused on the deliberate revival of those classical ideas during the Renaissance.

2

Renaissance Republicanism

Introduction

The Renaissance was characterised by the revival of ancient ideas and the recovery of classical texts under the notion that they were worthy of imitation.[1] As part of this process, the period witnessed the revivification of republican politics that encompassed ideas about self-governing communities, an understanding of liberty as the antonym of slavery, and the celebration of a moral philosophy that emphasised active political participation, prioritisation of the common good over private interests, and the inculcation of key virtues in rulers and citizens alike. While humanist scholarship and culture were key to the revival of republican politics, the political circumstances of the time were also crucial.

Renaissance republicanism has traditionally been presented as reaching its height in late fourteenth- and early fifteenth-century Florence, having been provoked by the conflict between republican Florence and autocratic Milan and, later, by Florence's rivalry with the other leading republican state of the time, Venice.[2] Various aspects of this account have subsequently been challenged. John Najemy has presented the development of civic humanism as the product of domestic rather than foreign policy concerns.[3] Quentin Skinner has challenged the timing. Building on the work of Paul Kristeller, he has shown that the political circumstances in the Italian peninsula shifted in the direction of self-governing communities as early as the twelfth century. This meant that theories of republicanism drawn from ancient sources were already well established by the time Leonardo Bruni (1370–1444) and Niccolò Machiavelli (1469–1527) were writing.

While Renaissance thinkers tended to emphasise the continuities between the ancient world and the present one, they could not ignore the significant changes that had taken place since the Roman republic. The rise of Christianity, in particular, presented problems for republican authors, since many regarded Christian religion as less obviously compatible with republican ideology than the polytheistic, patriotic religions of the ancient world. Thus one new element, distinctive to Renaissance republicanism, was the attempt to reconcile ancient republican thought with Christian belief.

Given the large chronological scope of Renaissance republicanism, it is perhaps not surprising that it exhibited a significant diversity. By drawing on both Greek and Roman sources, by adapting ancient ideas to new political circumstances, and by using republican arguments in a variety of political, historical, and moral debates, Renaissance writers developed republicanism in diverse and interesting ways. They also left a rich and complex legacy for future generations to exploit.

This chapter will offer an overview of the complicated story of the development of republican ideas during the Renaissance. It will begin by sketching both the political background that inspired this development and the cultural context out of which it emerged – not least, the very particular approach to history that was adopted by humanist scholars. Attention will then be paid to the various themes that were central to Renaissance republicanism and to areas of tension or contention.

The Political and Intellectual Background to Renaissance Republicanism

The Politics of Renaissance Italy

The city-states of the Italian peninsula were already evolving distinctive political systems that gave impetus to the revival and development of republican ideas from as early as the closing years of the eleventh century. Starting with Pisa in 1085, several cities challenged the jurisdiction of imperial power by establishing their own 'consuls', to whom they gave supreme authority. Before the end of the 1140s Milan, Genoa, Arezzo, Bologna, Padua, Florence, and Siena had all adopted this form of consular rule.[4] During the twelfth century a further development took place: these consuls were replaced by ruling councils, chaired by elected officials called *podestà*. By the end of the century Parma, Padua, Milan, Piacenza, Florence, Pisa, Siena, and Arezzo were all ruled in this way. These self-governing city-states were distinctive at a time when most of Italy formed part of the Holy Roman Empire and when government was commonly regarded as God-given rather than derived from the popular will. But they were encouraged by the collapse of Hohenstaufen rule in Italy in the mid-thirteenth century. Nevertheless, these states did not continue to be ruled by *podestà* for long: by 1300 the wisdom of elected systems was being questioned, and some Italian states began to shift back towards a single ruler or hereditary prince.

Florence and Venice, of course, continued as self-governing communities through the fourteenth century and beyond. A contrast was drawn between Florence's rather 'popular' form of republican rule, which grew out of its guild system, and the aristocratic character of the Venetian model. Yet Najemy's work makes clear that, from the late fourteenth century on, Florentine republicanism, too, became more oligarchic than before. He places particular emphasis on the Ciompi rebellion, which saw the rise to power of new guilds – particularly guilds of cloth workers who had previously been denied corporate association. That rebellion led to the almost complete exclusion of elite families from political office in 1378–82. It was this experience of true popular politics and the assertion of class interests, Najemy argues, that led the elite families and non-elite major guildsmen to embrace civic humanism.[5] In this context, the emphasis on the need to place the public good above private interests was a deliberate attempt to undercut traditional guild republicanism and the competition between rival interests that lay at its heart. The good citizen no longer belonged to or represented a group, but rather the entire community, and the emphasis on virtue replaced the representation of particular views.[6]

While emphasising the importance of domestic affairs, Najemy acknowledges a link to foreign policy. Factional conflicts at home made the republic more vulnerable to foreign tyrants. From the 1380s on, the Florentines were in danger from the Visconti family of Milan, who succeeded in bringing an end to the independence of many Italian city-states and intended to unite much of Italy under their rule.[7] During the fifteenth century, Florentine liberty was also endangered by the rise of the Medici, a wealthy Florentine banking family that sought political power to match its own economic status. The exile of the Medici in 1492, in the aftermath of the French invasion of Italy, led to a brief revival of the institutions and ideology of republicanism that was prompted by Girolamo

Savonarola (1452–98). This revival included some experimentation with a Venetian-style Grand Council, but on a much more popular footing. The council acquired the right to appoint the city's judges and to confirm laws proposed by executive bodies. The Medici returned in 1512, but republican arguments persisted. Thinkers such as Pietro Paolo Vergerio the elder (c. 1498–1565), Donato Giannotti (1492–1573), and Francesco Guicciardini (1483–1540) used the idea of an aristocratic republic, as reflected in the Venetian system, to challenge the Medici rule,[8] Around the same time, in *The Discourses on the First Ten Books of Livy* (written around 1517), Machiavelli reignited the more traditional case for a popular Florentine republic, albeit with his own idiosyncratic additions. In 1527 the Medici were exiled once more, giving the Florentine republic one last brief period of respite before their final return in 1530. The Venetian republic, which will be explored in detail in the next chapter, survived longer, continuing to exist until the invasion of French troops in 1797. Given this history, it is not surprising that it was in Florence and Venice that the bulk of the republican writings of the later Italian Renaissance were produced; but those writings were also inspired and coloured by the long history of self-governing communities in the Italian peninsula.

Greek versus Roman Thought

A number of thinkers contributed to the development of the ideas used to justify the existence of the Italian city-state republics. Traditionally, Greek political thought and theories, especially those of Aristotle, were seen as crucial to the development of Renaissance republicanism. John Pocock deemed the 'theory of the polis' essential to the constitutional theory of Italian city-states, while Nicolai Rubinstein declared that Aristotle's *Politics* 'provided a unique key to the new works of urban politics' and that 'no such guide had existed before the rediscovery of his works' – a rediscovery prompted by William of Moerbeke's Latin translations of the *Politics* and *Nicomachean Ethics* in the late thirteenth century.[9] This view also led to the contention that Renaissance republicanism only began to flourish in the fourteenth and fifteenth centuries. Skinner has challenged both of these claims. While accepting that the revival of Aristotelianism contributed to the evolution of Renaissance republican thought, giving Renaissance writers a new confidence and new tools, he rejected the suggestion that it provided the origins of that discourse.[10]

Skinner suggests instead that the roots of Renaissance republicanism can be traced back to the twelfth century, when Italian universities emerged as centres for the teaching of Roman law.[11] He places particular emphasis on two sets of Roman sources that were used by the early – or, as he calls them, 'pre-humanist' – defenders of self-governing republics. First there was Roman law itself, which was examined in compendia and glosses such as those by Azo of Bologna (c. 1150–1225). Secondly, there were the writings of Roman moralists and historians, especially Sallust, Seneca, and Cicero, and these works exercised a significant influence on rhetorical textbooks and on advice books for city magistrates, which were particularly common in the thirteenth and fourteenth centuries.[12] Brunetto Latini's *Li Livres dou trésor*, written in the mid-1260s, is a good example of this genre. In Skinner's view it was these texts that provided the crucial foundations of Renaissance republicanism: 'It was from these humble origins, far more than from the impact of Aristotelianism, that the classical republicanism of Machiavelli, Guicciardini and their contemporaries originally stemmed. The political theory of the Renaissance, at all phases of its history, owes a far deeper debt to Rome than to Greece.'[13]

William Stenhouse has, however, cautioned against lurching from one extreme to the other.[14] While accepting that the dominant view is now to see the Roman influence on the Renaissance as more significant than the Greek, Stenhouse – together with Eric Nelson – reminds us that Greek examples were also common in Renaissance writings and served important functions.[15] Bruni studied Greek and was influenced by Greek sources, modelling his panegyric to Florence on a Greek text – Aristides's *Panathenaicus* – and translating into Latin various Greek works, including Aristotle's *Politics*. Renaissance thinkers also made use of other Greek sources, for example Plutarch and Xenophon.

This mixture, then, of Greek and Roman, ancient and modern texts provided the foundations for the works of leading Renaissance republicans of the fourteenth to the sixteenth centuries. These included accounts of Venice and its associated myth, such as those by Henry of Rimini (fl. c. 1300) and Pietro Paolo Vergerio the younger (fl. c. 1400), and culminated in *De magistratibus venetorum*, by Gasparo Contarini (1483–1542), which was written in the 1520s and published posthumously, in 1543. Florentine citizens and magistrates produced important works too. Those of Coluccio Salutati (1331–1406), while not inherently republican, highlight important shifts within Renaissance humanism. Salutati's protégé and successor as Florentine chancellor, Bruni, although born in Arezzo and working for a time in Rome, adopted Florence as his home. Both he and Machiavelli explicitly celebrated the republicanism of the Florentine state. By contrast, Guicciardini preferred the narrower Venetian system.[16] As Bernardo, his mouthpiece in the *Dialogue on the Government of Florence*, acknowledged, Guicciardini's proposed model 'bears a very close resemblance to the Venetian government, which, if I'm not mistaken, is the finest and best government ever enjoyed by a city, not only in our times, but also perhaps in ancient times'.[17] While drawing on the earlier works and developing many of their key themes, these later writers were generally more self-conscious in how they approached historical models and texts than their predecessors were.

History

The Renaissance approach to history comprised several distinct elements, but it has tended to be most closely associated with the didactic approach learned from the ancients, whereby history is a storehouse of examples for use in the present. The works of Bruni were typical of this attitude. As Jacques Bos has argued, 'for Bruni history is a continuous space of examples and comparisons, not to be examined in its own terms, but in the light of its usefulness for present action'.[18] However, Machiavelli argued that there was a tendency simply to admire the great deeds of antiquity rather than to imitate them.[19] One of Machiavelli's aims, then, in the *Discourses* was to facilitate this move away from mere admiration and towards imitation, '[s]o that those who read what I have to say may the more easily draw those practical lessons which one should seek to obtain from the study of history'.[20] This attitude was dependent on an assumption that the past and the present were essentially the same:

> If the present be compared with the remote past, it is easily seen that in all cities and in all peoples there are the same desires and passions as there always were. So that, if one examines with diligence the past, it is easy to foresee the future of any commonwealth, and to apply those remedies which were used of old; or if one does not find that remedies were used, to devise new ones owing to the similarity between events.[21]

Given this attitude, it is easy to understand how, in the political circumstances described here, Renaissance writers showed renewed interest in the republican ideas and models of antiquity. In this context, the history of republican Rome was seen as particularly pertinent, and was used both to explain the origins of Renaissance states and as an important point of comparison with those states.[22] Central to Bruni's panegyric to the city of Florence – a piece titled

Laudatio florentinae urbis – was the idea that Florence was founded by the ancient Romans and that this justified its central political and cultural role.[23] Even his *History of the Florentine People*, which focused more on the Etruscan than on the Roman origins of the city and criticised Roman rule, still drew a close parallel between it and contemporary Florence.[24] Moreover, Bruni developed a vocabulary of 'civic humanism' that was inspired by republican Rome and that he used to explain how political liberty could be maintained in Renaissance Florence.[25] Similarly, Machiavelli used the history of Rome, as presented by Livy, to provide guidance for contemporary Florence.

The writings of Machiavelli's contemporary and rival, Guicciardini, have been deemed to mark the beginning of a shift in historical outlook whereby more emphasis was being placed on change and mutability.[26] While Machiavelli saw history predominantly as a recurring process, Guicciardini emphasised the uniqueness of each historical act and judgement and adopted a methodology that placed greater weight on the careful use of sources and on factual accuracy. Indeed, Guicciardini explicitly criticised Machiavelli's use of Roman examples, given his sense that the past was different from the present. Already, then, in terms of sources and historical methodology we can see differences in attitudes among Renaissance republican authors. If we turn to the content of their ideas, we find that those differences in approach produced a variety of Renaissance republicanisms.

Self-Governing Republics

The distinctive contribution of Renaissance humanism to early modern political thought, according to Skinner, was the notion of *civitas libera*, the free state – a self-governing community in which the will of the citizens is the basis of law and government. At the heart of this idea was the contrast between citizen and subject. The former prescribes laws for him- or herself, whereas the latter is subject to laws established by kingly overlords. This idea was in turn based on the distinction, within Roman law, between freeman and slave and on the associated definition of liberty as absence of slavery – or absence of dependence on someone else's will. For those seeking to justify the existence of the independent, self-governing communities in the Italian peninsula, this notion of freedom as absence of slavery was important both at the individual level and at the level of the state.

Skinner shows that, even as early as in the thirteenth century, Azo of Bologna was writing to defend both the de facto independence of the Italian city-states and the popular sovereignty that lay at their heart. He insisted that the ultimate power to make laws lay with the people, and that they could continue to claim that power even after the establishment of a prince. 'My own view is that the people never transferred this power except in such a way that they were at the same time able to retain it themselves.'[27] Implicit here is both a continued right of resistance for the people and the idea that rulers were only there for the convenience of those over whom they ruled. In making this claim, Azo was drawing on the distinction between conceiving of people as individuals (*ut singularis*) and conceiving of them as a body (*ut universis*). No single individual had greater power than the ruler, but equally no ruler had greater power than the people as a body.

Leading republicans of the later Renaissance continued to emphasise the value of a free state. In his panegyric, Bruni attributed Florence's civic grandeur to its liberty and to the fact that the community was not dependent on anyone else's will. He traced Florentine interest in liberty and self-government back to its Roman origins.[28] He also linked the flourishing of culture in both ancient Rome and modern Florence to the possession of liberty.[29] His explanation was that liberty gave human beings the opportunity to use and perfect their talents:

> For when men are given the hope of attaining honor in the state, they take courage and raise themselves to a higher plane; if this hope is lost, they grow lazy and stagnate. Since such hope and opportunity are held out in our commonwealth, we need not be surprised that talent and diligence excel here in the highest degree.[30]

Acknowledging that Florence's civic independence and the liberty of its citizens were threatened by both external and internal forces, Bruni offered measures against both. He advocated the use of strong military power to prevent foreign conquest and presented the mixed republican constitution as the key to preventing subjection to internal tyranny. Indeed, for him the contrast between (Florentine) liberty and (Milanese) tyranny was crucial.

Just like Bruni, Machiavelli sought to offer a revised defence of traditional self-governing republics.[31] He noted that the Roman state was dependent on no one and presented this characteristic as a key factor in its success. He also suggested that cities never increased in power or wealth except when they maintained a state of liberty, and insisted that the safeguarding of liberty within a republic is crucial.[32] Machiavelli also followed Bruni in recognising the threat of both external conquest and internal tyranny and placed particular emphasis on protection against the former. This could best be achieved by engaging a strong citizen army, inculcated with good military discipline, rather than by relying on mercenaries for defence – a view for which he argued on the grounds that an army that fights for its own glory is more effective than one motivated by ambition.[33] Mercenaries, he observed, 'have no cause to stand firm when attacked, apart from the small pay which you give them', and this alone would not make them loyal or persuade them to die for the state, as well-trained and well-disciplined citizen soldiers would be prepared to do.[34] On this basis, Machiavelli challenged the common-place that money is the sinews of war, making the point that it is good soldiers that are crucial. He also noted that this was one respect in which the moderns tended to differ from the ancients, as it was much more common in his own time for states to entrust people other than their own citizens with military matters.[35]

A similar degree of care and vigilance was required to protect the state from internal tyranny: 'so great is the ambition of the great that unless in a city they are kept down by various ways and means, that city will soon be brought to ruin'.[36] Machiavelli noted that, while a republic needed to have citizens of good repute in order to be well governed, control needed to be exercised to ensure that the reputation of a citizen was helpful rather than harmful to the city. On this he cited the example of Spurius Maelius, a rich Roman who kept a private supply of corn that he distributed to the *plebs*, to gain its gratitude. Perceiving the potential danger this raised, the senate appointed a dictator who immediately put Maelius to death.[37] Other measures, such as the regular rotation of rulers and generals and the encouragement of popular vigilance, were also crucial in this regard.

The Beginnings of Republican Exclusivism

While Renaissance republicans were generally united in their commitment to the self-governing state and most (if not all) continued to adopt a pluralist position, the logic of their ideas did begin to point in a more exclusivist direction.[38] The term *respublica* was little used during the Italian Renaissance. When it was, it tended to describe the best regime rather than one that was non-monarchical; for example Bruni used it to describe 'any legitimate form of government serving the common good'.[39] Yet, as Skinner notes, it was only a short step from criticising kingly or princely rule to repudiating the idea of monarchy in any form. Moreover, while earlier, pre-humanist writers often assumed the presence of a single figure at the head of the system, their successors insisted that power at the top should be held jointly by a group of leaders collectively known as the *signoria*, 'the governing authority', whose power was carefully restricted: 'They can hold office for brief and statutory periods of time. They can only be elected with the consent of the citizen body as a whole. While in office, they can only exercise authority in accordance with the existing laws and customs of the commune.'[40] Here, then, it was the laws that ruled rather than particular individuals. What such a system promised was the most effective, and therefore potentially the most successful, form of state.

Several texts that advised city magistrates emphasised the superiority of self-governing states over princely ones, even if they did not explicitly use the term 'republic' to describe the former.[41] Latini, for example, declared that '[t]here are three types of government, one being rule by kings, the second by the leading men, the third rule by communes themselves. And of these, the third is far better than the rest.'[42] Another writer who seems to have been moving in the direction of republican exclusivism in the late thirteenth and early fourteenth centuries was Ptolemy of Lucca. The second part of his *De regimen principum* conflated regal and despotic rule to such a degree that monarchy itself appears inherently despotic.[43] He also drew a distinction between constitutional rule directed towards the common good and royal rule in the interest of the ruler, though historians have disagreed as to whether he conceived of the latter as necessarily the rule of one.[44] In his *Laudatio*, Bruni was also pushing in the direction of republican exclusivism through his insistence that the preservation of liberty depended on the maintenance of a mixed form of republican government.[45]

On Hankins's account, however, true republican exclusivism requires not just the rejection of monarchy or a preference for elected self-government, but the explicit use of the term *respublica* to describe that form. While insisting that most political writers of the Italian Renaissance were not republican exclusivists, he points out that some did begin to use the term *respublica* to denote non-monarchical regimes; and he presents this as a key precondition for the later rise of republican exclusivism and for the sense of monarchy as an inherently illegitimate form of government.[46] Crucial to this linguistic development were the Renaissance translations of Aristotle's works, in particular his *Politics*. In part this was due to a distinction between Latin and Greek. In classical Latin the term *respublica* tended to have a general use whereby it also connoted 'affairs of the state' or 'the public good'. It did not necessarily imply government by the people. Consequently, as Hankins demonstrates, not only was it not generally used by the Romans as a formal name or descriptor of their state, but there was no clear distinction between the Roman republic and the Roman Empire either.[47] In Greek, the term *politeia* was more directly connected to popular rule. In his version of Aristotle's *Politics*, Bruni translated *politeia* with *respublica*, taken both in the general sense of a government for the common good and in the more specific sense of popular rule. Moreover, *politeia* was replaced by *respublica* not just in the text itself, but also in Thomas Aquinas's commentary.[48] At the same time, in his role as chancellor of Florence, Bruni continued the practice of using *respublica nostra* as a way to refer to the Florentine state in official letters, thereby encouraging the association of this Latin term with existing non-monarchical regimes – since *respublica* was more positive than *oligarchia*. Another author influential in promoting this exclusivist use of *respublica* was Francesco Patrizi. He used the term to refer to popular government, aristocracy, or oligarchy but not to monarchy, tyranny, or the rule of the mob. Thus in the late fifteenth century republics and monarchies were frequently seen as binary opposites, though Hankins also notes a significant backlash by supporters of princely regimes who also began to label their systems as *respublicae*.[49]

Hankins is also cautious in his claims in another regard. While he acknowledges that Ptolemy of Lucca and Bruni might appear to embrace the full implications of republican exclusivism – including the sense of monarchical rule as inherently illegitimate – he remains unconvinced that such a position is held consistently by any author before the seventeenth century. While Bruni's *Oration for the Funeral of Nanni Strozzi* does hint at a position of this sort, Hankins suggests that it does not reflect Bruni's settled view, but was a consequence of the highly charged political moment in which that work was written.[50] Ptolemy, as well as not being explicit in his association of royal rule with the rule of one man, also restricted his advocacy of republican government to the city-states of northern Italy, accepting that even despotism could be a legitimate form of government under certain circumstances. He thereby maintained a relativist position.

By the time Machiavelli was writing, then, two distinct understandings of the term 'republic' were emerging. One was 'republic' as a self-governing state ruled in the common interest; the other was 'republic' as an antonym of 'monarchy'. These two senses of 'republic' had already been articulated, but few (if any) authors went so far as to make the associated claim that monarchies were inherently illegitimate forms of government. Machiavelli, too, continued to reflect both positions. While particularly interested in states that were self-governing rather than being subject to a foreign power, he nonetheless acknowledged that such states could be ruled either as republics or as principalities. Even in the *Discourses*, he discusses kingly rule, for example in relation to the early history of Rome.[51] He also acknowledges that a republic is not necessarily suitable for all states, noting that it is very difficult for a people accustomed to living under a prince to adopt a republican government and preserve its liberty, and that a people that has become corrupt cannot enjoy its freedom.[52] To illustrate the point, he considers the contrast between Rome after the expulsion of the Tarquins, when it was able to establish its freedom, and Rome in the very different situations after the killing of Caesar, Caligula, and Nero, when it was not. 'Results so diverse in one and the same city are caused by nought else but that in the time of the Tarquins the Roman populace was not yet corrupt, but in the later period was extremely corrupt.'[53]

Similarly, thinking about his own time, he declared Milan and Naples to be too corrupt to be ruled as free states, as was proved in Milan by what happened after the death of Filippo Visconti: '[i]t is on account of all this that it is difficult, or rather impossible, either to maintain a republican form of government in states which have become corrupt or to create such a form afresh'.[54] Elsewhere he offered further insight on this point, suggesting that it was impossible to set up a republic where equality did not exist. In Naples, in the Papal States, in the rest of Romagna, and in Lombardy, he noted, there were significant numbers of gentry living off their land without having to work. Consequently republican government was not suited to those states, 'for men born in such conditions are entirely inimical to any form of civic government'.[55] He therefore concluded:

> Let, then, a republic be constituted where there exists, or can be brought into being, notable equality; and a regime of the opposite type, i.e. a principality, where there is notable inequality. Otherwise what is done will lack proportion and will be of but short duration.[56]

Elsewhere in *Discourses*, however, Machiavelli does seem to hint at a newer, exclusivist understanding of what a republic is. He sets republics and principalities in contrast to each other and repeatedly suggests that a republic is a better form of government. He points out that cities that are independent and in which 'the populace is the prince' are much more able to expand their territory, and he adduces the examples of Athens after it liberated itself from the tyranny of Pisistratus and Rome after the expulsion of its kings, concluding: '[t]his can only be due to one thing: government by the populace is better than government by princes'.[57] There was good reason for the superiority of popular government: 'a republic has a fuller life and enjoys good fortune for a longer time than a principality, since it is better able to adapt itself to diverse circumstances owing to the diversity found among its citizens than a prince can do'.[58] Machiavelli had already explored the advantages of elected over hereditary rule earlier in the work. Rome's reliance on kings, he acknowledged in book 1, exposed it to danger, and even risked precipitating ruin if a weak king were to come to power. By expelling the kings, he pointed out, Rome removed the dangers associated with a weak or bad king.[59] Republics were generally more successful than principalities 'since, thanks to its practice of electing its rulers, it [*sc.* a republic] has not merely a succession of two highly virtuous rulers' (as could happen if one good king followed another) 'but an infinite number each succeeding the other; and this virtuous succession may always be kept up in a well ordered republic'.[60] Moreover, while Machiavelli did not deny that, in theory, a good prince could frame laws for the common good, he did believe that the interests of the prince and those of the community would usually be in opposition to each other, whereas for republican rulers it would be much easier – and therefore much more likely – to align their own interests with those of the common good: 'it is not the well-being of individuals that makes cities great, but the well-being of the community; and it is beyond question that it is only in republics that the common good is looked to properly in that all that promotes it is carried out'.[61] Machiavelli may not have been the first writer to hint at an exclusivist understanding of republicanism; he may not have done so consistently, but he played an important role in exporting this new understanding of the republic beyond Italy.[62]

Active Politics and the Importance of Virtue

Machiavelli's suggestion that the greater chance of securing the virtue of rulers under a republic than under a monarchy is what rendered the former the better form of government reflects the crucial importance of virtue in Renaissance republicanism. But what exactly did Renaissance thinkers mean when they spoke of virtue?

In broad terms, behaving in accordance with virtue meant putting the public good or the common good first. Renaissance writers took from Cicero two related ideas: that the magistrates must place the welfare of every citizen above their own advantage; and that they must look after the welfare of the whole body politic, not just of one part.[63] As Latini put it, it was necessary to 'place the common good above everything else'.[64] Similarly, Salutati made it clear that the laws of the community had to be directed towards the common good in order for liberty to be preserved.[65] Machiavelli too, as we have seen, linked the prioritising of the common good to the superiority of republics.[66] In principalities, by contrast, what the prince does in his own interest generally harms the city, and what is done for the good of the city harms the prince.

Subordinating one's own interests and desires to the common good was not an easy task, however, and therefore required wisdom and the practice of various specific virtues in order to be achieved. Their list included the contemplative or theological virtues of faith, hope, and charity, though these were not generally explored in great detail. More important were the active, cardinal, or political virtues: prudence, justice, courage, temperance – and, for those influenced by Seneca, magnanimity. Once again, Bruni's contribution was crucial, in that it articulated the need for these virtues and their connection to liberty. As Skinner acknowledges, 'Leonardo Bruni's vision in the *Laudatio* – a vision of the cardinal virtues as the key to liberty, and liberty as the key to civic greatness – exercised a profound influence over the development of Florentine political theory in the first half of the fifteenth century'.[67]

Of course, in a self-governing republic such qualities were required not just from the magistrates, but from the population as a whole, since all were involved in ruling the state. Thus, in some of the writings of the late fourteenth and early fifteenth centuries it is possible to see a shift of emphasis away from *otium* or contemplation as the ideal form of life and towards *negotium*, understood as active civic participation. While Petrarch had declared that the best kind of life for ordinary citizens was one of contemplation, Bruni and others of his generation condemned the behaviour associated with it as a dereliction of duty and instead insisted on the need to pursue an active political life, a lifestyle centred on *negotium*.[68] We can see the beginnings of this shift in Salutati's letter to his friend Pellegrino Zambeccari. He is not yet declaring the active life as superior to the contemplative, but is certainly moving in that direction:

> The contemplative life is better, I confess; nevertheless, it is not always to be chosen by everybody. The active life is inferior, but many times it is to be preferred. ...
>
> To conclude shortly, let us grant that the contemplative life is better, more divine and sublime; yet it must be mixed with action and cannot always remain at the height of speculation.[69]

Salutati also engaged in debate with Petrarch on this issue. In response to Petrarch's horror at Cicero's insistence on active citizenship, he asserted: 'in a time of civic strife the citizen who sides with neither part and desires to continue his private life is unfaithful and must be expelled from his city'.[70] Bruni developed this idea by using Cicero as an embodiment or symbol of the idea that individual human perfection can be attained only via the active political life.[71]

Machiavelli agreed that virtue was required not just of the ruler: it must be instilled in the entire population. And, as Skinner has shown, in many respects his account of virtue is in line with that of earlier Renaissance thinkers. Machiavelli insisted that citizens must place the common good above their own interests, must perform political and military service, and must curb their desire for material wealth.[72] He also acknowledged that the people were not naturally public spirited and so it was essential that the state introduce measures designed to encourage virtue – for example civic education, military training, or civil religion – and also to use the rewards of honour and glory. Yet once again we can see Machiavelli looking in two directions simultaneously.[73] He certainly attributed the greatness of Rome, in part, to the superb virtue of the Roman people.[74] He acknowledged that virtue tends to be stronger when people act out of necessity rather than choice, and therefore made the point that, if the state was established in a good fertile spot (as was sensible, if at all possible), it would be necessary to use laws to counter the idleness that such circumstances could bring. Strict training and firm discipline among citizen militias would be one way of achieving this end. Just like the Roman historians and moralists and their Renaissance followers, Machiavelli emphasised the crucial role that the cardinal virtues of courage, temperance, and prudence played in a successful republican government. Yet, while emphasising these virtues, Machiavelli did not accept the need for what, for Cicero and those influenced by him, had been the crowning virtue: justice, understood as the avoidance of both fraud and violence. Just as in *The Prince* Machiavelli acknowledged that a prince might sometimes have to act in an underhand or forceful way in order to maintain his status and attain glory, so in the *Discourses* he says that the rulers of republics might occasionally have to make use of fraud or force to bring about success in war or the greatness of the state: '[f]or when the safety of one's country wholly depends on the decision to be taken, no attention should be paid either to justice or injustice, to kindness or cruelty, or to its being praiseworthy or ignominious.'[75]

This view is exemplified most clearly in the treatment of Romulus: although Romulus is a king, Machiavelli regards him mainly as the founding legislator of Rome. He admits that the fact that Rome's founding figure killed his brother and brought about the death of another man might look like a bad sign, but he urges that, before judging these actions, we consider the ends for which Romulus committed murder. In this case, he argues, the ends justify the means. Romulus is absolved because he did what he did in the interests of the common good, and not out of personal ambition.[76] Something similar might be said about the actions of Brutus, who, after expelling the Tarquins from Rome, sat on the tribunal that condemned his own sons to death for not accepting the new regime, and was even present at their execution. This action, Machiavelli insists, was essential for the preservation of the new regime.[77] Thus Machiavelli is clear that republican rulers may need to adopt abnormal methods in order to make a state secure.[78] And he notes that Roman leaders did not fail to use fraud when necessary.[79]

Machiavelli's comparison between the generals Manlius Torquatus and Valerius Corvinus reveals the extent of his controversial and counterintuitive thinking on this issue. Both were hugely successful figures whom Machiavelli deems equal in their virtue, triumphs, and fame. Yet, while they treated the enemy in a very similar way, their respective attitudes towards their own troops were very different. Manlius adopted a policy of severity, whereas Valerius opted for a humane and considerate approach. Addressing the question of which one is more worthy of imitation, Machiavelli concludes that Valerius's gentle approach ought to be adopted by princes, but that republican rulers and generals would do better to imitate Manlius's behaviour. The reason, in his view, is that kind behaviour might be seen as arising out of private ambition – the desire to gain favour with the people, or to acquire partisans – whereas Manlius's behaviour is 'entirely in the public interest' and

> in no way affected by private ambition, for it is impossible to gain partisans if one is harsh in one's dealing with everybody and is wholly devoted to the common good ... Wherefore, than such a procedure none can be more advantageous or more desirable in a republic, since it neither fails to take account of the interests of the public nor does it suggest that personal power is in any way being sought.[80]

Constitutional Architecture

The idea that the practice of virtue would be difficult for rulers and citizens alike led some writers to put their faith in constitutional architecture rather than in the moral behaviour of even a

small number of ruling individuals. This has not always been fully
acknowledged, because of the tendency of those writing about republicanism to emphasise moral philosophy over constitutional models;
but Benjamin Straumann has shown that Rome's constitutional order
was almost as important for Renaissance republicans as Roman
ideas of liberty and virtue.[81] Straumann demonstrates that Ptolemy
of Lucca (c. 1236–c. 1327) accepted that it was Rome's constitution
rather than its particular virtues that set it apart and made it great.
'Ptolemy does not put his faith in the virtuous disposition of the
ruler. For better or worse, he prefers a system where the ruler is
constrained by law and puts the emphasis on legal constraints, not on
virtue.'[82] The same is true, Straumann claims, of Mario Salomonio:
'for Salomonio, then, no less than for Pomponius and Ptolemy, the
Roman Republic served as a model of a constitutional republicanism,
the distinct features of which lie, not in civic virtue, but rather in
higher-order rules which constrain ordinary legislation and politics'.[83]

Just like the Renaissance understanding of Roman liberty and
virtue, these accounts depended heavily on Cicero's views, reflected
in particular in *De republica*, *De legibus*, and *De officiis*. The first
of these works presented constitutional theory as the answer to the
problem of the deterioration of public institutions, while the *Laws*
provided a theory of constitutionalism and a set of constitutional
norms.

Machiavelli saw constitutionalism as a key factor, though in a
Polybian rather than Ciceronian fashion. He accepted Polybius's
notion of the cycle of governments and concluded that a mixed
constitution is best.[84] In more general terms, too, Machiavelli moved
away from the tendency of earlier Renaissance republicans to focus
on the need to inculcate civic virtue in the citizen body, admitting
that, when constituting and legislating for a commonwealth, it is
necessary to assume that all men are wicked.[85] The coercive power of
the law provides a crucial means of enforcing virtuous behaviour and
thereby protecting liberty. Machiavelli thus recognised, as a contributing factor in Rome's success, Rome's own acknowledgement of the
importance of preserving law and order and of making new laws in
order to address new circumstances and needs.[86] It was crucial, for
example, that laws were in place to prevent one person from gaining
a position of supreme authority for anything but a limited period
of time, and for specific ends. Nonetheless, he was clear that even a
good constitution and careful leadership of the state could not put
off the inevitable indefinitely: 'since no sure remedy can be prescribed
for such disorders, to which republics are liable, it follows that it is
impossible to constitute a republic that shall last for ever, since there

are a thousand unpredictable ways in which its downfall may be brought about'.[87]

Religion

Accommodating ancient republican politics with the Christian religion was no easy task and we should not be surprised if some Renaissance republicans avoided the problem rather than attempting to solve it. Nevertheless, others sought to square the circle by linking ancient and Christian virtues. For example, Salutati couches the debate between the relative merits of the contemplative and the active virtues in religious terms, pondering whether 'the contemplative hermit Paul' or the 'active man Abraham' would have been more pleasing to God. For Salutati the verdict is clear: 'just as there are incomparably more who are busy in secular affairs than who are concerned with spiritual matters alone, so far more of this kind of men are accepted by God than of that group who are interested in spiritual things alone'.[88] Moreover, Salutati then quotes Augustine in support of his arguments, concluding: 'I have quoted all these passages of father Augustine, so that you not keep flattering yourself about your man-constructed oratory or about your being closer to heavenly things, and that you not damn me for remaining in the world and justify yourself fleeing the world'.[89]

Machiavelli, too, insisted on the importance of religion to the success of a republic: '[a]nd, as the observance of divine worship is the cause of greatness in republics, so the neglect of it is the cause of their ruin'.[90] Religion, on Machiavelli's account, provided a useful means of persuading naturally self-interested citizens to defend their communal liberty and to put the public good above their own private interests. One crucial area in which religion could be used in this way was that of inspiring and encouraging citizen-soldiers. 'For, where there is religion, it is easy to teach men to use arms, but where there are arms, but no religion, it is with difficulty that it can be introduced.'[91] This was one reason for the huge success of Rome's armies. In his account of Rome's greatness, Machiavelli placed particular emphasis on Numa Pompilius and his clever use of civil religion to control the people of Rome.[92] Religion could also be used in civil affairs. Rome's citizens, he observed, were more afraid of breaking oaths than they were of breaking the law, thereby making it possible for the senate and great men to induce the people to act as they wanted.

Yet this was one lesson drawn from Rome that it was difficult for the Florentines to benefit from. Christianity, as Machiavelli acknowledged, was much less suited to inspiring patriotic action than its Roman forebear, on account of its focus on the next world rather than this one: '[f]or our religion, having taught us the truth and the true way of life, leads us to ascribe less esteem to worldly honour'.[93] Christianity, he went on, glorifies 'humble and contemplative men, rather than men of action', 'what it asks for is strength to suffer rather than strength to do bold things'.[94] Moreover, he believed that in his own time Christianity was approaching ruin and was, in fact, the cause of much irreligion. As should be clear, while Machiavelli strongly emphasised the importance of religion to the success of the state, there is much in his writings to suggest that his attitude was more about utility than genuine belief. This was the basis of Machiavelli's reputation as an irreligious thinker, or even as an atheist.[95]

Concord versus Tumults

If his outspoken attitude to religion was one way in which Machiavelli departed from other Renaissance republican thinkers, his willingness to embrace 'tumults' was another. While writers of the Italian Renaissance often acknowledged the benefits of foreign war, both in terms of expansion and as a means of preventing corruption,[96] they believed that an internally good government ought to bring concord and peace. This is overtly illustrated in the frescoes painted in the Sale dei Nove of the Palazzo Pubblico in Siena by the artist Ambrogio Lorenzetti. The figure of Pax is seated at the centre of the middle section of the middle painting of the cycle, which renders its place at the heart of the government.[97]

Machiavelli, however, like Sallust in ancient Rome, had a different view. While he attributed Rome's success partly to fortune and partly to its exceptional military organisation, he also insisted that the opposition between the senate and the *plebs*, along with the tumults that resulted from it, were crucial to the state's success. All republics, he noted, have two contrasting dispositions, that of the populace and that of the upper class, and 'all legislation favourable to liberty is brought about by the clash between them'.[98] The tumults in Rome did not harm the common good or lead to banishment or violence, but rather created laws and institutions of benefit to the public. 'Hence if tumults led to the creation of the tribunes, tumults deserve the highest praise, since, besides giving the populace a share in the administration, they served as the guardian of Roman liberties.'[99]

It is on this basis that John McCormick has questioned the characterisation of Machiavelli as a republican thinker.[100] McCormick argues that later republican thought owed more to Guicciardini than to Machiavelli, given its concern to guarantee the privileges of elites rather than to facilitate the political participation of the general populace. Guicciardini was more interested than Machiavelli in balancing the protection of liberty with the benefits of the rule of the wise, and was also famously dismissive of Machiavelli's theory of tumults in ancient Rome.[101] In this context, McCormick suggests that Machiavelli is better seen as an anti-elitist critic of republicanism who believed in the role of the people in holding the elites to account, and that he was a democrat rather than a republican. While McCormick's opponents have challenged his use of the label 'democrat' – on the grounds that Machiavelli thought that the populace could not be trusted to govern itself but needed continuous guidance from the elite – they do not fundamentally question McCormick's interpretation of Machiavelli's relationship to the wider history of republican thought.[102] It is certainly true that Machiavelli was sceptical of the capacity of any human beings, be they patricians or plebeians, to act consistently for the public good, without control and restraint. Whether this is sufficient grounds to deny his status as a republican is less clear. While Machiavelli's position may constitute a departure from the conventional position of Renaissance republicans, he was echoing ideas that were expressed in the ancient world by Polybius and that would become a persistent feature of republican thought from the seventeenth century onwards.

Machiavelli may have been at odds with other republicans on the question of internal peace, but his attitude towards external violence was more typically republican than theirs. Yet here, too, it is possible to identify at least two common 'republican' perspectives. Indeed, Machiavelli explicitly articulates the distinction between those republics that are aimed at founding an empire, as Rome did, and those that simply wish to maintain their status quo – like Sparta and Venice.[103] In the former case – that of republics for expansion, as he puts it – a large and well-armed population is required, and both defensive and offensive wars will have to be undertaken. Republics that are content to remain within a narrow territory, on the other hand, can maintain themselves more peacefully; but they have to avoid expanding their territory.[104] Moreover, Machiavelli even seems to link external to internal discord, suggesting that a republic for expansion will have to expect internal commotions precisely because of its need for a large, well-armed population. Nevertheless, this is the model he favours.

Conclusion

Among Renaissance republicans it is possible to identify a variety of positions and points of contention. Most of these writers celebrated self-governing communities and saw them as crucial to the preservation of liberty, both for the state and for the individual. Most of them understood liberty in the neo-Roman sense of not being subject to the will of anyone else. Most of them acknowledged that the maintenance of such communities – and therefore of this form of liberty – was dependent on the practice of virtuous behaviour by rulers and citizens alike. Yet at the same time there was great diversity with regard to the detail. Some drew more on Greek sources, others on Roman. The particular circumstances in which Renaissance writers were living also affected the details of their proposals. The two surviving republics of the fifteenth century, Florence and Venice, were frequently used as models in arguments in favour of a broader or narrower form of republican rule and in favour of expansion or preservation. This period also saw the emergence of a division between pluralist and exclusivist versions of republicanism; some writers started to hint that only non-monarchical government could be republican and that all monarchical government was illegitimate. While virtue among the people was highly regarded, there were fundamental disagreements over whether it could be best inculcated through education and the military training and discipline provided in citizen militias, or whether the process also required the imposition of legal constraints and religious institutions designed to control and shape behaviour.

One indication of Renaissance republicanism's lack of uniformity is the fact that perhaps the best known of all Renaissance republicans, Machiavelli, was at odds with his contemporaries on a number of issues. In particular, he insisted that one of the cardinal virtues deemed crucial by earlier writers, justice, not only was not essential to republican rule but could actually serve to undermine the survival and success of a republican state. Machiavelli also diverged from earlier thinkers in his rejection of internal peace as a crucial aim of republican government and in his pragmatic approach to religion as a useful tool for rulers. Rather than seeing these views as undermining Machiavelli's status as a republican, however, I suggest that they demonstrate that Renaissance republicanism was not a singular and static ideology, but rather one that was polyvalent, dynamic, and constantly changing.

3

The Emergence of Early Modern Republicanism

Introduction

While the Florentine republic came to a decisive end with the final return of the Medici in the early 1530s, its Venetian counterpart survived on through the early modern period, only being overthrown by French revolutionary troops in 1797. It was thus regarded as an ancient republic that survived into the modern world; and, as such, it provided a particularly potent model – and myth – for early modern republican thinkers. Another element of Renaissance republicanism that survived was, of course, the writings of Renaissance thinkers, and in particular those of Machiavelli and Guicciardini, which continued to be printed and translated throughout the sixteenth and seventeenth centuries. Alongside this Renaissance legacy, a number of new European republics emerged after 1500, the experiences of which were also crucial to the development of the concept. As a result, theorists were encouraged to write justifications of particular republican regimes, as well as to offer blueprints for more effective republican institutions. Crucially, these contemporary states were not simply static models to be analysed, understood, and possibly applied in other times and places. They were living examples of republicanism, and that lived experience stimulated reflection.

At least two distinct forms of republican government became prominent during the early modern period. The first was represented by the city-state republics that were seen as heirs to the Italian city-states of the Renaissance. The Venetian state was a crucial example of this phenomenon, but Geneva was another important model, whose influence was shaped by its position, from the mid-sixteenth century on, as a bastion of Protestantism – and, more especially, of Calvinism.

The second form of early modern republicanism was shaped by the increasing importance of republican leagues such as the United Provinces and Switzerland during this period. These states consisted not of a single city but of several, united together as a federation. In this capacity, they developed their own distinctive republican ideologies, which drew not just on the conventional ancient and Renaissance republican models but also on elements of the politics of the gothic tribes that had pre-dated and sometimes overthrown the Roman empire. Tribes such as the Batavians and Helevetians, along with the Saxons, had developed elective monarchies in which the prince was merely the first among equals and participatory assemblies that were regarded by many as the origins of later parliaments and estates.

While the Dutch and the Swiss republics were both leagues, they offered very different republican models. The scholarship on Dutch republicanism has shown it to be a distinctive variant, specifically tailored to local circumstances, with a more positive attitude towards commerce than was often found in classical or English republican writings, and with a moral philosophy of its own. Swiss republicanism has been studied in much less detail, but it, too, offered something distinctive: a form of republicanism that was both highly democratic and specifically adapted to a rural, pastoral state.

Even states that were not completely republican in character could be understood as incorporating important republican elements, and so made a contribution to republican thought during this period. The Polish–Lithuanian state, for example, with its elective monarchy, constituted a curious hybrid between more traditional monarchies and republican regimes, and this made it a useful resource for republican thinking.

This chapter will examine republican theory and practice during the early modern period. It will pay attention in turn to the Venetian, Genevan, Dutch, Swiss, and Polish–Lithuanian states as well as to the contributions made by those models and by various reflections on them to the contemporary understanding of republican government. First, however, it is necessary briefly to survey the extent to which classical sources continued to influence early modern thinking on republicanism.

Classical and Renaissance Influences

The degree to which classical 'republicanism' survived beyond the Renaissance has been the subject of some debate.[1] Various developments rendered the early modern world very different from what had gone before. These included ideological transformations, not least the rise of Christianity and the development of modern scientific practices; economic changes such as the global exploration and trade that had led to the rise of commercial society; and practical innovations, notably the invention of the printing press. Yet classical models, institutions, ideas, and texts remained prominent in Europe throughout the early modern period.[2] Arthur Weststeijn has demonstrated that Polybius's favourable interpretation of ancient Rome was rediscovered and became influential in late sixteenth- and throughout seventeenth-century Europe,[3] while others have emphasised the importance of Greek models.[4] Nor was it only the Spartan, Athenian, and Roman examples that were used by early modern thinkers. Jaap Nieuwstraten has demonstrated the utility of the Achaean League as a confederate model in seventeenth-century Dutch political debate.[5] And the Hebrew republic was an increasingly significant 'classical' model for sixteenth- and seventeenth-century republicans – one that, by the end of the period, was being treated, at least by some authors, in much the same way as more conventional ancient republics.[6]

One means by which early modern Europeans came to an understanding of the ancient republics was a series of cheap Latin political tracts published by the Leiden-based printer Elzevier between the 1620s and 1640s.[7] This series explored the geography, history, and politics of various states, and included among its titles composite works on the Greek and Roman republics (Ubbo Emmius's *Graecorum respublicae* and *Respublica romana*) and Petrus Cunaeus's *De republica hebraeorum*. Alongside the ancient texts, Elzevier also published two accounts of the one older republican city-state that had survived into the modern world: Venice.

Venice

Key accounts of the Venetian republic were offered, in the Elzevier series, by Gasparo Contarini and Donato Giannotti. These highlighted the fact that the Venetian state had remained largely unchanged for centuries, and attributed this longevity to its carefully balanced mixed constitution. The Venetian system combined elements (and therefore the benefits) of democracy, aristocracy, and monarchy, very much as Polybius's theory had advocated. As Contarini declared, this 'cite retayneth a princely souveraigntie, a government of the nobilitie, & a popular authority, so that the formes of them all seeme to be equally ballanced, as it were with a paire of weights'.[8] In fact this 'myth of Venice' dates back even further, to Pietro Paolo Vergerio's *De republica venata* (c. 1400), and even to the account offered by Henry of Rimini a century earlier.[9]

The democratic element of the Venetian constitution was represented by the Grand Council, which was composed of all the male citizens aged twenty-five or over whose family name appeared in the *Libro d'oro* (*Golden Book*), together with a smaller number admitted on the basis of lot from the age of twenty. The Grand Council enjoyed considerable powers: it ratified all laws and chose the magistrates, via a complex system of lot and election. On these grounds, a number of theorists emphasised Venice's democratic character,[10] but the requirement that the names of members appear in the *Libro d'oro* meant that the Grand Council was a largely closed group. Consequently, by 1581 the number of those eligible to sit in the Grand Council was only 1,843 out of a total population of 134,890 – in other words the membership of the Grand Council was just over 1 per cent of the population.[11] Moreover, owing to its large size, the Grand Council could not carry out many tasks itself.

In practice, then, the most powerful component of the regime was the Senate (which represented the aristocratic element in the mixed system). As Contarini said, '[t]he whole manner of the commonwealths government belongeth to the senate'.[12] The Senate had power over foreign affairs, war and peace, taxes and expenditure, legislation, and the appointment of new officers, magistrates, and ambassadors. Sixty senators were elected annually by the Grand Council; and those sixty would then have the power to select a further sixty. In addition, various officers and magistrates also had voting rights within the Senate, producing a full membership of over two hundred. Contarini also presented the Council of Ten, which was elected annually by the Grand Council, as part of the aristocratic element of the constitution.[13] It was designed to protect the safety of the commonwealth, rather like the Spartan ephors.

While most power lay with the Grand Council and the Senate, the Venetians welcomed the idea of a single figurehead at the apex of their system. This was the doge, who was elected for life, via a complex balloting process. Although he could exercise a vote in the Senate and two in the Grand Council apart from functioning as a ceremonial head of state, his powers were firmly under the control of the other elements of the system. Thus it was claimed that 'the Duke of *Venice* is deprived of all meanes, whereby he might abuse his authoritie, or become a tyrant'.[14] He was assisted by six councillors, one from each of the six tribes of the state, who held office for eight months at a time. While the majority of the councillors could act in the doge's absence and without his agreement, he could act only if at least four of them were present. When it came to major issues, he was also required to involve the College of Sages, a committee made up of sixteen members of the Senate chosen for a six-month period. Moreover, at the election of each doge, his powers were assessed and could be increased or decreased by a committee of the Grand Council. In times of emergency it would not be the doge who would assume special powers, but rather the Council of Ten.

The Venetian constitution was seen to have secured stability by removing internal sources of division and corruption, particularly those arising from the weaknesses of human character. Measures were taken to ensure that no individual or group held too much power. The Doge held his position for life, but this was tempered by the complex and careful procedure by which he was chosen and the severe restraints upon his power. Membership of the Grand Council was also for life and, of course, hereditary, but the most powerful offices within the state – membership of the Senate and most committee and magisterial positions – operated on the basis of either full or partial rotation of office. In addition, much care was taken to avoid faction, bribery, and corruption in elections, through the use of lot and a secret ballot.

Another distinctive aspect of the Venetian republic, and one that marked it off from Sparta, the ancient republic with which it was most commonly associated, was its emphasis on wealth and trade. William Bouwsma suggested that, owing to the republic's status as a trading nation, wealth was more important within it than lineage.[15] Machiavelli had criticised Venice as a state designed for preservation rather than expansion, Rome being the key contrast; but Weststeijn offers a different analysis, arguing that Venice participated in expansion via trade and commerce, whereas Rome did so by military might.[16]

One final important feature of the Venetian state was its independent attitude towards religion. As Bouwsma explains, '[j]ust as Venice insisted on her freedom from the emperor in temporal affairs, so she insisted – almost as firmly – on her freedom from the pope in the affairs of the church'.[17] Thus the church and the clergy were subject to state government to a much greater degree than was usual in Catholic countries at the time. The link between church and state was even more fundamental in another key city-state republic of the early modern period: Geneva.

Geneva

Geneva gained its independence in 1536, having been one of a number of prince bishoprics that had been loosely attached to powerful neighbours, in this case Savoy.[18] The Savoyards did not give up their claim easily and in 1602 Charles Emmanuel, son of the duke of Savoy, launched a surprise attack on the city at night, during which over a thousand troops used ladders to scale the city walls. The alarm was raised and the invaders repulsed, which resulted in the deaths of sixteen Genevans and two hundred Savoyards. The Escalade, as the surprise attack became known (with reference to the military technique of scaling city walls with ladders), continues to be celebrated every year on the weekend closest to 11 December. Children particularly enjoy the symbolic smashing of a chocolate cooking pot, which commemorates the story of one woman in the city who was cooking soup when she noticed the attackers below and poured the boiling liquid down on top of them. It is said that the noise this generated awakened the entire city and was crucial to the victory. Geneva survived as a separate city-state republic until 1798, when it was invaded and then annexed by French revolutionary forces. In the Treaty of Vienna of 1815, Geneva was made part of the federal republic of Switzerland. Its survival as a city-state republic during the early modern period owed much to the attitudes of its neighbours and to the fact that its independence suited their interests.[19]

While Geneva was not a theocracy, as political power was vested in laymen rather than ministers, religion was as important as republicanism to the Genevan sense of identity. The city's status as a Protestant state in the shadows of Catholic France was significant, and its association with the Protestant theologian and statesman Jean Calvin (1509–64) did much to shape its structure and purpose, as well as being seen as crucial to its survival. Calvin came to Geneva as a French refugee and quickly became involved in the leadership of the city, while writing there the first edition of his *Institutes of the Christian Religion* in 1536. This was his magnum opus, which he continuously revised throughout his life. Initially not everyone in Geneva agreed with Calvin's views, and in April 1538 the city council exiled him for being too rigid. After three years in Strasbourg he was called back to Geneva in 1541 and issued the *Ecclesiastical*

Ordinances of the Church of Geneva, a sort of constitution that set out both the foundational rules and organisation of the reformed church and its relations with the political authorities of the city. Apart from distinguishing four types of church ministry (pastors, doctors, elders, and deacons), the *Ordinances* also set out the terms of two key institutions: the company of pastors, which watched over the teachings of the pastors and admitted new members, and the consistory, which was responsible for preserving doctrinal and moral purity. Calvin was also keen to establish which powers belonged to the church and which to the city, excommunication (which he understood as a religious rather than a civil power) proving particularly contentious. The consistory sought to promote Calvin's version of the reformed faith, but was restricted by the fact that it was not a court and had no powers of judicial punishment.

Geneva's political system was equally complex. The population was divided into four distinct groups: citizens, bourgeois, *habitants*, and *natifs*. Citizens had to have been born in the city. They had a right to membership of the General Council and could hold higher offices within the city, but in order to exercise these rights they increasingly had to be wealthy, given the high tax requirements involved. The bourgeois, immigrants to the city who had paid for rights of citizenship, were also admitted to the General Council, but were not eligible for higher office. Their children, if born in Geneva, were entitled to full citizenship. *Habitants* ('dwellers') were those immigrants who had not paid for citizenship rights and hence could not participate in the political life of the city. Their children were known as *natifs* ('natives') and, in addition to being deprived of political rights, they could not exercise certain professions. In 1760 one *natif* talked about feeling like 'a sort of serf' in his own city.[20]

The city operated on the basis of a mixed system of government, with a strongly aristocratic flavour to it. There was no single figure at the top. The highest offices were those of four syndics, who represented the different quarters of the city and were elected by the General Council. That council formed the base of a pyramid of councils. It was composed of citizens and of bourgeois – the male heads of households who were over twenty-five years of age. Its functions included enacting legislation, electing officers, and voting on taxation; and, at least to begin with, this was the sovereign body within the state. Above it was the Great Council or the Two Hundred, which was controlled by a handful of families. Its powers included hearing appeals against sentences, granting pardons, and overseeing coinage. Originally there was also a Council of Sixty, but it soon lost significance. Day-to-day governance was undertaken by the Small Council or the Twenty-Five, a body that was elected out of the Two Hundred and met regularly.

Over the course of the sixteenth and seventeenth centuries, this system adapted in various ways to the circumstances that arose. In particular, there was a definite shift in the direction of oligarchy. Initially refugees had been welcomed and their participation in citizenship through the purchase of bourgeois status encouraged but, with the increasing persecution of Protestants in Louis XIV's France from the 1680s on, Geneva was confronted with more refugees than it could easily accommodate. In the late part of that decade it was sometimes receiving as many as 1,000 refugees a week;[21] thus citizenship became more closed, and the price of entry rose significantly. As a result, the gulf between citizens and bourgeois on the one hand, *habitants* and *natifs* on the other increased too. At the same time, different trends in family size meant that those who were not able to exercise political rights came to outnumber those who were. Also, from as early as the 1570s, more power was allowed to pass from the General Council to the smaller councils. The Great Council became the main seat of power, while the Small Council's control over day-to-day government ensured its significance.

In addition to its oligarchical flavour, Genevan republicanism was characterised by a strict sense of morality, injected by Calvinism. At the same time commerce was viewed as crucial to the state's economic and political survival and therefore also coloured its republicanism. These same characteristics were prominent within Dutch republicanism.

The United Provinces

The Dutch Revolt of the 1580s, the first stadtholderless period between 1650 and 1672, and the Dutch Patriot reform movement of the 1770s and 1780s, all contributed to the development of Dutch republicanism. Yet Dutch theorists were not operating in national isolation. Eco Haitsma Mulier has demonstrated the important impact that Venice exercised on Dutch thought, and Wyger Velema has shown that the Dutch drew not just on ancient and Renaissance republicanism, but also on Huguenot theories of resistance.[22]

In 1555 Philip II of Spain became the new sovereign of the Low Countries. He was an unpopular ruler and opposition blossomed into revolt in the 1580s; these events culminated in the formal renunciation of Philip in the Act of Abjuration of 1581, which in turn led to a long period of war. The revolt reinforced the long-standing Dutch commitment to liberty.[23] The Grand Privilege of 1477 had secured the centrality of self-governing independence to Dutch political thought and practice. Liberty was guaranteed by privileges, and those privileges were in turn protected by the states. Philip II's rule was seen as a threat to this system, and so the right to resist tyrannical rule was used to justify the revolt. The anonymous pamphlet *Political Education* of 1582 drew on ancient republican ideas, particularly those of Cicero, in order to make this argument. It insisted that the purpose of government is to ensure the welfare and prosperity of the community, and that a prince should act with justice in the interests of that community. Therefore a prince who simply served his own interests could be deemed a tyrant and, as Cicero had made clear, tyrants should be dethroned.[24] The work also insisted that, despite his position, a prince ought to remain subject to the law rather than placing himself above it.[25]

The Dutch also developed the Batavian myth so as to bolster and support the idea of Dutch liberty. This myth presented the Dutch as descendants of the Germanic Batavian tribe, which was renowned for its independence, valour, and simplicity. Circulating from the fifteenth century, the myth was developed in the seventeenth by Hugo Grotius, who declared that Batavians were superior to both Athenians and Romans and had defended their liberty without falling prey to 'the lust for domination that was connected with the pursuit of liberty'.[26]

While up to that point most republicans had tended to be pluralistic about constitutional form, Dutch republicanism firmly rejected monarchical rule from an early stage, though the position of stadtholder ensured that in practice some ambiguity remained. The death of William II in November 1650 marked the beginning of the first stadtholderless period. The ruler's son, William III, was born a week after his father's death; hence he was in no position to rule, and the power that William II had exerted in his conflict with the state of Holland earlier that year made people wary of the role. This period lasted until 1672, when William III restored the political power of the House of Orange, and produced some of the most influential works of Dutch republicanism, not least in the writings of the brothers Johann and Pieter de la Court and of Baruch Spinoza. Opponents of the stadtholder tended to equate this position with monarchy, in order to reject it. His supporters, on the other hand, presented him not as a monarch but as a crucial element in a mixed republican system.

Anti-monarchism was particularly strong in the works of the de la Court brothers. The two brothers adopted a Hobbesian vision of the state of nature, but insisted that the community would not entrust its safety and well-being to a single individual. Consequently, monarchy could have been instituted only through violence or fraud. They also enunciated all the disadvantages of monarchical rule, from its tendency to bankrupt the nation and the problem of succession to its inclination towards pursuing offensive wars. The de la Court brothers used these arguments to try to convince the Dutch not to reinstate the stadtholder. The de la Court brothers distinguished themselves also by being strongly critical of ancient republican models. This was due in part to their preference for a commercial over an agrarian economy and to their belief that commerce had not been fully developed in the ancient world.[27] Unlike those who, being influenced by the Spartan model, saw commerce as a potential threat to civic virtue, the brothers were more optimistic, noting its centrality to the Dutch economy. Owing to the emphasis on concord and commerce at the expense of warfare, Eco Haitsma Mulier, using Machiavelli's terminology, characterised the Dutch republic as a state for preservation rather than a state for increase. More recently, however, Arthur Weststeijn has challenged this view, suggesting that the Dutch were intent on expansion but, like the Venetians, they used industry and commerce rather than the more conventional method of war in order to achieve this goal.[28]

Despite embracing commerce, the Dutch did express concerns about morality and the threat of corruption. The de la Court brothers' understanding of human nature was strongly influenced by the ideas of René Descartes and, in particular, by the notion that humans are dominated by strong passions. Although they accepted that passions could be tamed through reason, virtue, and education, they did not think that passions could be completely controlled, and therefore they rejected any form of government that relied on the political virtue of the citizens or rulers in order to function. Instead, they insisted that constitutional orders and self-interest needed to be used if the common good was to be promoted. On this point they had much in common with Spinoza, who also insisted on the important role that state institutions could play in controlling the passions.

The Swiss Federation

The Swiss model has tended to play a less important role in our thought about the early modern republics than the Venetian, Genevan and Dutch models. Thomas Maissen's work does, however, show that, particularly after the Peace of Westphalia in 1648, the

Swiss began to see themselves as republicans and to look to contemporary and ancient republics for inspiration.[29]

The Roman republic was celebrated in the house of Johann Carl Balthasar in an elaborate ceiling fresco that was completed around 1690. It depicted the heroes of the Roman republic together with personifications of Rome, Venice, the United Provinces, and the Swiss, with the motto 'Rome teaches the wonderful liberty of the republic'.[30] The Roman hero Lucius Junius Brutus, who had been responsible for driving the Tarquins out of Rome, also assumed particular importance for the Swiss, being likened to William Tell and to local heroes such as Rudolf Bruni, Zurich's founding father. The town hall in Zurich sported busts of various ancient Greek and Roman heroes, including one of Brutus, as a way of reminding magistrates to put republican virtues before other concerns.[31] Around the same time, the Swiss adopted the ancient tribe of the Helvetians as their ancestors, solidifying a sense of themselves as one people with firm classical roots. This offered a parallel to the Dutch Batavian myth.

Yet, as Maissen notes, the Swiss engagement with past republican concepts and heroes actually served to differentiate Swiss republicanism from other versions: 'the references to the classical past eventually helped the Swiss to become something that neither Rome nor the Confederation had ever been: a democratic nation-state'.[32] This also constrained the extent to which other early modern republicans drew on the Swiss model: while the Dutch recognised certain similarities between themselves and the Swiss, not least because both were confederations and placed great emphasis on participation, in general the Dutch saw the Swiss model as too democratic and not well suited to the demographics, economics, and worldly ambitions of the Dutch.

Poland–Lithuania

Although it was an elective monarchy throughout the early modern period, the Polish–Lithuanian state was known as the Republic of Two Nations, and the citizen body (made up of the nobility) viewed it in those terms. The author of *Libera respublica* of 1606 set that state firmly in the tradition of ancient republics:

> And here is the proper form of that Republic which we call free and ... of which there have only been three in the world: Rome ... from which it passed to the Venetians, where it has lasted until our own time. Our ancestors *ad normam* that of Venice have set up the third for us.[33]

Polybius's theory of mixed government provides a useful tool for understanding the Polish state as a republic. From the late sixteenth century the government comprised three estates: the king, the senate, and the House of Nuncios – the latter retaining most of the power.[34] As several commentators have emphasised, freedom was in many ways the crucial concept for the Polish nobility – it was much more important than who was or was not head of state – and the mixed system was seen as the best means of protecting it.[35]

The Polish nobility's understanding of liberty included both a civil and a political element. It was partly about the protection of basic rights and privileges. The civil liberties of the nobility dated back to 1430, when, under the principle *Neminem captivabimus nisi iure victum* ('We will not arrest anyone without a court verdict'), it was decreed that no member of the nobility could be imprisoned unless a judicial sentence had been passed against him or her. A further reform followed in 1578, when judicial power was taken away from the king and placed under tribunals that consisted of judges elected by the nobility.[36] It was also important to members of the nobility that they could participate in the political life of the state. The right to engage freely in political debates had long been seen as part of the right and duty of a good citizen, and was acknowledged as crucial to the preservation of liberty.[37] As one sixteenth-century political expert put it,

> great is that public liberty, since my lord does not govern me as he likes or as he sees fit, nor does any person without credit, but it is my brother who does ... and, as a free man, I prefer to put up with what my brother, raised alongside me, himself sanctions.[38]

The same idea was still being endorsed in the *Katechizm narodowy* of 1791: 'Political liberty is the state of the nation which prescribes laws for itself.'[39]

Republican virtue also played an important role in the Republic of Two Nations. The Polish nobility was familiar with the works of ancient authors such as Livy, Sallust, and Cicero and emphasised the importance of prioritising the public good and of cultivating civic virtues and virtuous citizens.[40] But, from the seventeenth century on, liberty and equality began to be seen as more crucial to the survival of the state than civic virtues, and tensions also arose around the position of the king within the state.

As part of its political role, the nobility had enjoyed the right to elect the king ever since 1573.[41] Royal power was limited in other ways too. The king was not considered to be the source of the law, but was rather bound by the laws of the country that were guaranteed by the articles of agreement – *pacta conventa*. If the king broke that agreement, the citizens would have the right to rise up against him.[42] In this respect the Poles saw their system as being distinct from that of other European monarchies. By electing their kings and maintaining a right of resistance against them, they protected the nation from the threats such a figure could pose.[43] Yet, as time wore on, the king increasingly came to be seen as a potential threat to liberty.

Conclusion

Early modern republics were diverse and fluid, both in terms of constitutional form and in the values they sought to promote and develop. Alongside city-state republics such as Venice and Geneva, this period witnessed the rise of successful federal republics in the United Provinces and Switzerland. By drawing together multiple cities, these republics covered a wider territory, and therefore a larger citizen body, than their counterparts that were focused on a single urban area. The same was true of elective monarchies like Poland–Lithuania.

The understanding of the Polish–Lithuanian state as a kind of republic was possible because many in early modern Europe remained committed to the Ciceronian ideal of *res publica*, which did not necessarily exclude the presence of a single figurehead. The more exclusivist understanding was rapidly gaining ground, however, and anti-monarchical sentiment ran particularly deep in the Dutch republic from the sixteenth century onwards.

Another contrast that continued to prove significant was between those who accepted the need for aristocratic leadership of the republic and those who were more inclined to emphasise the importance of democratic participation. A contrast here can be drawn between Venice, Geneva, the United Provinces, and Poland–Lithuania – all of which were characterised at least at certain points as aristocratic republics – and the more democratic character of the Swiss confederation. Yet this was a conflict that occurred *within* as much as *between* states, as oligarchs and democrats opposed each other at various times in the United Provinces, Geneva, and Switzerland.

Diversity is also in evidence with regard to attitudes towards commerce, wealth, and luxury. The Venetian and Dutch republics, and to a lesser extent Geneva, all relied on trade and, as a result, were positively disposed towards it. Rather than seeing commerce as a poison that would corrupt the citizens, they presented it instead as providing a welcome alternative to war. In a Swiss context, however, emphasis on simplicity and frugality prevailed. Attitudes to virtue also varied: some continued to insist on the need for virtuous rulers and citizens, while others placed greater emphasis on controlling human behaviour through constitutional mechanisms or by balancing competing interests. Variations also occurred with regard to religion. While this period saw the rise of an association between republicanism and Protestantism, particularly in the Dutch and Genevan contexts, Catholic republics continued to exist and the Dutch and Genevan models differed from each other, not least in their attitude to dissent and in the degree of toleration they were willing to grant.

There is, of course, another important example of an early modern Protestant republic that has not featured in this chapter. Approximately sixty years after the Dutch Revolt, another revolutionary movement shook Europe. On 22 August 1642 Charles I, king of England, Scotland, and Ireland, raised his standard and embarked on war with his Parliament. Just over six years later, on 30 January 1649, Charles I was executed by his subjects, ushering in a short but significant period of republican rule. This English Revolution and the republicanism it generated will be the focus of the next chapter.

4

The English Revolution

Introduction

Mid-seventeenth-century England constitutes a watershed moment in the history of republicanism, for two important reasons. In the first place, May 1649 saw the self-conscious creation of a 'Commonwealth and Free State' in a large nation that had traditionally been ruled monarchically.[1] England in the 1650s witnessed the putting into practice of the kind of republican exclusivism that had first emerged, purely as a theoretical construct, in the Renaissance. Secondly, the build-up to, and aftermath of, the creation of the English Commonwealth produced an outpouring of republican writings. These writings subsequently came to be viewed as a republican canon (many of their authors gained symbolic status) and were reprinted and redeployed at later republican moments in Britain and beyond. Moreover, the English republican canon has itself become the subject of a further outpouring of printed matter, this time by late twentieth and early twenty-first-century scholars. English republicanism has perhaps received more attention than any other part of the general history of republicanism and has sparked the interest not just of intellectual historians but also of those interested in political, cultural, religious, and literary history.[2]

The result of this attention and of this interest, however, is far from providing us with a simple and uncontested vision of English republicanism; they have rather served to complicate our understanding of it and to generate controversy. Although parliament declared England to be a 'Commonwealth and Free State' on 19

May 1649, that declaration was a response to the fact that the king had been tried and executed. Rather than being a product of English republicanism, the founding of the English republic was instead a consequence of the regicide; and this had not come about because of republican fervour. The new republic was not, in any meaningful sense, a constitutional form that had been actively sought by the population. Moreover, it was not even a bold and immediate response to the regicide, but rather a belated last resort; the English were reluctant republicans. Partly because of this, the eleven years of the Interregnum witnessed a range of different regimes. Two written constitutions were produced and implemented during that period, and the composition and organisation of the legislative body changed a number of times. Both election and nomination were experimented with, and both unicameral (single-chamber) and bicameral (double-chamber) systems were implemented.

The relationship between the English republic and English republicanism is also complex. Few English authors wrote in favour of an English republic prior to 1649. Most of what we now think of as the canon of English republican writings was written when England was already a republic (or looked back to a time when it had been one). Just as the decision to establish the republic was a consequence rather than a cause of the regicide, so English republican writings were more a consequence than a cause of the establishment of the republic. Furthermore, relatively few of these works were entirely supportive of the English republic as it existed in the 1650s – in any of its manifestations. Most advocated at least minor improvements, if not major reform.

Furthermore, the wealth of republican writings (and of scholarly work on those writings) has complicated our understanding of what constituted English republicanism and what its key characteristics were. While historians looking back have tended to see the distinction between royalists and republicans as fundamental, that does not appear to be how it was seen at the time. For example, in 1659–60, in a moment of crisis for the English Republic when its supporters ought to have been rallying together, we find them instead arguing among themselves – James Harrington attacking Sir Henry Vane, John Rogers, and Henry Stubbe, while Rogers, Stubbe, and John Milton challenged Harrington's ideas in return.[3] In recent years scholars have come to realise that those searching for the essence of English republicanism – for a single coherent definition of it – search in vain. The original sense of English republicanism as a form of 'classical' republicanism has been largely discredited and divisions among English republicans are widely acknowledged.

Rather 'English republicanism', if it means anything at all, must be used to refer to a spectrum of competing discourses that had some elements in common but differed fundamentally in other respects.

This chapter will attempt to sketch out this complex picture. It will begin by tracing the establishment of the English republic, the controversy surrounding its institution, the various regimes that it engendered, and its relationship with English republican writings. In the second half of the chapter attention will be paid to the various figures who wrote the works that make up what is now regarded as the English republican canon. The spectrum of views constituting English republicanism will be set out, and some of the debates that occurred among its advocates will be explored.

The Establishment of the English Republic

Far from being a bold and deliberate move on the part of the victorious parliamentarians and their New Model Army of 1645, the English republic was established almost by default, and from the outset its grounds for legitimacy were extremely thin. A breakdown in relations between King Charles I and his parliament had brought civil war between 1642 and 1646. After the cessation of hostilities, the defeated king was held in captivity, first being detained by the Scots, to whom he had surrendered, and then, from early 1647 on, being under parliamentary control. Despite parliament's resounding victory, few on that side were intent on replacing Charles I, let alone the monarchy. What they sought was rather a negotiated settlement that would see a shift in power from king to parliament and would secure certain religious guarantees. However, a series of failed peace treaties, some brokered by parliament, others by the army, together with what is known as 'the king's Engagement' – an agreement with the Scots signed in 1648 – and the subsequent revival of fighting in the Second Civil War made the prospect of reaching a settlement acceptable to all the sides increasingly unlikely. Parliament's response was to offer greater concessions, in a bid simply to bring the conflict to a close; and on 15 November the House of Commons voted to move forward with the fruits of the latest negotiations – the Newport Treaty. The army, however, felt that parliament was allowing the king to dictate terms and, in response, it issued *A Remonstrance of General Fairfax and the Council of Officers*, which called for, and justified, an end to negotiations with Charles I and proposed that he be brought to trial as an enemy of the people. Parliament refused to discuss the *Remonstrance* and instead pushed forward with the treaty. The army responded by purging the parliament of those members who were considered to be in favour of coming to a settlement with the king. Pride's Purge, on 6 December 1648, saw troops at Westminster arresting some MPs and physically preventing others from entering the Chamber. By the end of the day, forty-five MPs had been arrested and one hundred and eighty-six excluded from the House of Commons. A further eighty-six left in protest over the next few days, leaving a 'Rump' of around two hundred sitting in the House.

In recent years there has been some debate among historians as to whether the execution of Charles I was the outcome of a deliberate plot originating in the army, or whether it was actually more of an unintended consequence of the actions taken by each side. Sean Kelsey put forward the controversial argument that, far from being a kangaroo court designed to give a thin veil of legitimacy to the regicide, the trial of Charles I was actually a final and extended attempt at a negotiated settlement that went badly wrong only because Charles I refused to play the game and would not plead.[4] Kelsey's argument, though welcomed and accepted by some historians, was firmly rebuffed by others. In particular, Clive Holmes challenged Kelsey's reading of various pieces of evidence, insisting that the charge against the king was clear and that there was little room for anything but a guilty verdict. Holmes suggests that the spinning out of the trial was less about giving the king full opportunity to plead, as Kelsey claimed, than about ensuring that his alleged misdemeanours were given a full and public exposition.[5]

While the question of whether the regicide was intended or not may be a genuine matter for debate, there is more consensus on the idea that the regicide did not inevitably lead to the creation of a republic – let alone the fact that no one had a clear plan for the kind of republic that should be established. The chronology of early 1649 provides strong evidence that an English republic was by no means a carefully planned outcome of the events of early January and that other options were still being considered well into the spring. Charles was executed on 30 January, yet it was almost two months later, on 17 March, that '[t]he Act Abolishing the Office of King' was finally passed.[6] In fact it was passed at this point only because parliament was concerned about the threat of revenge from royalists on the continent and felt it necessary to clarify the existing situation. Moreover, even though the Commons had already been purged, many of those who remained absented themselves from the debate and the Act was passed by a very thin house. Nonetheless the wording of the Act reads as though it was designed to compensate for the shaky support it received, the office of king being deemed 'dangerous and burdensome to the people of England'.[7] Abolishing the monarchy in this way effectively created a republic by default; but that is, still, rather different from positively choosing to establish such a regime. It was a further two months before 'An Act Declaring England to Be a Commonwealth' was finally passed.[8] Moreover, that document is extremely short, just over one hundred words, and has no preamble, which according to the historian Blair Worden indicates that there was disagreement among MPs.[9]

Yet, despite its brevity, the Act did embody several key elements of republican ideology. First, it embraced the idea of popular sovereignty, albeit exercised via parliament, by declaring that England and its territories would henceforth be governed 'by the supreme authority of this nation, the representatives of the people in Parliament, and by such as they shall appoint and constitute as officers and ministers under them'.[10] Secondly, the etymology of the terms 'republic' or 'commonwealth' was invoked in the statement that government would be carried out 'for the good of the people'. Finally, the Act affirmed that this government would operate 'without any King or House of Lords'. The positioning of this clause right at the end, and the suggestion that it was an additional feature of this particular 'Commonwealth and Free State' rather than an inherent feature of all such states, reminds us that, while exclusivist republicanism may have begun to take hold by that time, it was by no means the only understanding of the concept – or even an unquestionable one.

Once again, far from bringing an immediate and deliberate change in the regime, 'An Act Declaring England to be a Commonwealth' was simply used to justify the existing arrangement, namely the rule of the Rump of the Long Parliament (those who had not been permanently excluded during Pride's Purge). Under this system, sovereign power lay in a unicameral parliament consisting of just over two hundred MPs. A council of state was established on 7 February to assist with executive tasks, but it was very much an agent of the Rump rather than a distinct body. Thirty-one of its forty-one members were sitting MPs, each sitting for just one year.

The Rump faced many difficulties during its period of rule. It had to settle a nation torn apart by civil war; it had a huge financial bill to settle, not least with regard to the army, which had chalked up massive arrears and was also still working to establish control over Scotland and Ireland; and it had to try to establish itself as a legitimate ruling body. This last task was particularly difficult given the way in which the Rump had come into existence, its role in the king's trial and execution, and its dependence on the army.

The Rump also had to create a whole new iconography for the state, one that should replace the traditional regal iconography. New coins had to be minted, new ceremonial state paraphernalia had to be produced – and, of course, all this needed to be done very quickly in order for the state to be able to function effectively. For this reason, it is perhaps not surprising that, as Sean Kelsey has argued, much of the new iconography was remarkably conservative – a matter of recasting old models (in some cases just by removing the crown) and reinventing traditional pomp rather than inventing completely new forms.[11] Ultimately, Kelsey claims, it did not display an ideology of kingless republicanism as much as it revealed the 'gentry republic' that operated beneath the monarchy.

The seal of the commonwealth produced in 1649 is a good illustration of the need to invent new iconography. In the first place, the seal had to be produced quickly, as it was required in order for the Rump's decisions to be disseminated in official form. Consequently, the design had already been thought out by 9 January 1649, just a day after the preliminaries for the king's trial had begun, and Thomas Simon was paid to produce it on 26 January, before the king had been executed. This ensured that it was ready for use just a week after the regicide.

The design of the seal was also significant. One side depicted a map of the British Isles (though without Scotland, which was not yet under the Rump's control). The other was more problematic. A royal seal would traditionally show the monarch's head. In its place, the seal of the commonwealth shows the House of Commons in session – the sovereign parliament in place of the sovereign monarch. Around the edge were printed the words 'In the First Yeare of Freedome by God's Blessing Restored 1648'. At first sight, this statement is arresting: it seems to prefigure Year 1 in the French revolutionary calendar. There is perhaps something in this, since the idea did catch on more broadly. A number of books published in 1649 were dated Year 1 of Liberty. This dating was still being used by some a decade later. At the end of the preface to his 1659 work *Diapoliteia*, the Fifth Monarchist and republican sympathiser John Rogers noted that the work was written from his house in Aldersgate Street on 14 July 1659, or '14. Of the 5. Month (called July) 1659 in the 1. Year of our second Deliverance or Return to the Liberty of a Free-State'.[12] This revealed Rogers' preference for the Rump and his opposition to the Protectorate. However, this practice is not quite as revolutionary as it might seem. At this time there were two conventional systems of dating in operation. Anno Domini was, of course, one, but events would also – and often – be dated according to the year of the reign in which they occurred, for example 'in the thirteenth year of the reign of our sovereign lord Charles I'. Without a single ruler in 1649, this was no longer an option, and so 'the first year of freedom' provided an obvious alternative.

Despite the best efforts of the Rump to establish its legitimacy and create a convincing iconography, its rule did not last long. On 20 April 1653, Oliver Cromwell entered the chamber and forcibly closed the sitting. In its place, in an attempt to impose godly rule, he instituted the nominated assembly. This was a body of 140 men (though it was modelled on the smaller Jewish Sanhedrin), all chosen on account of their reputation for godliness. Despite the method of selection and Cromwell's insistence that this body was not a parliament, it soon became known as 'the Barebones' Parliament'; the name carried a reference to Praise-God Barbon, a London merchant and member of an independent congregation who was deemed to epitomise its membership. Its reign was short. It first met on 4 July 1653 and abdicated less than six months later. It was replaced by the Protectorate, which was founded on the first written constitution in English history, 'The Instrument of Government'.[13] Despite the originality of having a 'protector' rather than a monarch at the helm, the basic structure of this regime was more conventional than that of its two predecessors. Executive power now lay with the Lord Protector and his council of thirteen to twenty-one members, which was similar to the old Privy Council. Legislative power was held by the Lord Protector and parliament together, parliament being involved in all decisions except those to do with raising money in times of emergencies. Parliament's unicameral structure was maintained; and the Protectorship was given to Cromwell for life rather than being an hereditary office, but echoes of the old mixed monarchy were evident. The regime moved even closer to that model in 1657, when 'The Instrument of Government' was replaced by a new constitution, 'The Humble Petition and Advice'.[14] Under this document, the main components of the government were again the Protector, the council, and parliament, but the 'Other House' (a body of forty to seventy members who were to be nominated by Cromwell and approved by the Commons) was added to parliament, thereby re-establishing a bicameral system. Cromwell was given the right to appoint his successor – and it was in the end his son Richard who succeeded him. At one point the regime nearly came even closer to monarchy, since the original proposition from parliament was that Cromwell assume the crown. After some deliberation he rejected that aspect of the proposal (at least partly, no doubt, because of opposition within the army), but he has nonetheless been described by some as a king in all but name. The final year of the Interregnum was particularly chaotic institutionally: 1659 saw the return of the Rump Parliament not once but twice, as well as a brief period of direct army rule.

The Varieties of English Republicanism, I: Defences of the Regicide

It was against this background of shifting constitutional architecture that many of the works of the English republican canon were written. A small number of works were aimed at justifying or providing support for the regicide and for the republican government that emerged out of it. This was the case with several of Milton's writings, including *The Tenure of Kings and Magistrates* and *The Defence of the People of England*, and with Marchamont Nedham's *The Case of the Commonwealth of England, Stated*.

Milton, *The Tenure of Kings and Magistrates*

Within two weeks of the regicide, Milton published *The Tenure of Kings and Magistrates*, designed as a vindication of that act. The work attacked those Presbyterians who had opposed the king during the Civil War, but who now condemned Charles's execution. Jean Calvin had argued that, while inferior magistrates had a right of resistance against tyrannical rule, private persons did not. On this basis, the Presbyterians insisted that the army was merely a collection of private persons, thereby making its exercise of resistance unlawful. Milton responded that, since parliament as the inferior magistrate had not deposed and punished Charles, the army had the right to do so. The subtitle of the work made this clear: *The Tenure of Kings and Magistrates: Proving, That it is Lawfull, and hath been held so through all Ages, for any, who have the Power, to call to account a Tyrant, or wicked KING, and after due conviction, to depose, and put him to death; if the ordinary MAGISTRATE have neglected, or deny'd to doe it. And that they, who of late so much blame Deposing, are the Men that did it themselves.* The work was structured as a classical oration designed to persuade the reader of the truth of the argument that, if kings behave tyrannically, they 'may bee' 'lawfully depos'd and punish'd'.[15]

Milton grounded his argument in an account of the origins of government, which was designed to show that ultimate power lay with the people. Governments were instituted in the light of the Fall, he explained, for joint defence, powers being given to one or a few, but as deputies, not as masters. Over time it became clear that those rulers could not be trusted to behave dutifully towards the public good, so they had to be constrained by laws, counsellors, parliaments, and oaths, and that, 'if the King or Magistrate prov'd unfaithfull to his trust, the people would be disingag'd'.[16] Milton likened the covenant between kings and their subjects to all other covenants and considered kings to be subject to the laws in the same way as the others were.[17]

Milton had no doubt that Charles was guilty of tyranny; he defined a tyrant as one who 'regarding neither Law nor the common good, reigns onely for himself and his faction'.[18] But he went further, claiming that, since the king holds his authority from the people, they could depose him even if he was not behaving tyrannically: 'then may the people as oft as they shall judge it for the best, either choose him or reject him, retaine him or depose him though no Tyrant, meerly by the liberty and right of free born Men, to be govern'd as seems to them best'.[19] Without the right to abolish any supreme or subordinate governor, Milton asserted, the nation would be

> under tyranny and servitude; as wanting that power, which is the root and sourse of all liberty, to dispose and *oeconomize* in the Land which God hath giv'n them, as Maisters of Family in thir own house and free inheritance. Without which natural and essential power of a free Nation, though bearing high thir heads, they can in due esteem be thought no better than slaves and vassals born, in the tenure and occupation of another inheriting Lord. Whose government, though not illegal, or intolerable, hangs over them as a Lordly scourge, not as a free government.[20]

Milton, *Eikonoklastēs*, and *Pro populo anglicano defensio*

A month after the publication of *The Tenure*, Milton was appointed to an official position in the fledgling republic: the Council of State gave him the post of Secretary for Foreign Tongues. This involved his handling of diplomatic correspondence, but also led to his becoming a propagandist on behalf of the state, through works such as *Eikonoklastēs* and *Pro populo anglicano defensio*.

Eikonoklastēs (*The Image Breaker*) was the official refutation of *Eikōn basilikē* (*Royal Portrait*), an ingenious and innovative text published in the immediate aftermath of the regicide and said to be based on notes written by Charles while he was in prison. The *Eikōn*, which was probably largely the work of John Gauden, sought through a variety of visual and narrative techniques to turn Charles from failed monarch into a martyr, and the regicide from a royalist disaster to a more enduring victory.[21] Despite Milton's literary and poetical skills, his response failed to meet the challenge set by the royalist text; it was a rather pedestrian refutation, which failed to ignite the passions of its readers in the way that the *Eikōn basilikē* had done.[22]

Pro populo anglicano defensio (*Defence of the People of England*) also responded to a work that supported Charles I: *Defensio regia pro Carlo I* (*Defence of the Reign of Charles I*), written by the French scholar Claude Saumaise. Milton offered a line-by-line refutation of Saumaise's argument, deploying a wide range of evidence in the process – passages from the Old and New Testaments, the authority of the church fathers, ancient history and authorities, and English history, as well as the testimony of legal scholars – in order

> to defend the excellent deeds of my fellow countrymen against the mad and most spiteful rage of this raving sophist both at home and abroad, and to assert the common right of the people against the unjust domination of kings, not indeed out of hatred of kings, but of tyrants.[23]

As this quotation would suggest, Milton also made *ad hominem* attacks on Saumaise, criticising his linguistic skills, his ignorance – as a foreigner – of English practice, and inconsistencies both within *Defensio regia* and between it and his earlier works. As in *Tenure*, Milton emphasised that ultimate power lay with the people and that the king was appointed for their safety and security rather than the other way around.[24] On this basis he rejected Saumaise's reiterations that the king was above the law and kept pointing to the legality of the process whereby the English had judged their king and condemned him to death.[25]

While Milton was harsh in his opposition to tyrants and keen to defend the ultimate sovereignty of the people, his endorsement of an explicitly republican form of government in these works from the early 1650s is equivocal. For example, he uses biblical evidence to suggest that God favoured commonwealth government:

> God has decided then that the form of a commonwealth is more perfect than that of a monarchy as human conditions go, and of greater benefit to his own people: since he himself set up this form of government. He granted a monarchy only later at their request and then not willingly.[26]

According to Eric Nelson, Milton's interpretation of I Samuel 8 in the *Defence* constitutes the first presentation of an explicitly exclusivist commitment to republican government coming from an

Englishman.[27] Yet elsewhere in this text Milton seems to suggest that a king, if properly constrained, could be equally acceptable: 'If those kings who are undecided about this matter will listen to me and let themselves be bounded by the laws, then instead of the uncertain, weak and violent power which they now possess, full of cares and fears, they will preserve for themselves a completely stable, peaceful and long-lasting one'.[28] Given this, it is really only in *The Readie and Easie Way to Establish a Free Commonwealth* of 1660 that Milton stated an uncompromising exclusivist republican position: 'I doubt not but all ingenuous and knowing men will easily agree with me, that a free Commonwealth without single person or house of lords, is by far the best government if it can be had.'[29]

Nedham, *The Case of the Commonwealth of England, Stated*

Nedham's *The Case of the Commonwealth of England, Stated* appeared in early May 1650. Its aim, like that of Milton's *Tenure*, was clearly stated on the title page. The work was designed to demonstrate '[t]he *Equity*, *Utility*, and *Necessity* of a Submission to the Present GOVERNMENT' and to refute the claims of those groups who opposed the Rump.

Nedham had had a chequered career. He had worked primarily as a journalist during the 1640s, writing from 1643 on behalf of Parliament in *Mercurius Britannicus* before he faced imprisonment for his writings and switched sides. In June 1647 he published *The Case of the Kingdom, Stated*, which led to his employment on the royalist newspaper *Mercurius Pragmaticus* later that year. After further imprisonment in 1649 he took the Engagement Oath and began writing *The Case of the Commonwealth of England, Stated*. The Engagement Oath was a loyalty oath designed to enforce commitment to the new and precarious republic. It was launched in the immediate aftermath of the regicide, but initially was to be taken only by leading public officials. However, from October 1649 it was extended to members of the armed forces and to those involved in local and national politics and in education, and in February 1650 it was extended once again to include all adult males. This prompted much debate, as well as the publication of a number of texts – by figures such as Francis Rous, Anthony Ascham and Thomas Hobbes – designed to demonstrate to the nation's citizens the legitimacy and potential benefits of taking the Engagement Oath.[30]

Whereas Milton, in *Tenure*, had sought to assert the right of the people to revolt against Charles I, Nedham's text had much more in common with these de facto theorists who, rather than engaging with the rights or wrongs of the regicide, simply urged the population to take the Engagement Oath and accept the new status quo. Nedham's aim of convincing a sceptical public was reflected in his strategy of dividing his work into two and addressing the first part to 'the conscientious man' and the second to 'the worldling'. The former focused on what was just and equitable, while the latter outlined the inconveniences and dangers that would follow from opposing the settlement. Nedham's final chapter, however, supplemented this de facto justification with a more positive endorsement of the new regime.

Nedham began by acknowledging the constant tendency of governments to degenerate and shift. 'Hence it comes to pass that the best established and mightiest governments of the world have been but temporary.'[31] On this basis, the recent collapse of the English monarchy should not come as any great surprise, and it would be more profitable to work with this divine judgement than to struggle against it. Like Milton in *Tenure*, Nedham then turned to the origins of government, but offered a very different and much cruder analysis. Power did not originally lie with the people, as Milton had argued, but was derived from the rule of fathers over their families. Population expansion rendered this insufficient: 'there was need of someone more potent than the rest that might restrain them by force'.[32] Consequently, the power of the sword brought the establishment of 'the first monarchy and indeed the first political form of government that ever was'. Nedham then surveyed ancient and modern history to prove that the power of the sword has always been 'the Foundation of All Titles to Government', whether monarchies or republics. On this basis Nedham concluded

> That those whose title is supposed unlawful and founded merely upon force, yet being possessed of authority, may lawfully be obeyed. Nor *may* they only, but they *must*; else by the judgement of civilians such as refuse may be punished as seditious and traitorous ... Whosoever therefore shall refuse submission to an established government upon pretence of conscience in regard of former allegiances, oaths, and covenants, or upon supposition that it is by the sword unlawfully erected, deserves none but the character of peevish, and a man obstinate against the reason and custom of the whole world.[33]

Citing Hugo Grotius, Nedham argued that the king had lost his title in war and the lords their interests and privileges through their compliance with the enemies and invaders of the nation, 'and so the whole authority devolved naturally into the hands of the commons'.[34]

It was this, rather than any call from the people, that justified the new regime. There was no need, in the aftermath of civil war, for people to express positive consent – tacit or implicit consent was sufficient.[35] Having addressed the government's right to rule, Nedham turned to those who refused submission in the name of their conscience and former obligations – most notably the royalists who invoked the Oath of Allegiance and the Presbyterians who invoked the Solemn League and Covenant. Since allegiance served political ends, such ends could be altered by new circumstances, Nedham explained. Moreover, the religious prohibition on resistance to the established regime rendered opposition to the commonwealth unlawful.

The second part of the work considered the various groups who were opposing the regime: royalists, Scots, Presbyterians, and Levellers. In each case Nedham demonstrated the improbability of their designs being implemented and the inconveniences arising if they were. In his final chapter Nedham argued for 'the Excellency of a Free State above a Kingly Government'.[36] A free state, he asserted, is the only means of protection against both tyranny and confusion; more positively, it is a means of protecting the valuable treasure of liberty. Citing ancient authors and Machiavelli, and referring to past examples, he claimed that free government is 'the most commodious and profitable': best suited to expansion and to the honour and profit of the nation, and most likely to produce virtuous men and excellent heroes.

While Milton and Nedham both wrote to defend the English Commonwealth arising out of the regicide, they did so on very different grounds. Where Milton sought to justify the regicide and believed that ultimate power lay with the people, giving them the right to resist any tyrant and in principle any ruling power with whom they were dissatisfied, Nedham offered a more pragmatic defence of the new regime. This was grounded not in popular sovereignty, but in the wisdom of submitting to the established authority. Furthermore, these texts seem to echo the tentative and somewhat uncertain nature of that regime. As Rachel Foxley has suggested, the republican writings of the 1650s are balanced upon a knife edge between critique and propaganda.[37] *The Case of the Commonwealth* opens with Nedham's acknowledgement that he has only recently come round to thinking this way. Similarly, Milton, though bold in his opposition to tyranny, expresses a more ambivalent attitude to monarchy, at least until 1660, and offers little positive endorsement for republican architecture.

As *Tenure* did to Milton, *The Case of the Commonwealth* brought Nedham an official position. On 24 May 1650 the government authorised a payment of £50 to him for 'service already done', as well as an annual payment of £100 'whereby he may subsist while endeavouring to serve the commonwealth'.[38] Soon after this, Nedham began editing the parliamentarian newspaper *Mercurius Politicus*, in which extracts from *The Case of the Commonwealth* were reprinted. Editorials he produced for *Mercurius Politicus* in 1651–2 developed the more positive justification of a republican government that he had set out in the final chapter of his earlier work and provided him with the basis of his second major republican publication: *The Excellency of a Free State*, which appeared in 1656.

Nedham, *The Excellencie of a Free State*

The Excellencie moved away from de facto argument and placed the emphasis instead on the positive attributes of commonwealth government, particularly one based on the popular possession of arms and on a 'due and orderly succession of the Supreme Authority in the hands of the People's Representatives'.[39] Drawing heavily on ancient examples – especially that of Rome – and on the teachings of Machiavelli, Nedham began by celebrating liberty as a great prize or jewel that the English people had won through their victory in the Civil War. To preserve that liberty, it was necessary to ensure that not just 'the name King' but also 'the thing king' – in other words kingly power – was banished from the realm. This required not only that people not be subject to the will of a single person, but also that they be subject only to laws to which they had consented. In insisting on this point, Nedham was articulating the neo-Roman theory of liberty, as described by Skinner. Thus Nedham made it clear that power must be in people's hands; and he offered twelve reasons why people are the best keepers of their liberties. He also argued that, in order to prevent those representing the people from becoming corrupt, it was essential that members of the representative assembly be renewed on a regular basis. Having set out his twelve reasons for the superiority of popular government, which invoked both reason and example, he concluded:

> Let this serve to manifest, that a Government by a free Election and Consent of the People, setled in a due and orderly succession of their supreme Assemblies, is more consonant to the light of Nature and Reason, and consequently much more excellent than any Hereditary standing Power whatsoever.[40]

The rest of the work was taken up with responding to objections to popular rule, demonstrating the historical basis of popular government, and examining various errors of policy. Nedham continued working on behalf of the government throughout much of the Interregnum; he only abandoned his editorial role in May 1659, when the Protectorate was replaced by the revived Rump Parliament.

The Varieties of English Republicanism, II: Critiques of the Protectorate

The shift from commonwealth to protectorate in 1653 brought a change of focus to republican writings. Works appeared that, rather than justifying and supporting the new regime, were more openly critical of it or were designed to offer better alternatives to it, since the Protectorate was judged, at least by some republicans, to undermine key republican values. Both Sir Henry Vane and James Harrington, for example, shared Oliver Cromwell's ultimate aim of healing and settling the nation, but neither was convinced that his regime offered the best means of doing so. In *A Healing Question*, Vane went so far as to suggest that in recent years the government had operated on the basis of private and selfish interests rather than according to the common good.[41] Harrington's precise attitude to Cromwell has been the subject of some debate among historians. According to John Toland, who edited Harrington's works and produced an account of his life, Cromwell had tried to stop Harrington's *The Commonwealth of Oceana* from being published. Harrington managed to get the work printed only by going to see Cromwell and allegedly threatening to hold his granddaughter to ransom.[42] Whether or not the story is true, *Oceana* set out an account of how Cromwell ought to have behaved after the dissolution of the Rump in 1653 that was starkly at odds with what he had actually done – so much so that Blair Worden has described the work's dedication to Cromwell as an anti-dedication and Harrington's Cromwell figure, Lord Archon, as an anti-Cromwell.[43] Yet Jonathan Scott has challenged Worden's conclusions, suggesting that *Oceana* only makes proper sense if it is viewed as a work of counsel for the Lord Protector, advising him on how to set his regime on a proper footing so as to achieve his ultimate aim of healing and settling.[44]

Harrington's *The Commonwealth of Oceana*

Whatever the motivations behind it, *Oceana* certainly offered an alternative to the English republic as it existed in the 1650s.[45] It proposed a detailed and somewhat idiosyncratic system, based on several crucial elements.

In the first place, Harrington put forward a new and distinctive argument, which would resonate with later republican thinkers: that the possession of political power is determined by the ownership of land. The reason why civil war had broken out in England in 1642 was that the actions of Henry VII and Henry VIII had shifted most of the land in the nation from the aristocracy to the gentry: the result of this process was that the balance of property within the country was no longer in line with that required to support a traditional mixed monarchy – bearing in mind that in those days wealth flowed from the ownership of land. However, simply implementing a common-wealth, as the English had done in 1649, was not sufficient to rectify the situation. First, it was important to fix the balance of property so that the latter could not shift out of the hands of the gentry again, thereby destabilising the English polity. This was to be done by means of an agrarian law, which placed limits on the inheritance of land.

Alongside this fixing of the foundations, Harrington was also keen to ensure that what he called the 'superstructures' of the system guaranteed rule in the interests of the public and protected the state against corruption – in other words to ensure the pursuit of the public good by those in positions of power. He advocated three key mechanisms for this purpose. First, the process of legislation was to be divided between the two houses of a bicameral parliament, the upper house or senate debating and proposing legislation, while the lower house or the popular assembly voted (without any debate) to accept or reject the senate's proposals. Harrington regarded this as a means of ensuring that the senate would not be able to act in its own interest to the detriment of the public as a whole. Secondly, he advocated a system of rotation of office for both chambers and for most other councils and offices within the commonwealth. In most cases this would mean the renewal of one third of a body each year, each member serving for a total of three years and then being required to spend three years out of office before becoming eligible for office once again. Thirdly, Harrington borrowed from the Venetian republic a complex balloting system that was secret and was designed to avoid corruption during electoral proceedings.

Opposition to Harringtonian Republicanism

Several of Harrington's specific measures echoed ideas expressed in a less developed form by Nedham.[46] By republishing in 1656 the editorials he had originally written for *Mercurius Politicus* in 1650–2, which celebrated popular government, Nedham could be seen as offering a critique of the Protectorate and of the direction it was taking. There was even an explicit passage in which he warned against raising one man to power in a republic in which a monarchy had recently been overthrown. Yet by the spring of 1647 Nedham seems to have been distancing himself from Harrington's position, which in many respects he appears to have prefigured. In March 1657 he wrote four editorials in *Mercurius Politicus* in which he satirised the philosophers and political theorists, including Harrington, who were speculating on alternative forms of government and veered back, towards the position he had adopted in *The Case of the Commonwealth*, according to which the right course was to submit to de facto authority.[47]

While earlier historians, such as Zera Fink and J. G. A. Pocock, were content to present Harrington as an archetypal English republican, more recent scholarship has highlighted the fact that, on a number of issues, Harrington was directly at odds with many of his republican contemporaries. Jonathan Scott has argued that Harrington's republicanism was atypical in that it placed confidence in constitutional architecture rather than in virtuous rulers, called for an agrarian law, and denied the value of 'tumults'.[48] Similarly, Paul Rahe has explicitly distinguished between the 'classical republicanism' of Milton and the Hobbesian republicanism of Harrington.[49]

The conflict between Harrington and his fellow republicans can be seen most starkly in the publications produced during the turbulent period between May 1659 and May 1660. Not surprisingly, the combination of absence of a permanent regime (the Rump returned to power in early May 1659, but was supposed to be there only for a fixed term, in order to decide how best to settle the nation) and the conflicts between different political and religious groups that characterised that year served to encourage the publication of pamphlets that advocated settlements of various kinds. The works of 'republican' authors were prominent among these publications. Vane, Stubbe, Rogers, and Milton all produced works during this period that set out their vision for the English Commonwealth. Harrington alone wrote no fewer than eight separate pamphlets, and these were complemented by further Harringtonian pamphlets authored by his friends and followers.[50] Yet what is striking about this outburst of republican pamphleteering is that, far from presenting a unified call for the preservation of republican government, most of the pamphlets were directed against each other.

Most English republicans of the time shared a belief in the need for both civil and ecclesiastical liberty, and insisted that both would be better secured under a commonwealth or popular state than under any other form of government.[51] They also agreed that government needed to operate in the interest of the public rather than in the interest of private individuals and that virtuous government was therefore essential to the success of republican rule. It was on the question of how virtuous rule might best be secured, however, that divisions emerged.

Milton, Vane, Rogers, and Stubbe retained a belief in at least the possibility of virtuous rule, thereby insisting that the key lay in selecting the right people for office. Milton was keen to apply the rule of reason and believed that the means of doing so was to institute a 'general councel of ablest men, chosen by the people to consult of public affairs from time to time for the common good'.[52] At one level, this might not appear all that different from Harrington's notion of a 'natural aristocracy', superior to the rest, which ought to take on the role of senators and debate and propose legislation.[53] However, a few distinguishing features separate Milton's 'Councel of ablest men' and Vane's 'well qualified' from Harrington's 'natural aristocracy'. First, Vane's group in particular was distinguished on account of its religious views. The wisest and best, on Vane's account, were synonymous with the godly. Rogers, too, insisted that those chosen as rulers should be not only 'wise' and 'of the highest capacity, reason and latitude' but also 'holy', 'pious', and 'of the liveliest courage for the cause and interest of our dearest Jesus'.[54] Similarly Stubbe, in *A Letter to an Officer of the Army*, set out his preference for a select senate, the members of which would be elected for life from 'the several parties in the nation leagued in the establishment of a commonwealth, viz. Independents, Anabaptists, Fifth Monarchy Men, and Quakers'.[55] Harrington, by contrast, deplored the rule of saints: '[b]ut they of all the rest are the most dangerous who, holding that the saints must govern, go about to reduce the commonwealth unto a party'. Noting that in scripture saints were commanded to submit to higher powers and be subject to human laws, he went on: '[a]nd that men pretending under the notion of saints or religion unto civil power have hitherto never failed to dishonour that profession, the world is full of examples'.[56]

This also resulted in different views as to how long rulers should remain in power. Both Milton and Vane were keen to harness the wisdom and skill of the 'ablest' and 'well qualified' persons, and so both proposed the establishment of offices for life. Vane's standing Council of State would be 'setled for life',[57] and Milton thought that his Grand Council needed to be perpetual, so that the nation may benefit from the growing skills and experience of its members. Harrington, by contrast, did not trust his natural aristocrats to resist corruption if they were given too much power or were able to retain it for too long. This is why he required that the senate and councils be subject to rotation of office and asserted that, while the senate could debate and propose legislation, those proposals would only be passed into law if they were approved by the popular assembly. Despite acknowledging the potential risk that those who were not given office may become ambitious and those who were may become corrupt, Milton still rejected Harrington's idea of rotation, on the grounds that this would involve putting good men out of office and bringing in inexperienced ones.[58] Rogers expressed the same view in less measured language. Rotation would, he observed, '*Boult* or fling out the best and ablest in the Commonwealth, for *Bran*, leaving the worst behind *In,* of all others'.[59] Ultimately, then, Milton, Vane, Rogers, and Stubbe felt it necessary to entrust the good men with the rule of the common good and with a flourishing commonwealth. Harrington, on the other hand, considered such a policy to be at odds with human nature. He pithily explained this view in *Aphorisms Political*:

> X. To light upon a good man, may be in Chance; but to be sure of an Assembly of good men, is not in Prudence.

Moreover, even good men were likely to become corrupt, particularly when holding a position of power:

> XIII. Where the Security is in the Persons, the Government maketh good men evil; where the Security is in the Form, the Government maketh evil men good.[60]

Therefore, rather than relying on a virtuous elite, Harrington placed his faith in laws, designing a system that would neutralise individual self-interest, or even turn it to positive ends. In his attitude towards human nature, Harrington had more in common with Hobbes, that arch-opponent of republicanism, than with other republican authors of the time. In *Oceana* he contrasted the maxim of a demagogue – '[g]ive us good men and they will make us good laws' – with that of a legislator – 'give us good orders, and they will make us good men'.[61] Both Rogers and Stubbe challenged this principle directly. As Rogers explained to his readers, '[n]or can we trust that Maxime of his (p. 48 Oceana,) Give us good orders, and they will make us good men! So much, as give us good men, & they will give us good orders; and Government too, with Gods blessing.'[62] Similarly, Stubbe asserted: 'Good orders do not secure a Commonwealth wherein the major or active part is not spirited for such a form.'[63]

Precisely because he relied on laws rather than men, Harrington could afford to be more indulgent when it came to who might be included in the citizen body, and at the same time more optimistic about the potential for long-term stability and survival. He firmly believed that the decisions and actions of citizens would be constrained by the laws and institutions of the system. Thus Harrington was almost alone among the republicans of his time in his suggestion that even royalists should be allowed to vote. For Stubbe, this suggestion constituted a key weakness of Harrington's model; and it was the main reason why, despite admiring many aspects of it, he could not endorse it himself.[64] As he explains, 'the *universality of this nation is not to be trusted with liberty at present*, that an *equal Commonwealth* is that whereunto we ought and may prudently grow, but which we cannot at once fabrice, without running an extraordinary hazard of being again enslaved'.[65]

Harrington was also led to a very different view of the religious dimension of the commonwealth from those of other republicans with whom he engaged in debate. Vane, Rogers, Stubbe, and Milton all insisted that liberty of conscience could best be achieved by abandoning the national system and instituting a complete separation between church and state. In *A Healing Question*, Vane had declared that Christ was the 'sole Lord and Ruler in and over conscience', and therefore the government and civil magistrates should not interfere at all in religious matters.[66] Similarly, Stubbe advised that, 'things *Civil* and *Spiritual* being of a different nature, and not *subordinate*, so as he who is deputed to administer the *former*, is not thereby empowered to intermeddle with the *latter* any way'.[67] Harrington, by contrast, was once again closer to Hobbes than to his fellow republicans in his reliance on a form of civil religion – an Erastian church settlement that combined a national church with toleration for Protestant sects.[68] His notion of a civil religion was central to his vision of the commonwealth and demonstrates the importance of religion within his wider political and philosophical thought.[69]

Conclusion

The English Commonwealth was groundbreaking in being the first republic to be established in a large nation-state and in bringing into practice, for the first time, the idea of republic as an antonym of monarchy. Yet it was established reluctantly, out of necessity rather than by choice; a succession of different regimes operated under its aegis; and its life was short. These ambivalences and shortcomings are reflected in the body of republican writings that emerged from the Interregnum.

Even in their attitude to monarchical government, English republicans held ambiguous and contrasting views. Milton did eventually commit to a non-monarchical regime, but his earlier works were characterised by a negative approach of attacking tyranny and absolute monarchy. Others condemned monarchy, but not all forms of single-person rule. Vane asserted the need to separate the legislative from the executive powers, but acknowledged that the latter could be ascribed to a single person if the legislative power thought this best.[70] Harrington, too, was not averse to having a single figurehead at the top of his system. In the Corollary of his *Oceana*, Olphaus Megaletor (Harrington's Cromwell figure) takes on that role and remains in it for more than forty years.[71] Moreover, Harrington suggested that it would have been possible for Charles – or for Oliver or Richard Cromwell – to retain his position within the English system, had he only altered his powers in acknowledgement of the new balance of property.[72]

On other matters English republicans were at odds with one another. They disagreed on such issues as the role of virtue and the best means of securing the public good, the correct relationship between church and state, and whether a commonwealth could incorporate different views and yet remain stable and durable. Indeed, in 1659–60 their disputes on such themes were louder and more ferocious than those they conducted against advocates of monarchy.

There was, then, not one single English republican position, but a variety of overlapping and competing views, among which shifting alliances formed. While this makes it difficult to define the essence of English republicanism, it highlights the fact that those writings that emerged out of the English republican experiment of the 1650s provided a rich and diverse legacy that could – and did – appeal to a wide range of later political thinkers and activists, both in Britain and abroad.

5

Post-Revolutionary English Republicanism

Introduction

While English republicanism may have been a consequence rather than a cause of the establishment of an English republic, the ideas generated at that time long outlived the immediate context from which they emerged. Charles II was restored to the throne in May 1660 and the monarchy has remained in place ever since. Yet, while English republicans and their ideas were driven abroad and underground in the immediate aftermath of the Restoration, they did not disappear entirely.[1] During the Exclusion Crisis (1679–81) and the Glorious Revolution (1688–9), they resurfaced and were crystallised into a 'tradition' around the turn of the century by a loose coalition of opposition writers known as 'the Country Party'. Many of these were Old Whigs – or, as they called themselves, 'Real Whigs' – but a few were Tories. Moreover, as Caroline Robbins argued, this English republican tradition was perpetuated and developed over several generations.[2] These so-called commonwealth men presented themselves as heirs to the seventeenth-century republicans; and both John Toland at the turn of the century and Thomas Hollis and Richard Baron several decades later republished large numbers of the original writings in lavish editions that kept the ideas alive and brought them to the attention of new audiences.

These commonwealth men were, of course, living under different circumstances and had different preoccupations by comparison with their intellectual ancestors. As a result, they adapted republican arguments to suit their purposes. For example, they invoked republican ideas against standing armies in the controversy of the 1690s, and applied them in support of their anti-clerical and freethinking religious views. Since they were writing after the Restoration, their republicanism was generally pluralist rather than exclusivist. Yet, given what has already been shown regarding the ambivalent attitude to monarchy of some Civil War republicans, this can be described as a development rather than a complete reversal of earlier thinking. Moreover, the commonwealth men did not always agree with one another any more than had their predecessors.

This chapter will begin by examining the attempts of republican writers in the late seventeenth and eighteenth centuries to perpetuate (perhaps even to create) a republican tradition. Following this, various debates will be explored. In each case attention will be paid to what later republicans took from their predecessors, how they developed their ideas, and where they agreed – and disagreed – among themselves. Finally, brief attention will be paid to the continued influence these ideas exercised in the second half of the eighteenth century.

The Creation of the Canon

The Exclusion Crisis and Glorious Revolution

In terms of personalities, the connection between the mid-seventeenth-century republicans and their late seventeenth- and eighteenth-century successors was direct. Some of those who had been active during the Interregnum, such as Henry Neville and Algernon Sidney, continued to write 'republican' texts during the Restoration. Both men were in exile in the 1660s, but subsequently returned to England and English politics. They were particularly active during the Exclusion Crisis, when attempts were made to exclude Charles II's brother James from the throne on account of his Catholicism. Neville, who had been a close friend of Harrington, adapted the principles and ideas of *Oceana* to this context, in works such as his *Plato redivivus* of 1681. Sidney, who had been a soldier and a statesman under the common-wealth, was working on his *Discourses Concerning Government* in May 1683, when he was arrested for his alleged involvement in the Rye House Plot. This was a Whig conspiracy to assassinate Charles II and his brother in order to secure the succession of the Protestant duke of Monmouth, Charles's illegitimate son. The *Discourses* was a refutation of *Patriarcha*, Robert Filmer's defence of divine right monarchy. Sidney drew on natural rights, republican, and ancient constitutionalist arguments to make the case for rebellion.[3] The death sentence that was subsequently passed depended in part on the manuscript of the work that was found on his desk and used as a witness against him.

In the end, the attempts at exclusion failed and James II acceded to the throne in 1685. Nevertheless opposition continued, and was increased after the birth of a son to James's second wife, Mary of Modena, which raised the threat of not just one Catholic monarch but a whole line of them. The Glorious Revolution that followed saw James II deposed in favour of William of Orange, the husband of James's daughter Mary. William and Mary were installed as king and queen in 1688 and a bill of rights was issued laying out the extent and limits of their powers.

Toland's Publishing Campaign and the Country Party

In the aftermath of the Glorious Revolution and at a time when the revolutionary generation was dying out, a further appeal was made to the earlier period of the English Revolution, via a publishing campaign launched by Toland. Toland's efforts helped to create the notion of a republican canon by associating various seventeenth-century figures with one another. Apart from Neville's being friends with Harrington, the personal relations between John Milton, Marchamont Nedham, and Andrew Marvell were close.[4] However, as the debates of 1659 reveal, mid-seventeenth-century republicans were not always in agreement. The association that modern scholars have drawn between Milton and Harrington (who were on opposing sides in those debates) is, at least partly, a consequence of Toland's campaign. *A Complete Collection of the Historical, Political and Miscellaneous Works of John Milton*, prefaced by Toland's 'Life' of Milton, appeared in Amsterdam in 1698 and in London the following year. It was quickly followed by his editions of other key works, including *The Oceana of James Harrington* (1700), which was also prefaced by a 'Life' of the author.[5] Moreover, Toland referred explicitly to his edition of Milton at the beginning of his preface to Harrington's works.

These texts became ammunition in Toland's own political campaigns against tyranny in politics and religion. He enhanced them with fancy frontispieces and prefatory material, and was not averse to interfering with the text in order to address current circumstances,[6] or to shape how they were read.[7]

Toland had a number of friends and associates who held similar political views and used seventeenth-century republican ideas for their own ends. One of these was Robert Molesworth, who set out the political principles of the group in the preface to the 1721 edition of his translation of François Hotman's *Franco-Gallia*; that work was later published separately, under the title *The Principles of a Real Whig*.[8] Molesworth stressed the importance of parliament as a representative body and called for a more equal distribution of parliamentary seats (as well as a more equal union between England, Scotland, and Ireland); annual or at least triennial parliaments; and an end to corrupt practices such as executive control over parliamentary seats and pensions and bribery in elections. He also emphasised the importance of a free press and of freedom of religion as essential foundations of a free state. Militarily he rejected the maintenance of a standing army in peacetime and instead insisted that the nation should be defended at home by a citizen militia. He called for a restraint of monopolies on trade and was in favour of parliamentary support for public works; and he rejected the current policy of peace with France. Molesworth also celebrated the Glorious Revolution and claimed that the revolution settlement provided the best framework in which to enshrine his principles.

As well as being a friend of Toland, Molesworth was also linked to John Trenchard and Thomas Gordon.[9] Trenchard also knew Walter Moyle; the two of them had associated with Neville at the Grecian Coffeehouse in London during the early 1690s, where ancient models and republican ideas were discussed. Anthony Ashley Cooper, the earl of Shaftesbury, was another close associate of both Molesworth and Toland.

Yet not all of those who expressed these views were Real Whigs. On the face of it, Henry St John, Viscount Bolingbroke, had little in common with the Toland–Molesworth circle. He was a Tory, had Jacobite links; and, while he was an MP, he supported peace with France and promoted legislation against the dissenters (despite having attended a dissenting academy himself).[10] Yet on the threat posed by corruption and the encroachment of the executive on the legislative, his views were very close to theirs. As he acknowledged in *A Dissertation upon Parties*, the older division between Whigs and Tories had been superseded by that between Court and Country, the latter being made up of an alliance of Tories and Old (or Real) Whigs.[11]

The Publication Campaign of Hollis and Baron

These ideas remained influential well into the eighteenth century. The men behind the second – and in some ways even more ambitious – republican publishing campaign shared similar views.

The self-confessed republican Thomas Hollis conceived of his plan to promote liberty and oppose tyranny in 1754,[12] and by the 1760s was pursuing it alongside his friend Richard Baron.[13] As well as explicitly endorsing Molesworth's principles, Hollis praised Toland, describing him as 'a man of great genius and learning, a staunch asserter of liberty', and he both drew on Toland's editions and made clear the connections between them and his own efforts.[14] In 1761 Hollis republished Toland's *Life of Milton*; and his own 1763 edition of Sidney's *Discourses Concerning Government* was based on Toland's version and included a direct reference to Toland's campaign.[15] Hollis also helped to bring Neville into the canon, republishing *Plato redivivus* in 1763. Baron had already begun editing commonwealth works before he met Hollis in 1756.[16] He was responsible for editions of *The Memoirs of Edmund Ludlow* in 1751, a collection of the religious writings of Thomas Gordon entitled *A Cordial for Low Spirits* and published in 1751 and 1763, *The Works of John Milton* in 1753, and Nedham's *The Excellencie of a Free State* in 1767. He, too, linked his project directly to the seventeenth-century struggle, describing his desire 'to strengthen and support' the 'Good old Cause'.[17] Moreover, in his prefaces he emphasised the connections among the seventeenth-century figures and highlighted their relevance to the present. In the preface to his edition of Milton he declared:

> Many circumstances at present loudly call upon us to exert ourselves. Venality and corruption have well-nigh extinguished all principles of Liberty ...
> One remedy for these evils is to revive the reading of our old Writers, of which we have good store, and the study whereof would fortify our youth against the blandishments of pleasure and the arts of Corruption. MILTON in particular ought to be read and studied by all our young Gentlemen as an oracle.[18]

He then went on to associate Milton directly with Sidney.

Hollis's and Baron's publishing ventures, like Toland's, were not merely isolated or purely antiquarian endeavours; they were central to a bold political campaign that involved both a broader range of characters and a wider set of activities. Alongside the republication of older commonwealth works, new ones also appeared. The Real Whigs were all prolific authors themselves and later in the century new writers took up the baton in works such as Obadiah Hulme's *An Historical Essay on the English Constitution* (1771), James Burgh's *Political Disquisitions* (1774), Major John Cartwright's *Take your Choice!* (1774), and Catharine Macaulay's *History of England* (1763–83). Hollis was impressed with the first volume of Macaulay's *History* and subsequently bought tracts relating to the Civil War and presented them to her anonymously.[19] Macaulay and Hollis, together with her brother John Sawbridge and his brother-in-law Stephenson, were identified by Horace Walpole as 'the chiefs' of a 'very small republican party' that was in existence in the late 1760s.[20] These figures were also directly associated with the flamboyant journalist and politician John Wilkes, whose campaigns promoted liberty of various kinds in the 1760s and 1770s. Hollis even sought to embark on a political career himself. On returning from his second Grand Tour in the early 1750s, he attempted to get elected to parliament. After he failed, he devoted himself to the collection and dissemination of books and other artefacts, 'for the purpose of illustrating and upholding liberty, and preserving the memory of its champions, to render tyranny and its abettors odious, to extend science and art, to keep alive the honour and estimation of their patrons and protectors and to make the whole as useful as possible'.[21] He declared that, by gathering the works of past authors and reflecting on them, 'I am always animated' 'to walk after them in that path of virtue'.[22] Alongside the books, he also commissioned prints and had medals struck commemorating both individuals and events that stood as symbols of liberty.

The dissemination of these books and artefacts was as central to Hollis's project as collecting and commissioning them. He sent collections of books, prints, and medals to numerous institutions in various countries – for example to the British Museum, Christ's College Cambridge, Harvard University, the Berne Public Library, the Leyden Public Library, even the Vatican Library in Rome – and in cities such as Zurich, Geneva, Basel, Leipzig, Groningen, Göttingen, Hamburg, Stockholm, Uppsala, Cortona, and Venice.[23] Many of these donations were anonymous and were made through the agency of others, for example Mr Valtravers.[24] This was the case with the collection of books sent to Berne. An inscription in the catalogue that accompanies that donation gives some indication of the purpose behind it:

> An Englishman, a lover of liberty, his country, and its excellent consti-
> tution, as most nobly restored at the happy Revolution, is desirous
> of having the honour to present the following books to the library at
> Berne, as a small testimony of his unfeigned respect for that canton,
> and for the brave, worthy, and free people of Switzerland.[25]

Later Campaigns

The 1780s and 1790s witnessed a further adaptation of the publication campaigns. The Society for Constitutional Information (SCI), established in 1780, was primarily concerned with promoting parliamentary reform, but in pursuit of this end Capel Lofft (1751–1824) was entrusted with compiling extracts of political works for dissemination; the goal was to improve the political education of the population. In total they are said to have distributed 98,000 copies of thirty-three different works.[26] Among these extracts, English republican works figured prominently.

A similar strategy was adopted in the 1790s by the Newcastle-born London radical printer Thomas Spence. Spence's *Pig's Meat, or Food for the Swinish Multitude*, the title of which ridiculed Edmund Burke's derogatory phrase likening the working classes to swine, was composed of extracts from a range of works that Spence believed would be instructive for the public, including many republican texts. Moreover, like Hollis before him, Spence also issued medals and tokens celebrating both his ideas and other figures, thinkers, and events (see Figure 5.1).

Liberty

Liberty remained central to republicanism into the 1700s; and eighteenth-century republicans' particular understanding of civil liberty, religious liberty, and the relationship between the two deliberately echoed (and sometimes developed) the views of their predecessors.

Figure 5.1　Thomas Spence Halfpenny token, view of Bastille under assault by mob. Image © The Fitzwilliam Museum, Cambridge

In the first place, liberty was contrasted with slavery, in classic neo-Roman fashion. Moyle and Trenchard, in a jointly authored pamphlet, asserted that the English were lucky to be freemen not slaves, and Molesworth made much of the contrast between liberty and slavery in his *Account of Denmark*.[27] For some, this entailed a right to rebellion. Sidney pushed this idea particularly strongly, insisting that the people could alter the existing constitution or make a new one, not just in times of emergency but any time they wished.[28] This constituted a challenge to Harrington's attempt to create a stable and enduring system, but the idea owed much to Machiavelli's notion that dynamism, and even regular tumults, were crucial to republican success.

Whether favouring stability or dynamism, these thinkers also endorsed the related idea that liberty was threatened not only when it was actually violated but simply when rulers were in a position to violate it. Hollis stated his belief 'that the exercise of arbitrary and tyrannical power in a state is an infringement of the natural rights of mankind, and productive of intolerable mischiefs and inconveniences'.[29] The concern about the violation of liberty was behind the emphasis these men placed on the liberty of the press as an essential prerequisite to civil liberty.[30] Here too they were drawing on earlier ideas, in particular Milton's *Areopagitica*.[31]

These authors also insisted that civil and religious liberty went hand in hand and that one could not be secured without the other. Milton and Harrington had differences on other matters, but this was an issue on which they agreed.[32] Sidney, too, was obsessed with asserting liberty 'civil and spiritual' against arbitrary government of all kinds.[33] If anything, the eighteenth-century republicans went further in their emphasis on the primacy of religious liberty. In *Vindicius Liberius*, Toland insisted that 'where there is no *Liberty of Conscience* there can be no *Civil Liberty*'.[34] Similarly, Gordon commented in *Priestianity*: 'Is not the Liberty of the Mind preferable to the Liberty of the Body? If therefore we have preserved the One from Foreign Enemies at the Expense of our Blood and Treasure, we ought to secure the Other from Domestick Invaders.'[35] Moreover, in the *Independent Whig* he and Trenchard insisted on the need for men's minds to be free: 'our Judgment ought to be at no Man's Service nor our Minds controlled in religious Matters, but by God alone; for as no man's Soul can be saved by Proxy, so no Man ought to exercise his Faith by Proxy'.[36] Hollis, too, was keen to note that 'every man has an undoubted right to think and judge for himself, and ought to be tolerated in that way of worship which in his own conscience he believes to be right'.[37] These thinkers went further than their predecessors also in the range of views they were prepared to tolerate. Harrington had drawn the line at the boundaries of Protestantism, insisting that gathered churches could have full liberty of conscience as long as they were neither 'Popish, Jewish, nor idolatrous'.[38] Molesworth, however, did not respect such boundaries:

> as a Christian and a Whig, I must have Charity for those that differ from me in religious Opinions, whether Pagans, Turks, Jews, Papists, Quakers, Socinians, Presbyterians, or others. ... We ought no more to expect to be all of one Opinion, as to the Worship of the Deity, than to be all of one Colour or Stature. To stretch or narrow any Man's Conscience to the Standard of our own, is no less a Piece of Cruelty than that of Procrustes the Tyrant of Attica, who used to fit his Guests to the Length of his own Iron Bedsted, either by cutting them shorter, or racking them longer.[39]

As this quotation suggests, republicans were also concerned about attempts to hinder liberty of conscience, particularly by members of the clerical establishment. Repeatedly, they drew attention to the role of the clergy in shoring up the absolute power of princes, even encouraging tyranny. As Moyle bluntly put it, 'Priests and Tyrants have join'd their interest to enslave the World and share the Booty between them'.[40] Bolingbroke too blamed the persistence of 'the divine institution and right of kings' and the notion that a monarch was entitled to absolute power on 'an old alliance between ecclesiastic and civil policy'.[41] As well as encouraging and supporting tyranny, priests were also deemed responsible for perpetuating ignorance among the population and thereby corrupting morals and customs. As Toland explained, 'so from ignorance thus establish'd under the management of Priests, whose interest leads them to continue it, no less naturally precede loose morals and savage customs. This is the genuine effect of priestly power in all places'.[42] Some went so far as to suggest that humanity would have been better off without the clergy. The English gentleman in Neville's *Plato redivivus* confesses: '[t]he truth is, *Doctor*, I could wish there had never been any; the purity of Christian Religion, as also the good and orderly Government of the World, had been much better provided for without them, as it was in Apostolical time, when we heard nothing of Clergy'.[43]

The republicans' commitment to extensive toleration, together with their opposition to clerical power, led several to praise simple forms of religion, such as that introduced into Rome by Numa and that which had supposedly been practised among primitive Christians. In his account of Rome, Moyle praised Numa's policy, which required citizens to acknowledge that the gods are the authors of all that is good for human beings and to accept that, to obtain this good, the Gods need to be worshipped through the practice of innocent, just, and good behaviour.[44] Toland showed his respect for Numa, whom he linked to republican leaders, by including him as one of the legislators represented on the temple to liberty on the frontispiece to his edition of Harrington (see Figure 1.1). Similarly, in *Nazarenus*, Toland looked back fondly to the simple and tolerant faith of the primitive Christians.[45]

While the commonwealth men ventured further on religious matters than did their predecessors, the seeds of their understanding of civil and religious liberty can be found in seventeenth-century writings, and perhaps especially in those of Harrington. Just as the problem of priestcraft was one that had been identified by him (he coined this word), so their proposed solution took his ideas as a starting point. For Harrington, the means of rooting out priest-craft was to return the power of ordination to the people, thereby destroying the clergy's special status and power.[46] Moyle used his analysis of the Roman system to make the same point: 'THIS wise Institution of an universal Liberty in Religion, seems to be owing to this single Cause, *viz.* "That the Government of the National Religion was lodged in the *Senate* and People."'[47] In the same vein, when describing Trenchard's 'Notions of God' and religion in the Preface to *Cato's Letters*, Gordon alluded to his friend's criticism of the clergy and his awareness of the dangers that would follow if clergymen were not subjected to the authority of a civil magistrate.[48] These authors not only were committed to liberty of conscience, but also believed that such liberty was best secured under a national religion in which the church and the clergy were firmly under state control.[49] Particularly telling in this regard is Hollis, who, despite not conforming to the Church of England himself, supported it since he recognised its utility to the state.[50]

Virtue

Virtue, too, understood as the subordination of private interests to the public good, continued to be deemed crucial to a flourishing republican state. Sidney insisted that the success of republican govern-ments in the past was due to their 'virtue and good order' and cited Machiavelli on the need for virtue in the preservation of liberty.[51] He also expressed his preference for rule by men of virtue, underlining the importance of being ruled by the wisest and best and asserting that, 'as the work of a magistrate, especially if he be supreme, is the highest, noblest, and most difficult, that can be committed to the charge of a man, a more excellent virtue is required in the person who is to be advanced to it, more than for any other.'[52]

Like their predecessors, however, the commonwealth men offered a variety of answers to the thorny question of how virtuous rulers and citizens could be secured, given the flawed and corruptible nature of human beings. Harrington had talked in detail about the constant battle between reason and passion in the heart of 'man', and a number of later republicans expressed similar views. Neville acknowledged that the passions are 'as natural to man as reason and virtue',[53] Sidney noted that '[e]very man has passions; few know how to moderate, and no one can wholly extinguish them',[54] and Gordon said of Trenchard that he was aware of 'what feeble Materials human Nature was made of'.[55] Yet he also made the point that a happy man must be 'a Master of his Passions'[56] and believed that, if the passions could be properly balanced, then people would act rationally.[57]

Various thinkers saw a role for the state in bringing this about. Sidney argued that the discipline imposed through law could restrain passion and sin, thereby ensuring government according to reason.[58] Moreover, he argued that virtue was more likely to be cultivated in a popular government, which was one reason why that form was preferable: 'all tyrannies have had their beginnings from corruption. … They must therefore endeavour to maintain or increase the corruption by which they attain their greatness,' and 'all popular and well-mixed governments: they are ever established by wise and good men, and can never be upheld otherwise than by virtue'.[59] Bolingbroke was closer to Harrington's more sceptical position; he felt that passion would have to be used to curb passion and that a system would have to be created in which it would be in the individual's own interest to act virtuously.[60]

Education, particularly in the principles of liberty, was seen as essential to the inculcation of virtue and was praised even by those who were sceptical about the human potential to achieve virtue. Toland's publishing and dissemination campaign was directed towards this end, and the concerns about the tendency of priests to keep the people in ignorance were also motivated by it. Yet few believed that education alone could secure virtue, and many of these thinkers turned instead to the mechanisms Harrington had prescribed to counter the effects of natural human self-interest. Neville, for example, insisted on the benefits of an Harringtonian rotation of office as a curb against corruption.[61] Similarly, Moyle praised the Roman laws on this issue: 'for nothing sooner dissolves a Commonwealth than the Continuance of Authority too long in the same Hands'. And Macaulay advocated rotation of office in her proposed constitution for Corsica.[62]

A number of these republicans also followed Harrington in the suggestion that corruption was material as much as moral. Early in *Plato redivivus* Neville described as crucial the idea that '*Empire is founded on Property*' and claimed that one aim of his work was to show that property determines power.[63] He also embraced Harrington's concomitant notion that changes in the apportionment of land would lead to changes in government (or, if not, then to confusion and corruption). Indeed, Neville's diagnosis of England's political problems in the early 1680s, and his suggestions as to how they might be cured, are grounded in a Harringtonian understanding of the relationship between property and power.[64] Moyle, too, accepted the theory about the relationship between land ownership and political power. The idea that an incorrect balance would bring corruption was central to his analysis of the Roman state, and he attributed the theory directly to Harrington.[65] Trenchard and Gordon also accepted that the distribution of property would determine the distribution of power and acknowledged the consequences of this idea for those committed to a free state, highlighting that a free people could only maintain its freedom through an equal distribution of property.[66] Similarly, in her proposals for Corsica, Macaulay called for an agrarian law designed to maintain the balance of property.[67]

In many ways the English republicans of the late seventeenth and early eighteenth centuries followed the trajectory set by their mid-seventeenth-century predecessors, even if in some cases they developed rather than simply repeating earlier ideas. There are, however, several issues on which the later republicans have been seen as enacting a clear break with the previous tradition. One of the most significant of these issues concerns the relationship between republicanism and anti-monarchism.

Republicanism, Monarchy, and the Mixed and Balanced Constitution

Contrary to Milton's point that what was required was 'a free Commonwealth without single person or house of lords',[68] later republicans dissociated the idea of a commonwealth from the regimes of the 1650s – and from anti-monarchism more generally. They believed rather that commonwealth principles were perfectly compatible with the reformed version of the English monarchy that had emerged from the Glorious Revolution. Gordon said of his friend Trenchard:

> As passionate as he was for Liberty, he was not for a Commonwealth in *England*. He neither believed it possible, nor wished for it. He thought that we were better as we were, than any practicable Change could make us, and seemed to apprehend that a neighbouring Republick was not far from some violent Shock.[69]

Similarly, Molesworth objected to the suggestion that he and his friends were haters of kingly government.[70] The essential problem, he asserted, lay in the popular understanding of the terms:

> A true Whig is not afraid of the Name of a *Commonwealthsman*, because so many foolish People, who know not what it means, run it down: The Anarchy and Confusion which these Nations fell into near Sixty Years ago, which was falsely called a Commonwealth, frightening them out of the true Construction of the Word. But Queen Elizabeth, and many other of our best Princes, were not scrupulous of calling our Government a Commonwealth, even in their solemn Speeches to Parliament. And indeed if it be not one, I cannot tell by what Name properly to call it: For where in the very Frame of the Constitution, the Good of the Whole is taken care of by the Whole (as 'tis in our Case) the having a King or Queen at the Head of it, alters not the Case; and the softening of it by calling it a Limited Monarchy, seems a Kind of Contradiction in Terms, invented to please some weak and doubting Persons.[71]

As on other points, Hollis shared Molesworth's view on this matter.[72]

Both Neville and Toland believed that Harrington's principles, in particular, were adaptable to post-Restoration England.[73] The possibility of conceiving of the rule of William and Mary as governed by Harringtonian principles is reflected in Toland's frontispiece to his edition of Harrington's works (see Figure 1.1). Hanging either side of the figure of liberty at the centre of the image are medallions depicting Lucius Junius Brutus and a laureled William III. This design highlights the fact that both had uprooted a dynasty of tyrannical kings (the Tarquins and the Stuarts), but the implication is also that William III's rule is not incompatible with a regime that places liberty at its heart – or even with the specific regime envisaged by Harrington. This idea is also enunciated in the preface. Acknowledging current concerns about attempts to introduce republican government into Britain, Toland reassured his readers that the commonwealth men had done much to secure the monarchy; and he presented the settlement of 1688–9 in a positive light. Given this, he believed rebellion against a wise and good king to be highly unlikely. Moreover, he continued:

> Now if a Commonwealth be a Government of Laws enacted for the common Good of all the People, not without their own Consent or Approbation; that they are not wholly excluded, as in absolute Monarchy, which is a Government of Men who forcibly rule over others for their own Privat Interest: Then it is undeniably manifest that the English Government is already a Commonwealth, the most free and best constituted in all the world.[74]

Just as Toland saw Harrington's ideas as being adaptable to monarchy, so Hollis pointed out that Milton's republicanism was not innate but was the consequence of his experience of tyranny:

> But Milton, or the warmest common-wealth man, never thought of altering the ancient form of government, till Charles the First had sinned flagrantly and repeatedly against it, and had destroyed it by his violences. On the contrary, there are several and very fine passages in his prose works, where he commends that ancient form exceedingly, and with highest justice.[75]

What was crucial for these commonwealth men, then, was not the presence or absence of a monarch, but rather the existence of a carefully mixed constitution and the maintenance of a proper balance between the different elements that could serve to create virtuous behaviour out of self-interested action. That balance could be threatened or corrupted in various ways. For one thing, the executive could encroach on the legislature through the use of places and pensions.[76] Toland condemned the filling of parliament with those who owed their places to the court, asking '[w]hether a Parliament can be a true Balance where all the Weight lies only in one Scale'.[77] That balance could also be threatened by the establishment of a standing army, an issue that came to the fore in the 1690s.

The Standing Army

The Treaty of Ryswick in September 1697 brought an end to the Nine Years War. Louis XIV withdrew his support for James II and recognised William III as king of England, promising peace and friendship to him and his successors. William's decision to maintain his standing army after the signing of this treaty prompted a strong reaction from republican writers, particularly in terms of the threat it posed to the balanced constitution, and therefore to the preservation of a free government.

Moyle and Trenchard, in their contribution to the debate, made reference to the theory of the balanced constitution and to a Harringtonian understanding of the relationship between property and power:

> [O]ur Constitution depending upon a due balance between King, Lords and Commons, and that Balance depending upon their mutual Occasions and Necessities they have of one another; if this Cement be once broke, there is an actual Dissolution of the Government. Now this Balance can never be preserved but by an Union of the natural and artificial Strength of the Kingdom, that is, by making the Militia to consist of the same Persons as have the Property; or otherwise the Government is violent and against Nature, and cannot possibly continue, but the Constitution must either break the Army, or the Army will destroy the Constitution: for it is universally true, that where-ever the Militia is, there is or will be the Government in a short time.[78]

This connection could be seen by observing present and past states. Toland noted: "'Tis well known, that all the World over, wherever the Sword is in the hands of the *People*, it is a free Government be it of one or of many; and on the contrary, all Tyrannies are supported by *Mercenaries*.'[79] The reason for this was not just the old Machiavellian argument that militiamen would be more strongly motivated – and therefore more effective – than mercenaries, but also that the presence of a militia would check the self-interested behaviour of the ruler. Having to rely on a citizen army would constrain the ruler to engage only in conflicts that were in the interests of the common good, since otherwise there was a risk that the soldiers would mutiny. Moyle and Trenchard insisted that, if the armed force was composed of the same elements as the government, it would be virtually 'impossible' for the army 'to act to the disadvantage of the Constitution'.[80] Similarly, Toland justified the idea that the freemen ought to form the armed force of the nation by stating that his aim was to prove that such a force 'can never be dangerous to our Liberty and Property at home, and will be infinitely more effectual against an Enemy attacking or invaded by us'.[81] A citizen militia could also serve an educative function. Andrew Fletcher argued that training in the militia would inculcate civic virtue and a concern for the public good in the population.[82]

Commercial Society

The political and military issues that surfaced during the 1690s were closely related to economic change and, in particular, to the increasing importance of commerce and trade within the economy. In his account of the commonwealth men, Pocock emphasised their antagonism towards commercial society.[83] Harrington had grounded his political system firmly in the land, with ownership of property as a crucial foundation of independent citizenship. While he acknowledged that governments could be based on money, he believed that this was true only of small trading states such as Holland or Genoa, dismissing the idea that money would ever overbalance land in England.[84] Yet in a relatively short time this prediction proved to be false.

While most thinkers of the time had little option but to accept these changes, Pocock argues that the later republicans – whom he labels neo-Harringtonians – were more anxious than most about the implications of this shift and of the subversion of real by mobile property. They thus developed what Pocock describes as a civic humanist denunciation of the corruption brought by the new finance and by the rise of a monied interest. At the heart of this denunciation was the concern that the new forms of wealth encouraged dependence in place of the independence grounded in landed property. It was members of this new rentier class who gained power by buying pensions and offices, meaning that they were dependent on the executive for their positions of power and could be induced to corrupt parliament by acting on behalf of their masters. Similarly, Fletcher noted that commerce and luxury brought greater opportunities for specialisation and consequently encouraged the delegation not just of political but also of military functions to others.

These concerns came to a head in the aftermath of the South Sea Bubble. In 1720 the House of Lords passed a bill allowing the South Sea Company a monopoly on trade with South America. The company underwrote the English national debt on a promise of 5 per cent interest from the government. This prompted wild speculation, as stocks spiralled on all kinds of schemes and many people made huge profits. Soon, however, the bubble burst. Trenchard and Gordon published *Cato's Letters* with the aim of identifying the causes of the crash and proposing a remedy for the national corruption it had revealed. The aim of the work, its authors declared, was to call 'for Publick Justice upon the wicked Managers of the late fatal *south-Sea* Scheme'.[85] They insisted on the need for equality in the distribution of property, expressed concern that the monied interest was perverting the balance of the constitution, and strongly opposed monopolies and heavy public debt. However, despite the fact that trade played an increasing part in British society, they offered little advice about how relative equality of property could be secured under such circumstances.

Pocock's interpretation of this issue has been significant for the current understanding of republicanism. On his account, republicanism contrasted with a form of liberalism that was more sympathetic to the growing commercial society of the eighteenth century. Owing to the tensions between them on this and other issues, republicanism and liberalism were initially presented by Pocock as incompatible discourses. But others have done much to challenge this assumption. Pocock tended to extrapolate from Harrington's position and to assume that republicans at all times had been hostile to commercial society. Yet, as Mark Jurdevic has shown, the idea that Renaissance republicans were hostile to commerce is based on a false reading of that period. In fact Renaissance civic humanism can be seen as the ideology of an 'ascendant merchant elite', which approved of commerce and the pursuit of private wealth as a means of building up a flourishing commonwealth.[86] Moreover, Hans Baron demonstrated that one of the key elements of civic humanism was the rejection of the Franciscan and Stoic ideals of poverty and the embracing of material wealth.[87] Similarly, Steve Pincus has argued that, while Harrington and Milton were hostile to commercial culture, seventeenth-century England was already experiencing an expansion of trade, and there were plenty of supporters of commonwealth government who defended the new commercial society.[88] The author of *The Grand Concernments of England*, for example, declared that '[t]rade is the very life and spirits of a common-wealth'.[89] These thinkers tended to place less emphasis on civic virtue and more on the politics of interest. Pincus argues that it was these views that were dominant in the late seventeenth and early eighteenth centuries, and that they provided the foundations for liberalism. 'These defenders of the English Commonwealth, then, melded republican conceptions of liberty to a commercial and modern political economy and conception of interest.'[90]

Responding to both Pocock and Pincus, Justin Champion has further complicated the picture.[91] Drawing on little known published writings and unpublished manuscripts produced by Toland and Molesworth, he suggests that these two and other eighteenth-century commonwealth men had a more subtle and sophisticated attitude to commerce than Pocock had suggested and that their economic concerns were largely motivated by political and social rather than purely monetary matters. These thinkers were worried about the corruption wrought by speculation, paper stocks, and credit, but they drew a clear distinction between credit that benefited the public and credit that furthered private interests and between a good merchant – industrious, dependable, and trustworthy – and a speculator or projector.[92]

Among Toland's papers there is a scheme for a national bank, which Champion suggests was probably written by Molesworth; its focus is not on speculative investment but on ensuring a healthy circulation of money. A similarly positive attitude to commerce and banks is evident in Toland's edition of Harrington's works. The volume is dedicated to the 'Lord Mayor, Aldermen, Sherifs, and Common Council of London' and Toland bestows great praise on London, particularly for 'its prodigious Trade and Commerce', which, it is said, is the 'true Spring' of its Liberty.[93] The fine houses of London's citizens are celebrated, but their wealth is also linked directly to the 'Splendor and Magnificence of the public Structures'. Particular praise is also lavished on the Bank of England, the constitution of which is described as coming 'the nearest of any Government to HARRINGTON's Model'.[94] Also of significance is the frontispiece to the work, which depicts, as foundations of the commonwealth, a rural scene placed under the title 'Opificio' (land, husbandry), but also an urban one labelled 'Commercio' (Figure 1.1).[95]

Several of Toland's papers also give an interesting insight into his own and his associates' attitude towards the South Sea scheme. A manuscript entitled 'The Secret History of the South-Sea Scheme' suggests, again, that his concern was not about the economic threat the scheme posed to agrarian values, but rather about political matters, especially the ways in which the scheme played upon and encouraged selfishness, deceit, and the pursuit of private interests at the expense of the public good.[96] Even more startling is a contract drawn up in June 1720, which reveals that Toland and Molesworth had invested money in the scheme.[97] While they were to oppose the bubble later on, Molesworth threatening to throw the South Sea directors into the Thames,[98] initially they thought that it was an 'honest Project', in which they were happy to invest.[99]

Money and credit, then, were fine when used for honest and positive purposes; what needed to be guarded against was their manipulation or use for purely private ends. Nor was this simply the view of Toland and Molesworth; a similar attitude is evident in *Cato's Letters*. That work accepted that public and private credit were important for society, but insisted that credit should operate in the right rather than the wrong way. As Trenchard and Gordon said of the South Sea scheme, '[i]t has changed honest Commerce into Bubbling; our Traders into Projectors; Industry into Tricking'.[100]

The Later Eighteenth Century

In late eighteenth-century Britain, the Wilkite movement, calls for parliamentary reform, and conflict with the North American colonies gave fresh impetus to the articulation and development of republican ideas. These developments raised key issues about the relationship between liberty and authority, the tendency for power to become corrupted, and the importance of representative government and free speech in countering that corruption. This was the background against which the publishing campaigns of Baron and Hollis took place and organisations such as the SCI were established. While many continued to speak with familiarity about places and pensions, militias versus standing armies, and religious toleration, the reform movement in particular raised new questions about the extent of political participation and the nature of the franchise.

In some of these writings we can see the extension of republican ideas towards universal suffrage and even social radicalism. Cartwright's *Take Your Choice!* began with the traditional republican appeal to liberty.[101] On this basis he emphasised the people's right to equal representation and the need for annual parliaments; he declared that these were not innovations but were principles embedded in the ancient constitution, having only recently been overturned by 'kingcraft and court policy'.[102] Neglecting these mechanisms had had a negative impact on the relationship between representatives and their constituents: 'our representatives, who are in fact our deputed servants, are taught to, assume the carriage and haughtiness of despotic masters; to think themselves unaccountable for their conduct; and to neglect their duty'.[103] Towards the end of the pamphlet he offered a plan for a new system that should have a more representative parliament, annual elections, and a secret ballot.[104] Cartwright also moved away from the persistent idea that property ownership should be regarded as a prerequisite for political participation:

> *every individual* ... whether possessed of what is vulgarly called property, or not, ought to have a vote in sending to parliament those men who are to act as his representatives; and who in an especial manner, are to be the guardians of *public freedom*; in which, the poor, surely, as well as the rich have an interest.[105]

Spence went even further. Where Cartwright sought to reform politics by cutting the link to property, Spence called instead for the reform of property ownership, in order to re-establish that link.[106] For him, what was required was a complete overhaul of the distribution and organisation of property. In the work of Spence and his followers we see the beginnings of a shift from republican ideas to socialism.

Conclusion

English republicanism survived the restoration of Charles II. Figures such as Neville, Toland, Molesworth, and their associates explicitly looked back to the English republicans of the mid-seventeenth century as a source of inspiration. Moreover, they shared an understanding of the importance of a particular conception of liberty, the need for virtue, and the threat posed by corruption – even if the question of how government in the public good could be secured tended to prompt anxiety rather than clear answers. At the same time, new issues and problems arose. The religious consequences of 1640–60 and the rise of commercial society proved particularly pressing in the late seventeenth and early eighteenth centuries. These ideas continued to exercise an influence in the second half of the eighteenth century thanks to the publication campaigns of Hollis and Baron. The eighteenth century was also the age of Enlightenment. The next chapter will consider the engagement with and development of republican ideas, in both theory and practice, in that context.

6

Republicanism during the Enlightenment

Introduction

The prospects for republican government at the beginning of the eighteenth century seemed far from hopeful. As was demonstrated in the last two chapters, the English republic had proved a failure; and, while republican ideas continued to be voiced in late seventeenth- and eighteenth-century Britain and applied to new circumstances, they appealed primarily to those in opposition rather than exerting a direct influence on government policy. In the United Provinces, the House of Orange had been restored to power under William III in 1672, curtailing some of the more radical republican theories that had circulated during the first stadtholderless period (1650–72). Venice and Geneva fared a little better, but this only served to reinforce the idea that republics were suited primarily to small states. Moreover, their experiences pointed to the tendency of republics to become dominated by oligarchies, and also revealed the dangers facing small states that were surrounded by larger and more powerful neighbours.[1] These problems were recognised by Enlightenment political thinkers, including the baron de Montesquieu and Jean-Jacques Rousseau. While they were sympathetic in many respects to republican government, they were under no illusions that a republic could easily be established in any of the large states of eighteenth-century Europe. Moreover, the Enlightenment also saw the rise of the idea and practice of *despotisme éclairé* or enlightened absolutism, which was designed to implement rule in the public interest by a means that was diametrically opposed to republican rule.

At the end of the century, however, this situation had been trans-formed. By 1795 new republics had been established in the United States of America and in France, and the French army had begun its campaign of republican conquest, 'liberating' various European states from monarchical oppression and imposing 'sister republics' from the Netherlands to Naples. The fact that the US and France were not small city-states but large nation-states – as well as the fact that in other respects they were very different from each other in their history and political topography – suggested that the suitability of republican government was not restricted to certain kinds of state, but could be applied anywhere. The ideas and practical experiences that led to this transformation are the subject of this chapter.

The chapter will examine the fate, during the eighteenth century, of two of the older republics that were discussed in Chapter 3: the United Provinces and Geneva. In discussing Geneva, consideration will also be given to the ideas of one of the thinkers who have been most closely associated with the theory of republics in the eighteenth century: Rousseau. His attitude towards republican government was profoundly influenced by the organisation and practices of his native city, though his relationship with Geneva was stormy. Of course Rousseau's ideas also exercised a profound influence in his adopted home of France, alongside those of French thinkers, notably Montesquieu and Gabriel Bonnot de Mably, whose thoughts on republican government will also be examined. The chapter will begin by considering the legacy of republican ideas bequeathed to the Enlightenment by ancient and Renaissance thinkers and by those who were writing during the seventeenth-century English Revolution.

The Legacy of Republican Ideas

Ancient republican models and ideas remained important through to the end of the eighteenth century and beyond.[2] Enlightenment thinkers wrote explicitly about ancient Sparta, Athens, and Rome, as well as being familiar with the works of Machiavelli and other Renaissance republican theorists. Yet the nature of these borrowings was far from straightforward. Ancient sources were put to divergent uses by thinkers of different political persuasions. For instance, Wyger Velema has shown how ancient sources proved equally appealing in the later eighteenth century both to Dutch patriots and to their opponents. Moreover, whereas for some they provided useful models for imitation and emulation, to others the vast gap between the ancient and modern world was itself instructive.[3] There was also an appreciation that much had changed since the Renaissance. Both political terminology and historical methodology were more sophisticated by the eighteenth century. The distinction between legislative and executive power was now well established, and historical causation had to be understood and explained rather than events being attributed to the vagaries of 'fortune'.

Enlightenment thinkers interested in republicanism could also benefit from the fruits of the English republican experiment. As early as the 1660s, English republican texts and ideas were already making their way to Europe, not least thanks to exiles such as Edmund Ludlow, Algernon Sidney, and Henry Neville, who escaped to Europe in order to preserve their lives.[4] There is also evidence of English republican works being read by some unlikely individuals. In 1665 the German-born orientalist Johann Michael Wansleben devoted time, after a failed diplomatic mission to Abyssinia, to producing, in manuscript, a digest of parts of five of Harrington's most substantial political works, brought together under the title 'The Fundations and Modell of a Perfect Commonwealth'.[5] Wansleben probably did not produce the work just for his own use, since, while the digest is in English, there are marginalia in German, Latin, and Italian. It is also significant that Wansleben focuses on the universal principles that can be drawn from these anglocentric publications. Fifty years later, English republican writings were beginning to exercise an influence in France. They were adopted initially by Huguenot authors and, later, by people who called for and enacted revolution. Once again, however, ideas became detached from their original context, not least by being used to support and advocate even more radical and democratic regimes than those favoured by their English authors.[6]

Eighteenth-century republicans drew on this legacy of works and ideas, but their understanding of republican government was also shaped, sometimes directly, by their own experience of republican rule. The United Provinces was one of several contemporary republics in existence in the eighteenth century.

Dutch Republicanism in the Eighteenth Century

According to Velema, the Dutch retained their republican reputation throughout the eighteenth century: '[t]o many eighteenth-century foreign observers ... the United Provinces remained a fascinating and extraordinary example of republican liberty'.[7] While Velema recognises the distinctive characteristics of Dutch republicanism, in particular the emphasis on concord and commerce at the expense of warfare, and the willingness of Dutch republicans to draw on interest theory, he also points out that Dutch republicanism cannot be reduced to a single model.[8] For example, while the de la Court brothers had moved away from veneration for antiquity, the work of Lieven de Beaufort – including his *Treatise on Liberty in Civil Society* of 1737 – was steeped in the classical tradition and demonstrated his particular interest in the Roman republic.[9] De Beaufort, who was a regent in Zeeland, wrote this work during the second stadtholderless period (1702–47), more specifically in the midst of particularly ferocious debates in the late 1730s between republicans (who supported the Dutch States Party) and Orangists. While both groups accepted the 1579 Union of Utrecht as the foundation of freedom and of a republican political order, republicans like de Beaufort challenged the supposed necessity of the monarchical element within the Dutch mixed constitution, suggesting that a synthesis of aristocracy and democracy would be preferable. De Beaufort associated the loss of liberty with luxury and ambition, but, in contrast to the de la Court brothers, he presented political virtue, civic equality, and religion – and not institutional mechanisms or the manipulation of self-interest – as the best way of restoring Dutch liberty.

The second stadtholderless period came to an end in 1747, when William IV was restored. He ruled as stadtholder for just four years, however, dying in 1751 and leaving his three-year-old son William as his successor. There followed a long period of regency government before William V took on the duties of stadtholder when he came of age in 1766.

The second half of the eighteenth century saw continued concerns about the decline of the Dutch republic. In the last quarter of the century both the supporters of the States Party (who now called themselves Patriots) and the Orangists recognised this decline.[10] Despite agreeing about it, however, the two groups had very different ideas about what action needed to be taken. Whereas the Orangists called for the strengthening of the stadtholderate, the patriots saw William V as a threat to liberty and called for some more fundamental reform. They combined older Dutch republican ideas with other strains of thought to produce what Velema has called 'an explosive and revolutionary mixture'.[11] As he notes, the Dutch patriot movement has often been presented in historiography as moderate rather than radical – obsessed with the past and with ancient constitutionalism. Yet this, Velema insists, is a false picture. While appeals to the Dutch past and the use of older Dutch republican and civic humanist ideas certainly formed an important part of Patriot ideology, this ideology was blended with ultra-Lockean radicalism and a radical reading of Montesquieu's *The Spirit of the Laws*. Such elements were used to attack the stadtholder and to argue for more participation of the people in politics.

Indeed, the patriots began to regard greater citizen participation in government as the solution to Dutch decline. They redefined liberty as the active and permanent sovereignty of the people and, on this basis, they declared that the existing republican order did not constitute a free state. Instead of placing the emphasis on mixed government, they placed it on the need to curb drastically the powers of the stadtholder while increasing those of a vigilant citizen body, which they sought to achieve through a free press, a strong petitioning movement, and a citizen militia. This shift occurred by and large during the 1780s and is traced by Velema in works that appeared in print during that decade. In 1783 patriots still stressed the rule of law and remained within the old constitutional framework. But a shift away from this state of affairs starts to be seen with works such as the *Constitutional Restoration* of 1784, which emphasised the right of a sovereign people not only to replace those who exercise power if they are not acting in the public interest, but also to change the form of government if they wished. *The Leyden Draft* of 1785 called for all governors to be elected by the citizens, and *The Patriot in Solitude* similarly insisted on the need for citizens to elect their own regents and hold them to account. Similarly, *The Aristocracy* acknowledged that much of the existing political system needed to be dismantled in order to secure a truly free republic.[12] This was eventually achieved, but only through foreign intervention. William V fled the Dutch republic on 18 January 1795. This event marked the end of the stadt-holderate and the establishment of the Batavian republic, which was inspired and initiated by the French.

Genevan Republicanism and the Genevan Revolution

During the eighteenth century Geneva faced two related problems that caused considerable conflict and instability, culminating in the failed revolution of 1782. In the first place, the small state struggled to maintain its independence in the face of the power and influence of Britain and France. In a situation where commerce was increasingly used to fund national defence, the size of the state was crucial and small republics were vulnerable. Geneva relied on the protection of France and various Swiss cantons for its survival, and yet risked becoming dominated by them, thereby having its political liberty undermined. At the same time, throughout much of the eighteenth century, debates raged over the balance between the different elements of the constitution and, in particular, over whether ultimate sovereignty lay with the General Council or with the smaller executive councils – the Two Hundred and the Twenty Five – or whether it was shared among all three. Several attempts were made to challenge the increasingly oligarchical character of the Genevan state, and accusations were launched that the ruling magistrates were being corrupted by their association with the French.

The first of these attempts was the uprising of 1707 led by Pierre Fatio. The rebels made four demands designed to wrest power away from the families that dominated the smaller councils and to return it to the General Council. They called for a limit to be placed on the number of members of the same family who could serve in the Two Hundred; for the establishment of a commission to oversee the revision of the legal code; for the General Council to meet annually; and for voting by secret ballot.[13] Fatio and his supporters thus touched on the key question of whether republican government required rule by the people themselves, or merely rule in what was taken to be their interests. Responding to the rebels, the syndic Jean-Robert Chouet demonstrated his very different views on this issue, drawing a clear distinction between enjoying a right and exercising it. He claimed that the Genevan people had delegated the powers of the General Council to the smaller councils in the interest of the common good; and he drew a parallel between this act and the kind of representative systems of government that operated in the Netherlands, in Germany, in Switzerland, and in England. He also pointed out that a full set of laws had been provided for Geneva in the sixteenth century, which meant that no further legislation was necessary (only minor regulations). This allowed him to argue that it was no longer essential for the General Council to play a major role.[14] Fatio responded that, if sovereignty was not exercised, then it was illusory; and he asserted that the General Council had not consented to having its powers taken away. Alarmed by the uprising, the Small Council called for help from Berne and Zurich and the rebels were suppressed by force. Fatio was charged with sedition and illegal assembly and condemned to death. He was shot in jail soon after.

This uprising led to a number of changes to the constitution. Those with concerns about the operation of government were given the right to make formal, written complaints or 'representations' as an alternative to the traditional method of gathering petitions. In 1712 it was agreed that new laws and taxes had to be put before the General Council for ratification, and the other two councils were to decide when to call it.

The following years saw further conflicts, in particular over the related issues of raising taxation and the building of fortifications. In November 1728 Jacques-Barthélemy Micheli du Crest put in writing his concerns about the decision that had been taken to build expensive fortifications around the city. He worried they would restrict the city's growth and would not necessarily provide adequate defence; but he also objected to the fact that the decision had been taken without the agreement of the General Council. The authorities seized all copies of his work, and he lost his position and his property. In 1731 he was declared a traitor and sentenced in his absence to perpetual imprisonment. Others would not remain silent, however, and in 1734 an unarmed crowd of bourgeois submitted representations to the four syndics and to the *procureur-général*, challenging the smaller councils' actions with regard to taxes and fortifications without the consent of the General Council and asking that the latter be summoned to address these issues. A General Council was called for 8 July. It voted in favour of the fortifications and for taxes to fund them. However, by insisting that the militias were not to be placed under the control of garrisons, it provided an important weapon for rebels – who, owing to their actions, started to become known as *représentants*. In December 1734 they drew on this new power to demand that those involved in activities against them be barred for life from membership of the higher councils. Thanks to the physical force behind the *représentants*, the Two Hundred gave in to their demands. In the following year Micheli du Crest inflamed attitudes still further by circulating his *Requête, avertissement, placet et mémoire*, which put the case for the sovereignty of the people. It was condemned and an effigy of him was executed by the authorities. In 1747, from his prison cell in Neuchâtel, he wrote *Maximes d'un républicain*, in which he lamented: '[n]othing is rarer today than a well-ordered republic where liberty reigns to a very high degree, one in which the people make the law, and the liberty of the great is curtailed'.[15]

By the time Micheli du Crest was writing his *Maximes*, violence had erupted once again. In August 1737 the *représentants* had again sought to get their views heard by means of force. Victory for the bourgeois militia prompted mediation involving France, Berne, and Zurich. The powers of the General Council over war and peace, taxation, fortifications, new laws, state borrowing, and the election of officers of state were recognised, and it was also agreed that no changes be made to the government and no troops admitted into the city without that body's consent. The Two Hundred was expanded by fifty members. The right of peaceful representation was also recognised, but the smaller councils were able to decide whether or not a matter was to be brought before the General Council, and the bourgeois lost their power to assemble the militia without orders from the syndics and from the Small Council.

In the 1750s and 1760s the *représentants*, under the leadership of Jacques-François Deluc, became more strongly organised, forming clubs known as *cercles* and producing written attacks on the oligarchic and francophone attitudes of the authorities. Yet by the 1760s the absence of formal mechanisms for opposition within the state meant that a stalemate had emerged.[16] The *représentants* would issue representations that they insisted should be put before the General Council, but the smaller councils would refuse to comply. As a result, party members became known as *négatifs*. The *représentants* then adopted the only means they could, and in November 1765 began withholding their ratification of government candidates for office. Initial attempts at mediation (again, facilitated by foreign intervention) failed, but in March 1768 the *représentants* gave up their rejection of candidates for high office in exchange for the right to remove four members of the Small Council and, on occasion, to elect directly their own nominees to the Two Hundred. At the same time the *natifs* – that is, the children of the incoming *habitants* who had been denied citizenship rights – were granted access to the professions and greater commercial rights, although they still lacked civil and political rights.

By 1770, however, discontent was bubbling up among the *natifs*. In line with similar claims that were made in colonial America, they objected to being expected to pay taxes to which they had not consented and to obey laws they had had no part in making. The threat was real, given that those not eligible to sit in the General Council now made up more than 80 per cent of the population. Initially the *représentants* worked with the government to restore order, but a proposal put forward by the French foreign minister, Charles Gravier, count de Vergennes, that threatened to undermine the gains made in 1768 brought the *représentants* into alliance with the *natifs*.

On 5 February 1781 the *représentants* built on a demonstration of the *natifs* and seized control of the city.[17] They asked for civil rights for *natifs* and for foreign powers to stop getting involved in Genevan affairs. Greater rights for *natifs* were subsequently established, but other problems remained unresolved. Consequently, on 8–9 April 1782 the *représentants* took control of the city once more, locked up the magistrates, and began to devise a new constitution. By the end of June, however, a combined military force of French, Bernese, and Savoyard troops had arrived in the city, calling for the magistrates to be reinstated and for the surrender of arms. The rebels, concerned that the city was in danger of being destroyed, voted 57 to 40 in favour of capitulation, and on 2 July the city fell without resistance; the *représentant* leaders fled. A new constitution was then established that gave even greater power to the magistrates, and on 21 November 1782 an edict, which became known as the Édit Noir (Black Edict), was passed. It removed the powers gained by the General Council in 1768, stifled dissent, and banished the leaders of the *représentants* from the city. Those leaders – Étienne Clavière, Antoine Du Roveray, and François d'Ivernois among them – turned their attention to other means of securing Genevan independence. These included reforming Europe's monarchies, arguing against mercantilist policies, and pushing instead for a commercial alliance between Britain and France.[18]

Rousseau

Jean-Jacques Rousseau was born in Geneva in 1712. His grandfather had been involved in Fatio's uprising of 1707, but Rousseau himself left the city at a young age and had not been involved in the subsequent political disputes. He made a name for himself by responding to the essay-writing competitions launched by the Academy of Dijon in 1749 and 1754. The work submitted to the second of these competitions, his *Discourse on Inequality*, was dedicated to his native city, whose principles, he believed, offered an alternative political model to that of the centralising monarchies of the eighteenth century, namely a polity ruled by virtue. After the publication of the *Discourse*, Rousseau returned to Geneva. He was readmitted to the Protestant Church after his youthful conversion to Catholicism, and he reclaimed his status as a citizen. In his *Lettre à d'Alembert* he set out an idealised vision of the Genevan state, a city of middling people living decent, modest, and hardworking lives and engaging in both the political and the military governance of their state.[19] But it was in *The Social Contract* of 1762 that he addressed directly the question of republican government. This work proved much less popular with his fellow citizens. Together with his novel *Émile*, which had been published in the same year, it was banned by the Small Council and condemned to be burned. Rousseau renounced his recently restored citizenship, in protest, in May 1763.

He could not, however, avoid the fallout that resulted from the Small Council's decision and was forced to engage in Genevan political debates. In September 1763 Jean-Robert Tronchin justified the condemnation of Rousseau's books in his *Lettres écrites de la campagne* and accused the *représentants* of undermining public order via their continued issuing of representations. This intervention has served to reinforce the assumption that Rousseau was firmly associated with the cause of the *représentants* and that *The Social Contract* was an expression of the latter's desire to return Geneva to its democratic constitutional origins. Yet the story is rather more complicated than this.[20] In part it was Tronchin himself who sought to turn Rousseau into a spokesperson for the *représentants*. And this notion was further encouraged by the *représentants'* insistence that Rousseau respond. Yet, while the resulting *Lettres écrites de la montagne* supported the idea that the sovereignty of the General Council ought to be asserted, as it accused the magistrates of threatening to overturn the crucial distinction between sovereignty and government within the city, Rousseau was equally concerned that the *représentants* themselves posed a threat to that distinction by seeking to make the government democratic. Consequently he supported the right of the smaller councils to a negative veto.

The crucial distinction between sovereignty (the making of laws) and government (their execution) was something that Rousseau had taken from the writings of Jean Bodin and had set out clearly in *The Social Contract*. It was on this basis that Rousseau argued that the definition of a republic is a state in which sovereignty lies with the people, but government could be exercised within such a state monarchically, aristocratically, or democratically.[21] While any of these governmental forms could constitute a republic, Rousseau's preference was for an aristocratic system, since he feared that democratic government was only suitable for gods.[22]

As a result of his belief that republican government required popular sovereignty, Rousseau argued that a true republic is possible only in a small state, where the whole population could gather together on a regular basis. 'The Sovereign, having no other force than the legislative power, acts only by means of the laws, and the laws being nothing but the authentic acts of the general will, the Sovereign can only act when the people is assembled.'[23] Moreover, he did not view representative government as an acceptable solution to this problem:

> Sovereignty cannot be represented for the same reason that it cannot be alienated; it consists essentially in the general will, and the will does not admit of it being represented: either it is the same or it is different; there is no middle ground. The deputies of the people therefore are

not and cannot be its representatives, they are merely its agents; they cannot conclude anything definitively. Any law which the People has not ratified in person is null; it is not a law.[24]

Nonetheless, in his *Considerations on the Government of Poland*, in which he was forced to engage with constitution building in a large state, Rousseau did offer some kind of solution to this problem, proposing that delegates who were subject to binding mandates could be used to convey the views of their constituents.[25]

Partly because of the significance he attributed to popular participation, Rousseau also emphasised the importance of civic virtue and insisted on the need to instil in the population the appropriate manners, virtues, and customs for this form of government.[26] One means of achieving this, Rousseau suggested, was via the figure of a great lawgiver (*Législateur*) – a figure of 'superior intelligence who saw all of man's passions and experienced none of them'.[27] While part of the lawgiver's task was to construct a constitution, he was also required, as Rousseau put it in *Considerations on the Government of Poland*, to foster 'bonds that might attach the Citizens to the fatherland and to one another'.[28]

Forging these bonds demanded that great inequalities between citizens were avoided: 'no citizen be so very rich that he can buy another, and none so poor that he is compelled to sell himself'.[29] Wealth and luxury, as he had argued in the *Discourse on Inequality*, exerted a corrupting influence, which would encourage citizens to put their own interests above those of the republic.

Also crucial was the careful use of public education and of honours and rewards. Rousseau dealt with education at length in *Considerations on the Government of Poland*, stating that '[i]t is education that must give souls the national form, and so direct their tastes and opinions that they will be patriotic by inclination, passion, necessity'.[30] He insisted that, if education was organised correctly, by the age of twenty a Pole would think of himself first and foremost as a Pole. To facilitate this, only Poles were to be allowed to work as teachers, and there should be no difference in education according to wealth. The rewarding of virtue was also key. 'I should wish all the patriotic virtues to be given luster by attaching to them honors and public rewards, the Citizens to be kept constantly occupied with the fatherland, for it to be made their principal business, for it to be continuously kept before their eyes.'[31] In place of courtly entertainments, public games should be held regularly. Rousseau insisted that these spectacles should take place in the open and should involve all citizens equally.[32]

Another crucial means of forging these bonds was religion. In speaking of the lawgiver and his task of appealing to the ordinary people, Rousseau claimed that he must 'have recourse to an authority of a different order, which might be able to rally without violence and to persuade without convincing'.[33] Rousseau cites Machiavelli on this point, but both were also looking back to Lycurgus, who had understood the importance of divine authority when establishing the Spartan constitution and from whom Rousseau also took the idea that, having accomplished his constitutional task, the lawgiver should step down from his position. At the end of the chapter on the lawgiver Rousseau makes clear that he believes that religion should be the servant of politics, an idea he elaborates on further in his chapter 'Civil Religion'.[34]

Rousseau identifies three ways in which religion and politics can be combined: 'the religion of the Priest', 'the religion of the Citizen', and 'the Religion of man'. The last, which reflects Christianity as it existed at the time of the apostolic church, has the greatest appeal. It could provide the fraternity among citizens required for a successful republic. It would also encourage the fulfilment of civic duties, a rejection of luxury and vanity, and the cultivation of virtuous magistrates and brave soldiers. Yet, by elevating the afterlife above life on earth, this form of religion presents problems for republican government. In its place, therefore, Rousseau offers his own version of a civil religion the tenets of which would be less 'dogmas of Religion' than 'sentiments of sociability', which encourage a love of civic duties.[35]

It is not surprising that Rousseau's unorthodox religious views (as well as his distinctive attitude to the relationship between sovereignty and government) presented problems for many in Geneva, including Deluc, the leader of the *représentants*. While Rousseau argued that the church had played a dangerous role in Geneva and called for a clear separation between church and state, Deluc continued to see the relationship between them as crucial.[36]

Despite all the attention he paid to the creation of virtuous manners, Rousseau remained sceptical on two counts. First, he drew a distinction between what was appropriate for men and what might be expected of women. On this point his ideas were challenged directly by Mary Wollstonecraft and, later, indirectly by the marquis de Condorcet and others.[37] Secondly, he questioned whether virtuous manners could be cultivated effectively in an old nation, where customs were already in place and prejudices deep-rooted, and especially one in which commerce and luxury had already taken hold.[38] On this basis he denied that the French were capable of the required regeneration. Where Rousseau remained sceptical about the potential for establishing republican government in France, several French thinkers drew on republican ideas, some even suggesting that those ideas could be of direct relevance to the French.

Montesquieu

Charles-Louis de Secondat, baron de La Brède et de Montesquieu (1689–1755), was born in the town of La Brède in south-western France. His major work *The Spirit of the Laws* was hugely influential, encompassing legal theory, comparative politics, and constitutional thought. One of Montesquieu's most important innovations lay in his development of an alternative typology of government designed to replace that originally developed by Aristotle. Against Aristotle's account of three good forms of government that operated in the public interest and three corresponding bad forms that were governed by the private interests of those in power, Montesquieu's typology distinguished just three main types, placing the fundamental distinction between moderate governments (which included republics and monarchies governed by laws) and despotisms:

> Republican government is that in which the people as a body, or only a part of the people have sovereign power; monarchical government is that in which one alone governs, but by fixed and established laws; whereas, in despotic government, one alone, without law and without rule, draws everything along by his will and his caprices.[39]

Montesquieu also added to Aristotle's typology by suggesting that the different forms of government could be characterised not only by their form, but also by their spirit or the principle that animated them:

> There is this difference between the nature of the government and its principle: the nature is that which makes it what it is, and its principle, that which makes it act. The one is its particular structure, and the other is the human passions that set it in motion.[40]

The principle of republican government, according to Montesquieu, was virtue, which he viewed in political rather than moral or religious terms and defined as love of the homeland and of equality.

There is some debate about whether Montesquieu himself ultimately favoured republican or monarchical government. While he certainly praised republics in theory, he did not believe such a form of government to be suited to the states of the modern world – least of all France. In part this was because he, like Rousseau, believed that republics were suited to relatively small states:

> It is in the nature of a republic to have only a small territory; otherwise, it can scarcely continue to exist. In a large republic, there are large fortunes, and consequently little moderation in spirits: the depositories are too large to put in the hands of a citizen; interests become particularised; at first a man feels he can be happy, great, and glorious without his homeland; and soon, that he can be great only on the ruins of his homeland. In a large republic, the common good is sacrificed to a thousand considerations; it is subordinated to exceptions; it depends upon accidents. In a small one, the public good is better felt, better known, lies nearer to each citizen; abuses are less extensive there and consequently less protected.[41]

Nonetheless Montesquieu did offer two potential solutions for those wishing to establish large republics. One was to make use of representation:

> As, in a free state, every man, considered to have a free soul, should be governed by himself, the people as a body should have legislative power; but, as this is impossible in large states and is subject to many drawbacks in small ones, the people must have their representatives do all that they themselves cannot do.[42]

The other was to adopt a federal system. Noting that small republics were at risk of being destroyed by external forces, whereas large republics were subject to internal corruption, Montesquieu proposed the federal republic as a solution to both problems. It could be created by many political bodies if they consented to become part of a larger state – which could be added to at any time. This model, Montesquieu argued, could combine the internal advantages of republican government with the external power of monarchy. 'This sort of republic, able to resist external force, can be maintained at its size without internal corruption: the form of this society curbs every drawback.'[43] It was for this idea of a federal republic as much as for his insistence on the separation of legislative, executive, and judicial powers that Montesquieu exercised a particular influence on American revolutionaries.

Mably

Less well known, but equally important as an eighteenth-century republican theorist, is Abbé Gabriel Bonnot de Mably (1709–85), whose contribution to French republicanism has been demonstrated by Keith Baker and Kent Wright.[44] Although Mably's ideal form of government was in line with the ancient republican tradition, his proposals for the reform of contemporary states were much more akin to those of the British republicans of the eighteenth century.[45]

Mably's ancient republicanism rested on two fundamental tenets: anti-monarchism and material equality. In his *Observations sur les grecs* he associated the emergence of liberty and independence in ancient Greece directly with the abolition of monarchical government. His emphasis on material equality led him to favour Sparta and to identify the rise of wealth and luxury as the most common cause of corruption within states. Speaking of Lycurgus, he said:

> What good would his establishment of order have been if the taste for riches and the love of luxury, which are always found together and which are always linked to the inequality of citizens because they make some tyrants and others slaves, had been allowed to silently unbalance the harmony of the government?[46]

It was this belief in equality as a key basis for republicanism that prompted him to insist, in *Des droits et des devoirs du citoyen*, that in his ideal state private property would be abolished and a community of goods established.[47]

Despite his commitment to this ancient republican ideal, however, Mably was clear that such a system could not be imposed in modern states such as Britain or France. As he explained through the persona of Milord Stanhope, who was the embodiment of a British commonwealth man and the central character in *Des droits et des devoirs du citoyen*, modern peoples were too attached to money and personal honour to bear a free and equal republic. Consequently, any political change that was to be enacted would need to be gradual; and, as was typical of eighteenth-century British republicans, he insisted that the abolition of monarchy was not essential to republican reform:

> Royalty is without doubt a vice in government, but it is necessary in a nation that has lost its primitive ideas of simplicity and equality, and is incapable of recovering them. With the unequal distribution of ranks, titles, riches, fortunes and dignities that there are in France, England and Sweden, is it possible to think there as one thinks in Switzerland?[48]

Through Stanhope, Mably offered an analysis of the British system of government that was typical of commonwealth thought. He combined admiration for the British constitution arising out of the Revolution of 1688–9 with a conviction that it had not gone far enough. He also called for an end to places and pensions, the introduction of frequent elections, and the replacement of the standing army with a citizen militia. Mably went further than his British counterparts in using the British experience as inspiration for a 'commonwealth' solution to France's political problems. This took the form of a *révolution ménagée* (managed revolution), in which the Estates-General would be recalled and its status at the heart of the French constitution fixed and sustained. Although Mably was writing around 1758, thirty years before the outbreak of the French Revolution, it has not escaped the notice of subsequent commentators that his proposals were not far removed from what actually occurred in 1788–9.[49]

Conclusion

Despite its unpromising opening, the eighteenth century in fact proved a fertile period for the development and application of republican ideas. Events in existing republics such as the United Provinces and Geneva inspired and sparked further deliberation on republican theory, not least about the role of a single figurehead within a republican constitution and about the degree to which republicanism necessitated popular participation in government. Against this background, the writings of Rousseau, Montesquieu, and Mably probed new issues and took republican thought in new directions. The question of whether republican government was only suited to small states or whether it could be expanded over a wider territory was particularly pertinent and generated different responses from key thinkers. The relationship of republicanism to anti-monarchism also continued to be debated. Mably was particularly interesting on this topic, presenting anti-monarchism as central to ancient republicanism, but admitting that the removal of royalty was not the priority for states like Britain or France, as they moved towards republican rule. It is also noteworthy that princely government remained at least a possibility according to Rousseau's rather strict characterisation of a republic. The role of virtue in republican government also remained crucial, Montesquieu seeing it as the 'principle' of republican government and Rousseau insisting on the importance of cultivating civic virtue among the population as an essential prerequisite to the establishment and survival of republican rule.

There can be no doubt that, by the end of the eighteenth century, the range of situations in which republican ideas were being discussed and to which they were being applied had broadened. They were not only used by supporters of republican states in places such as the United Provinces and Geneva, but also deployed by those who were living under absolute monarchies as a means of questioning that form of rule. In this way they no doubt helped to undermine popular faith in absolutist government and thereby contributed to the outbreak of revolution in North America and France. Moreover, as the next two chapters will demonstrate, those revolutions provided new opportunities for the dissemination and implementation of republican ideas, while also provoking fresh transformations in the ways in which such ideas were understood.

7

The American Revolution

Introduction

In late eighteenth-century North America as elsewhere, practical political experiences prompted reflection on political ideas. The rejection of British rule that was announced by the Declaration of Independence in July 1776, fought for during the War of Independence that followed, and cemented by the development and establishment first of the state constitutions and then, in 1787, of the Constitution of the United States of America generated much debate both in America and beyond. Few American revolutionaries were more prolific in their political thinking than the man who would become the second president of the United States: John Adams (1735–1826). His *A Defence of the Constitutions of the United States of America* (1787) epitomised this merging of the theoretical and the practical. Not only did it draw on both political thought and practical experience, but it used historical examples to identify the most appropriate model for new constitutions at both state and federal levels.

Adams's deep thinking on the nature of republican government led him to eschew any simple conception of the form. Part of the point of his survey of republican models, past and present, factual and fictitious, was to demonstrate that all republics are not the same, and his findings implied that in practice Cicero's equation of good government with republican government did not hold:

> The name republic is given to things, in their nature as different and contradictory as light and darkness, truth and falsehood, virtue and

vice, happiness and misery. There are free republics, and republics as tyrannical as an oriental despotism. A free republic is the best of governments, and the greatest blessing which mortals can aspire to. Republics which are not free, by the help of a multitude of rigorous checks, in very small states, and for very short spaces of time, have preserved some reverence for the laws, and been tolerable; but there have been oligarchies carried to such extremes of tyranny, that the despotism of Turkey, as far as the happiness of the nation at large is concerned, would perhaps be preferable. An empire of laws is a characteristic of a free republic only, and should never be applied to republics in general.[1]

It was not enough, then, for the Americans simply to establish republican government: it was crucial that they selected the right model. Moreover, the American revolutionaries also faced new geographical and cultural problems, specific to their situation, that had not troubled republicans of the past. The Americans were not, of course, the first to engage with the problem of creating a large, modern republic. The English had also grappled with how to establish a workable republic on a territory that covered thousands of square miles rather than being just a single city-state and had a population of 5 million rather than 200,000. But the scale of the American republic put it in a different league from its English predecessor and the notion of a movable frontier brought seemingly limitless space, but also fresh challenges. American republicans also followed their English predecessors in considering how to reconcile ancient republican values and ethics with Christianity as well as with the rise of commercial society. However, the Americans also had to wrestle with the presence of a native population and with the institution of slavery. Moreover, the English could hardly be said to have made a practical success of their endeavour. The English republic lasted little more than a decade, and throughout that period it was beset by divisions and instability. This is why it is the American Revolution rather than its English precursor that is widely seen as marking the birth of the modern republic.

Despite this, the American revolutionaries were aware of, and drew on, the writings and experiences of those who had gone before. As Bernard Bailyn demonstrated, classical education had provided the revolutionaries with a wealth of knowledge regarding the 'constitutions' and the history of ancient Greece and Rome, and they deployed that knowledge when addressing their own political situation. Bailyn also revealed the particularly significant influence exercised by the writings of the seventeenth-century English republicans and their eighteenth-century successors, at the beginning of the crisis as well as when it came to building the new republic. Earlier republican writings and models, then, were crucial both in prompting the outbreak of the American Revolution in 1776 and in determining and shaping the course of this revolution and the constitution that emerged from it. Yet, as Eric Nelson has demonstrated, it was not only republican models and ideas that American revolutionaries drew from England. They were also influenced by royalist writings from the seventeenth century; and it seems that these, too, were woven into the construction of the constitution.[2]

Nelson's revisionist account of the founding of the American republic derives not only from the attention he draws to the royalist sources of American republicanism, but also from his appreciation of the complexity of the concept of republicanism in the eighteenth century. As he pertinently states, '[a]ny satisfactory account of the republican turn in British North America must begin by acknowledging that "republicanism" in early modern Europe was no single thing'.[3] The Americans, of course, added to the complexity. As well as building on earlier models, writings, and ideas, they also exerted their own influence on republican thought. Their practical experience of revolution and constitution building led them to adapt existing republican ideas to suit their own circumstances and concerns and, effectively, to invent their own version of republicanism, fit for the particular context in which they found themselves. In fact it is probably truer to say that they invented not one American strain of republicanism, but several. Debates over the nature of republicanism abounded, and several competing republican discourses are evident in America during the revolutionary period and beyond.

This chapter will explore both the legacy of republican ideas that the American revolutionaries inherited and the way in which these people reshaped them, reimagining a republic suited to the circumstances of a newly liberated people, in a recently united state, with a vast expanse of land on its doorstep. Attention will be paid to the influence of the practical experience of separation from Britain and to the requirements that this separation generated, as well as to the specific debates that erupted in its aftermath.

The Ideological Origins of American Republicanism

The idea that the American Revolution and the republicanism that emerged from it had ideological origins is not new, but its lack of novelty has not resulted in consensus, since historians have disagreed as to which ideas were the most influential. In particular, debate has long raged over whether 'liberal' or 'republican' ideas played a greater role in determining the outbreak of the American Revolution and its subsequent outcomes. Moreover, Nelson's fresh argument about royalist influences on the American founders adds another strand to the debate, without challenging the underlying premise that ideas were fundamentally important.

Liberal versus Republican Origins

The liberal argument was exemplified in Louis Hartz's 1955 book *The Liberal Tradition in America*, which argued that Lockean ideas that were inherent in American society from the seventeenth century onwards shaped the entire revolutionary experience and, together with the absence of feudalism, helped to set the American Revolution apart from its French counterpart.[4] This argument was subsequently developed by authors such as Joyce Appleby and Thomas Pangle, who offered much greater detail on the nature of Locke's influence on the revolutionaries, and analysed the combination of liberal and capitalist ideas within revolutionary America.[5]

A decade after Hartz's book had appeared, Bernard Bailyn set out an alternative vision of the ideological origins of the American Revolution that was based on his extensive reading of a wealth of pamphlets published between 1750 and 1776. His four-volume edition of more than seventy of these pamphlets was prefaced by an introduction that was subsequently published separately under the title *The Ideological Origins of the American Revolution.*[6] It attempted to cut an explanatory path through this wealth of polemical literature. While confirming the 'rather old-fashioned view that the American Revolution was above all else an ideological, constitutional, political struggle and not primarily a controversy between social groups undertaken to force changes in the organisation of the society or the economy',[7] Bailyn's account of the content of this ideological struggle was innovative rather than old-fashioned. As a result of his research, Bailyn played down the natural rights philosophy that Hartz and others had assumed was central to the ideology of the revolutionaries and instead identified five discourses, or trains of thought, that he argued exercised a fundamental influence on the American colonists in the run-up to the Revolution. Moreover, he also made a persuasive case for the impact that ideas can have on events, demonstrating just how the works that the American colonists had been reading led them to interpret the actions of the British in a particular way, thereby propelling them into revolution.

The Classical Heritage

One of the five discourses identified by Bailyn was the 'heritage of classical antiquity'.[8] He noted that classical authors – Homer, Aristotle, Strabo, Polybius, Virgil, Seneca, Lucretius, Cato, and Suetonius – were frequently cited in the pamphlet literature. While much of the learning on display was superficial, Bailyn did find evidence of more detailed knowledge of and interest in Roman history between the first century BCE and the second century CE, a period that encompassed the writings of Plutarch, Livy, Cicero, Sallust, and Tacitus. The contrast between a corrupt and oppressive present and a virtuous, simple, and patriotic past found in the works of some of these writers seemed to the American pamphleteers to parallel their own story, and hence to be particularly pertinent to it.

The importance of the Roman model to American revolutionaries has also been highlighted by Eran Shalev.[9] He endorses the fact that, from 1776 on, the Americans focused in particular on the Roman republic as a model of virtue-based politics, comparing themselves to their Roman predecessors and imagining themselves to be Roman heroes. Yet Shalev also complicates this picture, noting a shift by the late 1780s, when the Roman model was seen as less relevant. By then many revolutionaries were suggesting that Carthage – a commercial republic – might be a better model for the leaders of the young American republic.

Shalev also notes the importance for America of the model of the Hebrew republic, which better fitted America's federal character and provided a method whereby powers might be effectively divided and balanced. The Hebrew model was also useful because it helped to bridge the difficult gap between republicanism and Christianity. Similarly useful in this regard were the social and political theories of New England Puritanism, which Bailyn argued were another important source of inspiration for the revolutionaries.[10] In particular, they embraced the idea that the colonisation of British America was part of God's plan, which facilitated the belief that their local conflicts and parochial concerns were relevant to, and in fact represented a critical moment in, a much broader cosmic history.

The British Commonwealth Tradition

Yet according to Bailyn neither of these two discourses (the heritage of classical antiquity and New England Puritanism) was the most important of the sources that influenced the American revolutionary pamphlets. That title went instead to the canon of republican works and ideas that sprang up in the aftermath of the English Revolution of the mid-seventeenth century, and to the late seventeenth- and eighteenth-century works inspired by that experience. The writings of Milton, Nedham, Harrington, Neville, Sidney, and especially Trenchard and Gordon were omnipresent in the pamphlets of the American Revolution. Quotations and longer excerpts from them found their way into these pamphlets. More generally, commonwealth writings such as *The Independent Whig*, *Cato's Letters*, and *The Craftsman* were used as models for American works; and the revolutionaries cited the names of these thinkers in their own works, used them as pseudonyms, and even named their children after them.

Moreover, the ideology at the heart of these texts was woven deeply into the minds of American revolutionaries. The colonists picked up on the fears voiced by these commonwealth authors regarding the precarious nature of liberty and its susceptibility to corruption and the abuse of power, whether through the executive's control over parliament – via places and pensions – or through the establishment of a standing army. Being imbued with these ideas caused the revolutionaries to be particularly sensitive to George III's erection, in the colonies, of new offices that were filled by people under his control and to his use of standing armies on American soil. Their extreme and explosive reactions can therefore be traced back to an understanding of the relationship between liberty and power and of the huge threat that the one posed to the other, as detailed in the commonwealth works.

Royalist Influences

Nelson agrees with Bailyn that these commonwealth ideas were fundamentally important in the first half of the eighteenth century up to the 1760s and that they prepared the foundations for the revolutionary generation. However, he insists that the behaviour of the British parliament over issues such as the Stamp Act and Townshend Duties prompted a shift in the attitude of many American revolutionaries. The domineering behaviour of parliament led colonists to conclude that the imbalance within the English constitution was not so much a matter of the king dominating parliament as one of parliament having usurped too many of the king's powers. Consequently they argued that prerogative powers should be restored to the king in order that he could fulfil his proper role in relation to the colonies.[11] It was only, Nelson argues, George III's refusal to act in this way that led the colonists to reject monarchy.[12]

As this would suggest, not only did a variety of ideas influence the American revolutionary generation, but also they viewed those earlier traditions differently from each other and were not averse to picking and choosing from them. In some cases divisions within the English republican canon were acknowledged and a discriminating attitude was in evidence. For example, Adams was extremely critical of Nedham's *The Excellencie of a Free State* and offered a scathing critique of it, presenting it as prefiguring the democratic ideas invoked by Jacques-Anne-Robert Turgot and his friends. By contrast, Harrington's works, and especially *Oceana*, were treated much more reverentially by Adams and used by him as a model for the Massachusetts state constitution.

The Break from Britain

The year 1776 marked a fundamental shift from theory to practice in American republicanism. With the Declaration of Independence, adopted on 2 July and signed two days later, the Americans separated themselves from Britain and, in doing so, released themselves from the authority of George III and his parliament. Since they did not appoint a new monarch, the state became a de facto republic. With hindsight, this may seem an obvious move, but at the time it was a step into the dark. As the American revolutionaries were well aware, the republican form of government was generally associated with small city-states – Athens and Rome among the ancients, Venice and Geneva in the modern world. The United Provinces did provide a model for a larger, federated republic, but it was not on the same scale as the thirteen colonies. Moreover, the two states that could in principle serve as models for a large state republic – Rome during its period of expansion and England in the mid-seventeenth century – looked more like cautionary tales than success stories. Many in the eighteenth century attributed Rome's ultimate decline and fall to its earlier expansion, arguing that it had extended its sphere of influence way beyond an area that a republic could reasonably control. Similarly, the fact that the English republic had lasted barely ten years, together with the failure of the English to find a durable and workable republican system and the frustration of many republican political theorists of the time meant that this model was also deemed problematic.

Paine's *Common Sense*

In this atmosphere of uncertainty, and given the absence of useful models, Thomas Paine's pamphlet *Common Sense*, which appeared in early 1776, was an important beacon of hope and possibility. Paine had been born in Thetford, Norfolk, in 1737. Thirty-seven years later, in 1774, he emigrated to America. His life up to that point had been largely unremarkable, but with the publication of *Common Sense* in Philadelphia on 10 January 1776 he was catapulted into the position of a professional revolutionary and 'Citizen of the World', as the plaque dedicated to him in his one-time home – the East Sussex town of Lewes – declares.

Common Sense combined two powerful arguments to make the case for revolution in America. In the first place, Paine presented an unequivocal call for, and justification of, American independence.[13] Addressing head on much contemporary concern, he explained that America gained no great advantage from being linked to Britain – not least because Britain was inclined to put its own interests first in that relationship. At the same time he argued that the distance between the two territories made it impractical for Britain to continue to rule the American colonies.

Paine's other crucial argument was his attack on monarchy and hereditary succession:

> There is something exceedingly ridiculous in the composition of Monarchy, it first excludes a man from the means of information yet empowers him to act in cases where the highest judgment is required. The state of a King shuts him from the World; yet the business of a King requires him to know it thoroughly: wherefore, the different parts by unnaturally opposing and destroying each other, prove the whole character to be absurd and useless.[14]

The same argument was used to attack hereditary rule generally, and therefore aristocracy as well as monarchy.

Clearly Paine, unlike some of his seventeenth-century predecessors, was firmly and unequivocally committed to an exclusivist view of republican government. Kings, whatever form they adopted and whatever powers they had, were wrong on Paine's account. This argument was based on a very particular reading of certain key biblical passages – not least I Samuel 8, where the Israelites asked God to give them a king like those of other nations. On this reading, the sin of the Israelites was not to ask for a specific type of king but to ask for any king at all, since by doing so they were effectively displacing God from his position of ultimate rule over them. They committed the sin of idolatry by seeking to give a mortal a royal position. Despite Paine's famous coyness about his sources, Nelson suggests that he drew this reading from Milton's *Pro populo*

anglicano defensio (*Defence of the People of England*), the first text
to introduce into Christian biblical exegesis this interpretation of I
Samuel 8, which derived from certain Jewish traditions.[15] Moreover,
as Nelson has suggested, Paine's powerful argument about the ills of
kingship thrust many patriots into a firmly anti-monarchical stance,
albeit one that still left room for a strong chief magistrate wielding
considerable prerogative powers.[16]

In place of monarchy Paine called for the establishment of a new
form of republicanism, suited to the modern world. One key element
of it was representation, which needed to be adopted as soon as a
state or colony had grown to a size where all members could no
longer meet together. Legislative decisions could then be taken by a
smaller group, chosen from the whole and made up of those 'who are
supposed to have the same concerns at stake which those have who
appointed them, and who will act in the same manner as the whole
body would act were they present.'[17] It was crucial, Paine insisted,
that regular elections were held, so that those elected did not effectively become a separate political class.

Paine sketched out his own vision of how such a system might
work in practice.[18] At its heart were the colonial assemblies – the
sovereign bodies for the purposes of domestic government. These
assemblies would be elected annually and would be subject to a
more equal representation than had previously been the case. At
the central level, the Continental Congress would provide oversight
of the colonial assemblies as well as acting as their spokesperson
with regard to foreign and diplomatic concerns. The members
of the Congress would not, however, be chosen directly by the
colonial assemblies. Rather, each colony would be divided into six
to ten convenient districts each of which would send delegates to the
Congress, so that each colony had at least thirty representatives. The
office of president of the Congress would rotate among the colonies
and its incumbent would be chosen by a method that combined lot
and a ballot.

As this system reveals, Paine firmly embraced the idea of popular
sovereignty, insisting that it should be the people who held ultimate
power within a state; and he used this idea to justify separation from
Britain. His commitment to popular rule was also reflected in the
style and approach of *Common Sense* itself. As the title suggests,
Paine's intention was to offer 'simple facts, plain arguments and
common sense'.[19] Unlike many political writers of the time, he
eschewed Latin tags and allusions to ancient myths and history, as
these required a grammar school education to be properly understood. Instead he urged his audience to use its own reason to engage

with political matters, and he made much use of repetition and of imagery and metaphor to render complex ideas clear and accessible to the ordinary reader.

Paine's pamphlet proved extremely popular. More than 100,000 copies had been sold by April 1776, which made it the most frequently printed pamphlet of the revolutionary period, and extracts also appeared in a range of colonial newspapers.[20] It was seen as giving the colonists the confidence they desperately needed to push forward with independence. Moreover, the model that was set out was not all that far removed from the system that emerged in 1776.

The State Constitutions and Articles of Confederation

The initial settlement, following the Declaration of Independence, did involve the bulk of the power remaining in the colonies or states, although there was much more variety than Paine had envisaged in the form adopted in the various state constitutions, since each assembly was responsible for drawing up its own constitution rather than a standard model being imposed on them all. In many cases the state constitution followed quite closely the previous colonial system of government. Consequently, in Massachusetts the notion of checks and balances between the powers of the one, the few, and the many remained key, as they had been under colonial rule. By contrast, the Pennsylvanian constitution provided for just a single unicameral assembly and a large degree of popular sovereignty.

The settlement of disputes between states and the representation of them in foreign matters was assigned to the Continental Congress under a new constitutional model, called the Articles of Confederation. It was drafted as early as mid-July 1776, but was not passed by the Continental Congress until 15 November 1777. Moreover, it took a further three and a half years before it was ratified and put into practice. The last state to ratify the Articles of Confederation was Maryland, and on 1 March 1781 the Confederation was formally announced.

The Articles of Confederation effectively created the 'United States of America' and, as a practical reflection of this, removed travel restrictions and trade barriers between states for the first time. Due to the Continental Congress's concerns about the dangers of strong central power, the Articles provided only for a loose federation. Each state would retain its sovereignty, freedom, and independence and much political power. The document was primarily a league of friendship between the states for their common defence and welfare. The only central force was the Continental Congress, the powers of which were strictly limited. It was to consist of just one legislative house with no executive or judicial power. It would be constituted of two to seven delegates from each state; and, regardless of the number of representatives it had, each state would be entitled to just one single vote in any debate. Congress would take on only those powers that had to be exercised centrally: control over foreign policy and diplomatic relations; acting as a court of appeal – particularly for settling disputes between states; the provision of a system of coinage, of standard weights and measures, and of a postal service; overseeing trade and other contacts with the Indian tribes; and providing an armed force for defence against external invasion. Any minor legislative acts passed by Congress had to be approved by at least seven of the thirteen states, and any major changes required the agreement of nine of them. Changes to the Articles themselves could be made only with the consent of all thirteen states.

In practice, the exercise of congressional power was severely restricted by the lack of executive authority. All congressional resolutions were conceived of simply as recommendations, since it was up to the states themselves to enforce them. Therefore it is not surprising that by the mid-1780s the Articles of Confederation were proving unworkable. As well as lacking an executive, Congress had no power to impose taxes or to regulate commerce. Moreover, some more traditional leaders had started to protest about the rise of new men to political power since 1776. As James Otis famously put it, 'when the pot boils the scum will rise'.

The Drawing up of the American Constitution

Within this climate of dissatisfaction, it was only a matter of time before the decision was taken to change the existing system. That moment came in May 1787, during a meeting in Philadelphia that had been prompted by a commercial dispute between Virginia and Maryland over the taxing of shipping on the Potomac River and in Chesapeake Bay. Delegates from twelve of the thirteen states attended the meeting (Rhode Island chose not to send delegates) and it was quickly decided that, rather than simply dealing with the immediate situation, it was necessary to take more drastic action and to draw up a new constitution. This text was drafted in the summer of 1787, signed on 17 September, and submitted to the Continental Congress for approval three days later.

The new constitution, which, famously, was deemed to have been produced in the name of the people, set out the legislative, executive, and judicial powers of the new central (federal) government. Legislative power was to reside in Congress, which would now adopt a bicameral structure. The members of the lower House of Representatives would be elected by the people in their states, while two senators would be elected by each state legislature. Congress, which would meet at least once a year, would exercise powers over taxation, common defence, and general welfare; and the Senate would also have the power of impeachment. All bills that had been passed by the House and by the Senate would then be presented to the president, and on being signed by him would become law. The president and his vice president would be the locus of executive power. The former would be commander in chief of the army and navy and would also have powers over foreign policy. The president would be chosen by an electoral college within the states, and both he and the vice president would serve a four-year term. The third power, alongside the legislative and executive, was judicial. It was to be lodged in the Supreme Court and the inferior courts across the country. Trial by jury was also enshrined in the constitution.

Though drawing up the constitution was itself a difficult task, completing that document did not mark the end of the story. In order for the constitution to be enacted it had to be ratified by at least nine of the thirteen states. Ratification was to take place not in the existing state legislatures but in specially convened conventions. Delaware was the first state to ratify the constitution, on 6 December 1787. The crucial ninth state was New Hampshire, which ratified the constitution on 21 June 1788. By August 1788 all but Rhode Island and North Carolina had completed the ratification process. Rhode Island was the last state to ratify the constitution, which it did on 28 May 1790. On 4 March 1789 the first United States Congress under the constitution met in New York, and on 30 April 1789 George Washington was inaugurated as first president of the United States of America. The American constitution was one of the most enduring documents of the eighteenth century. It remains in place today, with only a relatively small number of amendments.

American Debates, I: Arguments over the Mixed Constitution

Despite the enduring consequences of America's separation from Britain and its adoption of a republican government, the revolutionary period witnessed debate and division over a number of political and constitutional issues. One of the debates that divided

American revolutionaries was over whether the state and federal constitutions ought to adopt a unicameral or a bicameral structure.

Several European friends of the American revolutionaries – including the former French finance minister Turgot, his fellow countryman Mably, and the English dissenting minister Richard Price – insisted that a unicameral system was essential to the successful functioning of republican government. They argued that authority had to be focused in a single place and worried that some states were modelling their constitutions too closely on English customs, when what was required was a complete break from these. These writers attracted supporters in America, but they also prompted a lengthy and heated response from John Adams.

Adams's *A Defence of the Constitutions of Government of the United States of America* was explicitly designed as a forceful justification of the mixed and balanced constitutional form (as reflected in the state constitution of Adams's native Massachusetts) against the alternative vision of Turgot, Mably, and Price. Adams offered an exhaustive account of the constitutions of all republics, past and present, and of the views of political theorists, ancient and modern – an account designed to demonstrate decisively not only that a mixed and balanced system had been favoured in both theory and practice, but also that a system based on Turgot's model had never actually existed and would not be possible. At a number of points Adams broke off from his descriptive narrative to remind readers of his argument. After his description of the Swiss canton of Uri, for example, he remarked:

> Such a diminutive republic, in an obscure corner, and unknown, is interesting to Americans, not only because every spot of earth on which civil liberty flourishes deserves their esteem, but upon this occasion is particularly important, as it shows the impossibility of erecting even the smallest government, among the poorest people, without different orders, councils and balances.[21]

Adams also used his investigation into political theory and practice to justify the precise nature of the balance that was required. 'There can be,' he argued, 'in the nature of things, no balance without three powers.'[22] This meant that he placed weight on the seemingly controversial issue that there was a place (indeed, a need) for a single figurehead at the apex of a republican system of government:

> Among every people, and in every species of republics, we have constantly found *a first magistrate, a head, a chief*, under various denominations indeed, and with different degrees of authority ... in

every nation we have met with a distinguished officer: if there is no example in any free government, any more than in those which are not free, of a society without a principal personage, we may fairly conclude, that the body politic cannot subsist without one, any more than the animal body without a head.[23]

Adams also insisted that all republics required a council or a senate generally composed of those with most experience and power. His point was not simply that all republics, past and present, had been composed of these three elements; he was also keen to emphasise that their stability, and ultimately their success, were dependent on the institution and maintenance of the correct balance between them. Having written at length about the constitution and history of Geneva, he concluded:

> The history of this city deserves to be studied with anxious attention by every American citizen. The principles of government, the necessity of various orders, and the fatal effects of an imperfect balance, appear no where in a stronger light.[24]

Adams's emphasis on the importance of balance reflected his concerns regarding human nature. He was all too conscious of the corrupting effects of power, and therefore of the need for it to be checked and controlled. Turgot's system, Adams feared, relied too heavily on the virtue of those in positions of power. In all republics, of whatever size or shape, various measures were required to check the passions.[25] Adams was scathing about the assumption, inherent in Turgot's position, that only a single sovereign could behave tyrannically. 'It is an error to think it an uncontroulable maxim, that power is always safer lodged in many hands than in one.'[26]

Instead of Turgot's rejection of the English constitution, Adams expressed great praise for it:

> I only contend that the English constitution is, in theory, the most stupendous fabrick of human invention, both for the adjustment of the balance, and the prevention of its vibrations; and that the Americans ought to be applauded instead of censured, for imitating it, as far as they have.[27]

Unlike Paine, Adams was not even fundamentally opposed to the monarchical element in the English system, and did not deem it to be incompatible with republican government. In his *Novanglus Letters* he accepted that even a sovereign with sweeping prerogative powers could be compatible with freedom.[28] As Nelson has demonstrated, this position was based on a particular view of representative government, which was actually the one favoured by the royalists during the English Civil War. By contrast, in line with the standard parliamentarian line that a legitimate representative must be a good likeness of the represented, Nedham had insisted that only an assembly could represent the people. Paine's view, as discussed above, was very similar. Adams, however, believed that it was not necessary for the representative body to reflect the people it represented; in his view any person or agency authorised by the people to exercise political power could assume that role. On this reading, even an hereditary monarch could be deemed representative.

The whole question of what was meant by representation, how it ought to operate, and what its relationship was to republicanism also lay at the heart of the debate between Federalists and anti-Federalists over the constitution.

American Debates, II: Anti-Federalists versus Federalists

The protracted process of ratifying the American constitution generated much debate across the country, and in many states it was only ratified by a slim majority. Essentially the conflict was between anti-Federalists and Federalists: between those who feared that the proposed constitution threatened the rights and liberties that had been fought for in 1776 by placing too much power at the central level, and those who sought to defend the benefits of a strong central government as the best means of protecting those rights and liberties. Much of this debate was carried out in articles in local newspapers.

One series of anti-Federalist articles, which appeared under the pseudonym Centinel in two Philadelphia papers – the *Independent Gazeteer* and the *Freeman's Journal* – made an explicit reference to Adams's *Defence*. Rejecting Adams's mixed and balanced model, Centinel declared that the form of government that is best calculated to preserve individual freedom is the one that makes those entrusted with power responsible to their constituents to the utmost degree. Moreover, he asserted that the Pennsylvanian constitutional model, which comprised a single legislative body elected for a short term and had regular rotation of office, was the best possible form.[29] While this model was certainly closer to Turgot's ideal than to Adams's, Centinel argued that the proposed federal constitution met neither his own criteria for good government nor those laid down by Adams. Ultimately Centinel warned that '[t]he all prevailing power of taxation, and such extensive legislative and judicial powers are vested in the general government, as must in their operation, necessarily absorb the state legislatures and judicatories'. By removing responsibility, and even the possibility of accountability, from the people, the architects of the constitution had produced not a regular, balanced, government on Adams's model but an aristocracy.

The strongest statement of the alternative, Federalist, viewpoint was set out in a series of articles known collectively as *The Federalist Papers*, which were drawn up in an attempt to persuade the people of New York to ratify the constitution. Owing to New York's geographical location and political significance, its support for the new system was deemed crucial; but the governor of New York, George Clinton, was firmly opposed to it. Alexander Hamilton (c. 1755–1804) therefore came up with the idea of writing a series of articles in New York newspapers to explain and justify various elements of the new system. He enlisted the support of James Madison (1751–1836) and John Jay (1745–1829) and, together, they produced eighty-five articles under the collective name Publius. The first of these pieces appeared in the *New York Independent Journal* on 27 October 1787, and between that date and August 1788 articles by Publius appeared two or three times a week, in as many as four different New York newspapers. Broadly speaking, the first thirty-seven papers dealt with the problems and inadequacies of the Articles of Confederation. Papers 38–51 were concerned with the general principles of the constitution and the advantages of union. The remaining papers sought to explain and justify specific elements of the constitution: the House of Representatives (52–61); the Senate (62–6); the office of the president (67–77); and the judiciary (78–83).

While committed to the idea of a republic, the Federalists were quick to recognise the problems and limitations of popular government, not least on the basis of recent American experience. To remedy these problems, they advocated a strong centralised power; they put the case for representative government as a good in itself, and did so on the basis of a distinctive understanding of its operation and function; and, in the process, they shaped a new, modern understanding of republican government that was at odds with ancient practices and, once again, represented an adaptation of republican ideas to new circumstances.

In *Federalist X*, which has become the most famous of the eighty-five papers, Madison elucidated the features and advantages of this form of government. The focus of the article was on dealing with the problem of faction, which threatened to beset modern states. He argued that, since the causes of faction could not be removed, the only option was to control its effects; and that this meant ensuring either that the same passion or interest could not be held by a majority or that, if it was, its members should be prevented from oppressing the rest 'by their number and local situation'. The conclusion he drew from this analysis was that democracy on the ancient model had to be rejected.[30] Madison then went on to distinguish ancient democracy from what he called a republic:

> A republic, by which I mean a government in which the scheme of representation takes place, opens a different prospect and promises the cure for which we are seeking. Let us examine the points in which it varies from pure democracy, and we shall comprehend both the nature of the cure and the efficacy which it must derive from the Union. The two great points of difference between a democracy and a republic are: first, the delegation of the government, in the latter, to a smaller number of citizens elected by the rest; secondly, the greater number of citizens, and greater sphere of country over which the latter may be extended.[31]

Madison turned ancient wisdom upside down by insisting that a system of representation was in fact crucial to a successful republican government. Hamilton had already started to move in this direction, by coining the phrase 'representative democracy' in a letter he wrote in 1777.[32] Madison, however, added a clever twist to the argument by associating representation not with democracy, but with republicanism. This allowed the Federalists to claim the label 'republican' for themselves, forcing their opponents into defending the more problematic 'democratic' label and at the same time eschewing anti-Federalist attempts to condemn them as aristocrats.

Madison also trumped the anti-Federalist vision of representation as a necessary evil. He did so by depicting the representative system as a positive good, which had to be adopted by reason of America's size. The anti-Federalists used the mirror analogy to describe the role of representation, emphasising the need for the representative body to look like, or accurately reflect, the citizen body as a whole if it was to represent properly the views of its members. Against this conception, the Federalists adopted the idea of representation as a filter that would remove undesirable elements, ensuring both that the best individuals would be selected as representatives and that the best interests of the country would be protected and advanced as a result. Representation, Madison argued, would

> refine and enlarge the public views by passing them through the medium of a chosen body of citizens, whose wisdom may best discern the true interest of their country and whose patriotism and love

of justice will be least likely to sacrifice it to temporary or partial considerations. Under such a regulation it may well happen that the public voice, pronounced by the representatives of the people, will be more consonant to the public good than if pronounced by the people themselves, convened for the purpose.[33]

Moreover, Madison went on to argue that such a system also made a virtue of a large republic. Not only would a large republic mean a larger number of suitable candidates for representative office but, in addition,

as each representative will be chosen by a greater number of citizens in the large than in the small republic, it will be more difficult for unworthy candidates to practice with success the vicious arts by which elections are too often carried; and the suffrages of the people being more free, will be more likely to center on men who possess the most attractive merit and the most diffusive and established characters.[34]

He used this point to justify and endorse the constitution. 'Hence it clearly appears that the same advantage which a republic has over a democracy in controlling the effects of faction is enjoyed by a large over a small republic – is enjoyed by the Union over the States composing it.'[35]

While Madison was evidently adept at manipulating the terminology and the ideas, his adaptation of republican notions and concepts to fit new circumstances was in keeping with what republican theorists had been doing for centuries. Although he placed greater emphasis on legal and constitutional mechanisms than on the active participation of citizens, a similar tendency is evident in the writings of earlier thinkers. Moreover, Madison did not deny completely the importance of collective determination and the need for civic virtue: 'Is there no virtue among us? If there be not we are in a wretched situation. No theoretical checks, no form of government can render us secure. To suppose that any form of government will secure liberty or happiness without any virtue in the people, is a chimerical idea.'[36]

Conclusion

It is clear that ideas were crucial to the American Revolution, and republican ideas proved particularly potent. American revolutionaries were aware of, and drew on, republican ideas from the ancient world, and also from early modern thought and practice. The works inspired by the English Revolution of 1640–60, together with those that appeared in post-revolutionary England, were particularly crucial in determining how the colonists understood the political situation in the 1760s and 1770s and in propelling them towards revolution. In addition, Paine's uncompromising, exclusivist understanding of republican government not only helped to sway attitudes towards independence but also transformed the way in which republicanism was understood in America and beyond, ensuring that the pluralist interpretation would never again enjoy the dominant position it once had.

After the Declaration of Independence and the establishment of a republic by default, republican ideas continued to play a role in the political debates with which the fledgling nation engaged. Thinkers as diverse as Paine, Adams, Hamilton, and Madison had imbibed earlier republican thought and applied it in response to American circumstances. Yet the ways in which they did so differed greatly. This meant that key debates of the American revolutionary period, including the one over bicameral versus unicameral sovereignty and the one concerning the nature of representative government, often involved republican ideas being invoked on both sides.

One important debate that has not been explored in any detail here is that over slavery (it will be discussed in Chapter 9). While slavery remained in place in the United States until the 1860s, a century before that revolutionaries were well aware of the contradiction inherent in the idea of fighting for liberty and liberation for white citizens, while continuing to enslave blacks. Indeed, Robert G. Parkinson has argued that a fundamental tension between inclusion and exclusion is evident within the text of the Declaration of Independence itself.[37] That tension was equally inherent in the conflict between Federalists and anti-Federalists, which reflected a longer-running dispute, within republican circles, as to whether ordinary people could be trusted to exercise political power themselves, or whether they needed to be guided – even ruled – by those with greater wisdom, time, and expertise.

Ultimately, of course, the Federalists proved victorious. Yet, as Nelson has demonstrated, the outcome was rather curious. The debates of the 1770s had brought an end to the office of king, but the president inaugurated in 1789 wielded more power than any English monarch since William III.[38] In Nelson's formulation, the Americans had rejected monarchy but had ended up with what was, effectively, royal power. In fact the situation was even more complex because, while insisting on a centralised executive, the Americans still required the president to be accountable – and it had been the need for accountability, rather than the absence of a single figurehead, that was of greatest importance to the seventeenth-century critics of royal power. Nonetheless, there is an interesting contrast here between the eighteenth-century British commonwealth men – who were willing to accept an hereditary monarch as part of a 'republican' government as long as his or her power was strictly limited and constrained – and the American revolutionaries – who insisted on electing their president on a short term of office, but were prepared to give the person they elected much greater power. Given the complex history of republicanism detailed in this volume, we should perhaps not be all that surprised. As has been demonstrated, 'republic' and 'republicanism' are slippery terms that have been subject to different understandings and interpretations. Even in the eighteenth century, there was no one republican position, but rather a variety of different positions that could be taken on a number of key issues; and almost as many republican models emerged as there were republican thinkers. Moreover, republicanism was dynamic rather than static, constantly developing in line with, and in response to, events. The American revolutionaries simply joined this complex and fast moving story, applying the wealth of republican resources at their disposal to the specific problems and issues that confronted them. Nor were they the only ones to engage with republican sources or to devise republican solutions to political problems at the end of the eighteenth century. The next chapter will explore parallel debates and discussions that took place in revolutionary France.

8

The French Revolution

Introduction

The establishment of the French Republic in September 1792 was a bolder and more deliberate act than that of its English and American precursors. In France the creation of the republic preceded the regicide, which took place on 21 January 1793. The decision about how to deal with the former king then followed as a consequence of the founding of the republic rather than being its cause, as had happened in England. Another facet of this boldness was the French revolutionaries' sense that their actions marked the beginning of something completely new in the realms of politics and political thought. The innovative nature of the French political experiment lay, at least in part, in the immensity of the transformation that the revolutionaries enacted, which encompassed far more than just political change. The French attacked not simply the 'tyranny' of Louis XVI, but the whole hereditary and aristocratic system of rule that had evolved over many centuries, as well as the associated political culture. The notion that they were banishing the old and replacing it with something entirely new was embodied in their use of the label *ancien régime* to describe the period before the Revolution; in the erasure of old structures and privileges through the reorganisation of the political geography of France on a more rational basis; and, most obviously, in the resetting of the calendar to 'Year 1'.

Yet the revolutionaries' self-conscious claim about the deliberate and original nature of their act must not be allowed to obscure two important facts. First, while the creation of the French republic preceded the trial and execution of Louis XVI, there is little evidence to suggest that the establishment of a republic was the explicit intention of any more than a handful of activists when revolution broke out in 1789. Some revolutionaries, for example Jacques-Pierre Brissot (1754–93), Étienne Clavière (1735–93), Jean-Antoine-Nicolas de Caritat, marquis de Condorcet (1743–94), Jérôme Pétion (1756–93), and Camille Desmoulins (1760–94), were expressing firmly anti-monarchical views by 1789. They were, however, very much in the minority in the country as a whole, and other key figures, including Maximilian Robespierre (1758–94), were late converts to anti-monarchism.

Of course, whom we label as a republican during this period depends on our definition of the term. Jonathan Israel has argued that, while figures such as Honoré-Gabriel Riquetti, count de Mirabeau (1749–91), and Abbé Emmanuel-Joseph Sieyès (1748–1836) were not 'doctrinaire republicans', they were sympathetic to several aspects of the republican programme.[1] While they were willing to keep the monarch as a figurehead, they did so on the understanding that his powers would be severely curtailed. The constitutional monarchy established in 1790 was, Israel suggests, effectively a republic: a republic in practice if not in name.[2] Yet the unwillingness to change the name, or to overthrow the monarchy when so many other aspects of the regime were being dismantled, is itself significant. Equally revealing is the fact that Louis XVI's flight from Paris in June 1791, which exposed his willingness to ally himself with enemies of the Revolution, did not bring the end of the monarchy. Brissot and his associates certainly seized the opportunity as best they could: they established the Société des Républicains and its affiliated newspaper, *Le Républicain*, and clandestinely posted proclamations across Paris that called for the deposition of the king and for his replacement by a new republican order, based on universal suffrage. Moreover, the National Assembly's announcement, on 14 July 1791, that Louis was absolved from blame prompted popular anger and the drawing up of a mass petition that the king be put on trial. But, in the end, these forces were not strong enough to overthrow the regime at this point, and the constitutional monarchy remained in place for a further twelve months.

The second fact that we need to bear in mind is that the French revolutionaries' claim to be doing something entirely new did not mean that they were unaware of earlier republican examples, nor did it prevent them from drawing on such models and experiences. The ancient world, especially ancient Rome, and the previous republican experiments in England and America – as well as the writings of

Montesquieu, Rousseau, and Mably – all exercised an influence on French revolutionary republicanism. Moreover, because the French were able to draw from such a rich and diverse reservoir of republican thought, what emerged was not one single form of French revolutionary republicanism, but rather several distinct versions, which overlapped in various ways, but which also came at times into direct conflict with one another. This chapter will first survey the French revolutionaries' use of earlier republican ideas, then go on to examine the distinctive republican positions of the Girondins, Cordeliers, Jacobins, and Thermidoreans.

The Resources of Republican Thought

Classical Sources

The education of young, middle-class, and upper-class men in France in the eighteenth century was still grounded in the study of classics and classical authors. Thus the revolutionary generation was familiar with the philosophy of Aristotle, the letters and speeches of Cicero, and the accounts of Roman history by the likes of Livy and Tacitus. At various points in the eighteenth century, thinkers and activists looked back to their ancient models. Sparta, for example, was of particular interest during the 1760s. While Claude Helvétius was critical of its value as a model, both Mably and Rousseau viewed it more positively.[3] The Roman parallel was also particularly resonant in France, just like in England and America. A medal struck to commemorate the fall of the Bastille illustrated this connection through the appropriation of two Roman republican symbols.[4] First the fasces – a bundle of wooden sticks bound together with a blade: these represented the power and justice of the magistrate, a key symbol of authority in ancient Rome. Secondly, crowning the fasces, a Phrygian cap, the Roman symbol of liberty. Slaves in ancient Rome had their heads shaved, in indication of their servile status. Those who were released from slavery would be given a cap, to hide their bald head until the hair grew back. Hence the idea of a liberty cap or bonnet, which was a dominant symbol in revolutionary political culture.

There are also numerous references to revolutionaries reading or being influenced by classical sources. Desmoulins lamented: '[f]or many years, I have searched everywhere for republican souls, I despair at not having been born Greek or Roman'.[5] Similarly, Madame Roland (1754–93) supposedly wept when she first read

Plutarch, upset that she had not been born in ancient times. More disturbingly, Charlotte Corday (1768–93) is said to have read Plutarch the day before she murdered Jean-Paul Marat.[6] The painter Jacques-Louis David (1748–1825) frequently depicted ancient scenes in his paintings. In *Brutus and the Lictors* (1789), for example, he drew on a famous story from Roman history to explore the central themes of patriotism and the sacrifice of the individual for the good of the state (see Figure 8.1). Lucius Junius Brutus, who had been responsible for expelling the Tarquins from Rome, discovered that his sons had been acting to restore the monarchy. He prioritised the good of the state over his own family by sentencing his sons to death for treason. While David's picture captures the enormous weight of Brutus's sacrifice, the message is clear that he made the right decision.

English Republicanism

Ancient republican models were not the only ones on which the French revolutionaries could draw. The previous two centuries also provided ample republican source material. English republican works

Figure 8.1 Jacques-Louis David, *Brutus and the Lictors*. Reproduced thanks to the Getty's Open Content program

and ideas stirred considerable interest in revolutionary France.[7]
Initially the parallel drawn by the French revolutionaries was with
1688–9 rather than with 1640–60, and, while the emphasis at
this stage was not explicitly on republicanism, there was a strong
sense that the French had derived their commitment to liberty and
their hatred of despotism from the English.[8] However, the debate
concerning what should be done with Louis XVI after the declaration
of the First Republic in the autumn of 1792 caused parallels to be
drawn between Louis Capet and Charles Stuart, as the French looked
to the English example to decide how they should deal with their
former king.[9] Perhaps the most striking evidence of French interest
in the English revolution lies in the publications of the revolutionary
decade. Several works explicitly compared aspects of the history of
England in 1640–60 with events in France in the 1790s, and the
term 'revolution' was used by French revolutionaries to describe the
earlier period.[10] Most significant, as far as republican source material
is concerned, was the publication of translations of the works of
leading English republican writers: Algernon Sidney's *Discourses*,
John Milton's *Areopagitica* and *Pro populo anglicano defensio*,
Marchamont Nedham's *The Excellencie of a Free State*, Edmund
Ludlow's *Memoirs*, and several of James Harrington's works.[11]

The American Model

While it was widely acknowledged that North America constituted a
very different political landscape and that the United States' political
system could not simply be exported to France, it too was an
important source of republican inspiration for the French. The fact
that the American republican experiment was very recent led to the
idea of America and France as sister republics, a notion symbolised in
the nineteenth century by the French nation's gift to the United States
of the Statue of Liberty – *La Liberté éclairant le monde* (*Liberty
Enlightening the World*), as it was named – to commemorate the
centenary of the American Revolution.

The proximity in time between the two revolutions also meant
that the influence could be direct. The French joined the American
revolutionary war on the side of the colonists in 1778, this proving
crucial to their success. French soldiers, including General Lafayette
(1757–1834), were influenced by their experience of fighting in this
campaign. Lafayette was said to have fed American ideas directly into
his draft version of the Declaration of the Rights of Man in 1789.
Several American revolutionaries – including Benjamin Franklin,
Thomas Jefferson, and John Adams – spent time in France in the

1770s and 1780s, and Adams's *A Defence of the Constitutions of Government of the United States of America* was translated into French in 1792.

Francophone Sources

The French could also look closer to home for republican inspiration. The question of Rousseau's influence on revolutionary thought and action has been a topic of debate ever since the eighteenth century. In 1791 Louis-Sébastien Mercier (1740–1814) published a pamphlet entitled *Jean-Jacques Rousseau considéré comme l'un des premiers auteurs de la Révolution (Jean-Jacques Rousseau considered as one of the first authors of the Revolution).*[12] State acknowledgement of the legacy of Rousseau was reflected in the production and display of busts, statues, and other memorabilia commemorating the Genevan philosopher. A bust of Rousseau was placed in the meeting room of the National Assembly in the summer of 1790, and copies of his works were placed at its base. On the anniversary of the fall of the Bastille that year a bust, perhaps the same one, was carried in the procession and a hymn in praise of him was sung; and a street was named after him.[13] When Voltaire's remains were transferred to the Panthéon in July 1791, medals of Rousseau were carried in the procession; and, just over a month later, a petition demanding Rousseau's own pantheonisation, which had long been in the pipeline, was drawn up by Pierre-Louis Ginguené (1748–1815/16) and signed by various revolutionaries. The petition also asked that a pension be provided for Rousseau's widow, Thérèse, and called for a statue of him to be commissioned. The artist Baudon prepared a portrait of Rousseau together with portraits of Voltaire and Mirabeau, commemorating their status as key inspirations for the revolution.[14] Various revolutionaries have been described as followers of Rousseau – Robespierre, Desmoulins, Claude Fauchet (1744–93), and even Mirabeau. However, in most cases these claims have been qualified – for example in the case of Desmoulins, who became more critical of Rousseau over time, or in that of Fauchet, who disagreed with him on key points.[15]

This broad but ambiguous reverence for Rousseau among the revolutionaries was part of a wider veneration for Enlightenment thinkers, and especially for those with republican credentials. In an oration delivered at Mirabeau's internment in the Panthéon, Joseph-Antoine Cérutti (1738–92) included Rousseau, Montesquieu, and Mably on a list of figures who had prepared the way for the Revolution. The suggestion was also made that Montesquieu's remains be transferred to the Panthéon.[16] Yet, as in the case of the Enlightenment's influence on the American Revolution, here too it has been argued that the revolutionaries' use of Rousseau and other Enlightenment figures was often window dressing rather than reflecting a deep understanding of their ideas, let alone substantive commitment to them. Joan McDonald pointed out that Rousseau's name, works, and ideas were cited by those on both sides of the revolutionary divide; and she also demonstrated that the revolutionary understanding of Rousseau was determined primarily by the literary and personal cult generated by his novels *La Nouvelle Héloïse* and *Émile* and by his autobiographical *Confessions* rather than by his overtly political works. *The Social Contract*, for example, was little read before 1791.[17]

The Genevan and Dutch Models

The French revolutionaries also made alliances with, and drew on the experiences of, contemporary European states, especially the Genevan and Dutch republics. Clavière had been directly involved in the Genevan Revolution of 1782, and his friendship with both Mirabeau and Brissot was initially forged in Neuchâtel, where the *représentants* in exile employed the two Frenchmen to write propaganda materials for them.[18] During the French Revolution roles were reversed when various Genevan revolutionaries – including Clavière, Étienne Dumont, and Antoine Du Roveray – formed the 'atelier de Mirabeau', writing speeches and newspaper articles on his behalf. While Geneva was not a suitable republican model for France, Clavière's Genevan background served to forge his identity as a republican. It also revealed to him the importance of political economy, prompting him to lament that the French had neglected this subject. Richard Whatmore suggests that, in his writings of the early 1790s, Clavière developed a political economy for France that was similar to the one he had previously envisaged for Geneva, with an emphasis on morality and on markets that would serve those possessed of moderate wealth.[19] Like earlier exponents of republican political economy discussed in Chapter 5, Clavière insisted that trade was not immoral in itself, but that care needed to be taken over how it was pursued. Perhaps most importantly, Clavière's experience in Geneva instilled in him a hatred of aristocracy and a concern that nobles remained too dominant in French society.

Contemporary relations with the Genevan state were, however, complex. A revolution in January 1789, prompted by anger at the high price of bread, led to the establishment of a Genevan government more attractive to the *représentants*; but Clavière kept his distance. When a further uprising on 4 December 1792 brought supporters of revolutionary France to power in Geneva, his former associates accused him of having abandoned his commitment to protect small states.

Relations with the Dutch patriot movement reflected a similar mixture of sympathy and distancing. When Prussia invaded Holland in support of the besieged stadtholder in 1787, Mirabeau and Brissot were involved in writing articles for the *Analyse des papiers Anglais* that urged the Dutch to maintain their republican liberty. The same argument was further developed in *Aux bataves sur le stathouderat*, which appeared under Mirabeau's name in 1788. However, no commitment was made to provide direct French support. The hope was that the Dutch example (along with that of the American colonists) would inspire other weak states to stand up for themselves.[20]

The Brissotins–Girondins

The group of revolutionaries who congregated around Jacques-Pierre Brissot and consequently became known as Brissotins embraced 'advanced' ideas on a range of subjects, including the rights of women and the abolition of slavery. Included among members of the Brissotin coterie were Condorcet and Clavière (on whom Brissot became financially dependent during the 1780s); Thomas Paine also associated himself with the group while in France. Later on in the Revolution the Brissotins became linked to the deputies from the Gironde region, who formed the main opposition to the Jacobins in 1792–3.[21]

The Brissotins' early endorsement of republican government was part of their progressive stance. As early as July 1789, Marie-Joseph Chénier (1764–1811) was looking for an opportunity to stage his anti-monarchical and anti-Catholic play *Charles IX* and was supported in his endeavour by Brissot, who argued the case in his newspaper. The play was eventually performed on 4 November 1789.[22] At this point the organisation of the group largely centred around the Cercle Social, a political society that established its own publishing house so as to be able to promote its ideas more effectively.[23] The *Journal du Cercle Social* began appearing in January 1790. In October of that year the Cercle Social took on the leadership of a new society, the Confédération des amis de la vérité (Society of the Friends of Truth), which was comprised of former municipal politicians from Paris's communal assembly who had been ousted after the introduction of the new municipal plan. At the organisation's first meeting, which was held at the Palais Royal on 13 October 1790, an estimated 4,000 people listened to Abbé Fauchet's opening address. The avowed aim of this organisation was to unite the political and social ideas of the *philosophes* with the interests of the Third Estate. Its members sought to do so by undertaking a detailed analysis of Rousseau's *Social Contract* and by tapping into the will of the people, not least by providing opportunities for the public to express its views. To this end they erected at the group's headquarters an iron box into which members of the public could place ideas and comments. After the king's flight to Varennes in June 1791, this group led a strong republican reaction through the Société des Républicains and its newspaper, *Le Républicain*. Brissot, Clavière, and Condorcet were elected, alongside several of their associates, to the Legislative Assembly in the autumn of 1791 and then to the Convention in 1792.

The position of the Brissotin–Girondin group on the trial and execution of the former king was complex. They insisted that he should be put on trial and that proper legal processes should be followed, but many of them were opposed to the death penalty. As Condorcet said in his speech on 3 December 1792, '[t]o judge an accused king is a duty; to pardon him can be an act of prudence'.[24] Most Girondins favoured an appeal to the people on the king's fate, but they were defeated on 15 January 1793, and the following day a majority voted in favour of immediate execution. An attempt at a reprieve also failed.

After the regicide, several Brissotins took up official positions or influenced the government in more informal ways. Jean-Marie Roland (1734–93) was minister of the interior, Clavière, who had already been finance minister under the monarchy, continued in that role, and Condorcet was responsible for drawing up the 'Girondin constitution' that was debated in the Convention in the spring of 1793. Their influence was short-lived, however, since they soon came into conflict with Robespierre and his associates. Girondin deputies were arrested on 31 May 1793 and subsequently expelled from the Convention. Many, including Brissot and Clavière, did not survive the year.

Building on years of thought and practical experience, the Brissotins offered a sophisticated definition of republican government. In his newspaper *Le Patriote Français* Brissot declared: 'I understand, by republic, a government in which all the powers are, 1. Delegated or represented; 2. Elective among and by the people, or its representatives; 3. Temporary or removable'.[25] Brissot used this definition to deny the relevance of ancient republican models to late eighteenth-century France, pointing out that none of the ancient republics had managed to combine these three requirements within a single system. Rome had had an hereditary senate, Sparta hereditary kings, and Athens had been a pure democracy with no representation. A successful modern republic, the Brissotins observed, needed to address issues that simply had not been relevant to the ancients. Both the area and the population of modern states were much larger than their ancient counterparts. This was an advantage, since the eighteenth century, and especially Geneva's recent experience, had revealed the vulnerability of small republics, which had to rely on larger neighbours for protection. A large republic would be better able to maintain itself.[26] It did, however, mean that some form of representation was essential. It was also crucial that modern republicanism be compatible with commercial society. Drawing on ideas and practices from the new United States of America as well as from Geneva, the Brissotins advocated a representative government, designed to obviate the problem of the size of the French state; the reinforcement of republican manners among the population, for example through education; and an emphasis on Montesquieu's *commerce d'économie*.[27]

While the Brissotins' view that legislative power should lie ultimately with the people but that in a large modern nation-state it would have to be exercised by representatives was not unusual at the time, their ideas on the organisation of executive and constitutive power were more controversial. Despite their sympathy for Louis Capet, their understanding of republicanism was inherently anti-monarchical. This was made evident in the debate between Paine and Sieyès that took place in the aftermath of the king's flight to Varennes.

Sieyès alluded to Paine's assertion, made in *Le Républicain*, that republican government was government by representation and founded on the Declaration of Rights. Sieyès challenged this view by arguing that it was perfectly possible to have a representative government that was monarchical and that the new constitutional monarchy was firmly grounded in the Declaration of Rights and constituted the best system of representative government ever conceived. The crucial difference between republics and monarchies, Sieyès insisted, concerned where executive power lay. In a republic, executive power would be held by a council appointed by the people or the National Assembly. Just like legislative power, then, it too would ascend from the base to the apex of the system. In a monarchy, by contrast, while legislative power would ascend, executive power would descend from the top. An individual of superior rank would be the head of state and would install heads of departments or ministries, exercising the right to choose and dismiss them in the name of the people.

On this basis Sieyès went further, arguing that in fact republics and monarchies were not opposites. The antonym of 'monarchy' was not 'republic', he said, but 'polyarchy', which means 'rule of the many' (*poloi*), as opposed to the rule of one (*monos*). A republic, Sieyès argued, echoing Rousseau, was simply government in the public interest. The real question to be asked was: 'In a good Republic, is it better that the government should be Monarchic or Polyarchic?'.[28] In Sieyès's opinion, the answer to this question was straightforward. The government of one had the advantage of unity of action and clear responsibility for decision-making. While Sieyès was happy to label himself as a supporter of 'Monarchic Opinion' the debate was in many respects a rerun of that between an exclusivist and a pluralist republican government, with Paine and the Brissotins firmly on the exclusivist side.

As well as embracing exclusivist republicanism, the Brissotins also took a distinctive line in their attitude to constitutive power. While they were happy to employ representation for day-to-day legislation, they insisted that the underlying constitution, and any amendments to it, ought to be endorsed by the people. Richard Tuck has argued that, as early as 1789, future Girondins were already advocating the use of plebiscite as a means by which the entire citizen body might exercise constitutive power directly.[29] In this regard they supported a form of democratic sovereignty that was broad in terms of the numbers of people it embraced, but restricted as to the range of issues on which the citizen body could express its views directly. Pétion was one of the first to set out the modern form of a plebiscite that involved an appeal to the people without any reference to representatives at all. The debt to Rousseau is evident in the language used: '[t]he law ought to be the expression of the general will ... if each person can make known his particular will, the combination of all the wills will truly form the general will'.[30] This attitude was also reflected in debates over what to do with Louis Capet. The Brissotins–Girondins were of the opinion that, rather than being tried by the National Convention, he ought to be judged by the entire nation. 'The nation alone has that choice; it alone can be regarded as absolutely exempt from any interest other than the common interest, from any special bias.'[31] Their call for an appeal to the people to decide his fate was grounded in the same notion – that it was the public as a whole, rather than the representatives, that should take fundamental decisions. Similarly, by 1793 most Girondins insisted that the new constitution would have to be based on a direct popular vote. For Condorcet, this was the only means to 'preserve [the people's] sovereignty in its entirety'.[32]

Just as Sieyès challenged the Girondins on the organisation of executive power, he was also uncomfortable with the distinction they drew between legislative and constitutive power. Whereas the Girondins argued that the constitution of 1793 ought to be ratified by direct popular vote, Sieyès countered that in a large modern nation-state all political action (including constitutional decisions) should be directed via representatives. He argued that *le pouvoir constituant* (constituent power), as he described it, should be exercised by a group of representatives chosen especially for the task, or by an existing representative body acting in a distinctive fashion. The Constitution of Year III (1793) effectively embodied the Girondin position, requiring as it did ratification by plebiscite, whereas that of Year VIII (1799) reflected Sieyès's views.[33]

While Sieyès criticised the Girondins for giving too much power to the people, others believed that their system did not give it enough power. From the beginning of the Revolution, the Cordeliers had criticised the Brissotins on this point. By 1792 both they and the Jacobins had made the point that all laws should be enacted by the people and that any legislation could be recalled by the local assemblies. This, according to the Girondins, constituted a blurring of the important distinction between sovereignty and government.

The Cordeliers

The fact that members of the Cordeliers Club disagreed with the Brissotin–Girondin faction throughout the early 1790s is striking, given that the Cordeliers, too, were among the earliest and most vociferous opponents of monarchical government.[34] In 1789 Desmoulins asked: 'Do the facts not cry out that Monarchy is a detestable form of government?'[35] And he reversed the typical position of favouring monarchy but opposing a tyrannical king when he made this aphoristic declaration: 'I like Louis XVI himself, but Monarchy is no less odious to me'.[36] By 1790 Desmoulins had been joined in his anti-monarchism by other writers who, like him, were engaged in practical political activity, first in the Cordeliers district and later in the club. Two writings – *Du people et des rois*, by Louis de la Vicomterie (1746–1809) and *Républicanisme adapté à la France*, by Pierre-François-Joseph Robert (1763–1826) – were uncompromising in their commitment to republican government, which they defined in sharply anti-monarchical terms:

> Any institution other than republicanism is a crime of lèze-nation ...
> the apostles of royalty are either traitors or men stupidly misled which
> society must regard as its enemies. It is said at this time that France
> is free; what France is free! And a monarchy? We must not deceive
> ourselves; if France is free, she is not a monarchy, and if a monarchy,
> she is not free.[37]

Moreover, as the title of his work suggests, Robert was not simply
concerned with theoretical definitions but was intent on helping
his readers to overcome the psychological barriers to imagining a
French republic, and also on demonstrating just how this form of
government could be made applicable to late eighteenth-century
France. The first part of the work used a fictional dialogue between a
country priest and a parishioner to demonstrate that French opinion
was not an obstacle to the destruction of royalty. The second part
sought to prove that the French monarchy was incompatible with
liberty. The last section offered a proposal for a workable French
republic.

While Desmoulins and other Cordeliers worked with the Brissotins
at various points (not least in the Cercle Social), there were clear differences in their attitude to republicanism from the outset. They took up
different positions in the municipality of Paris in 1789 and continued
to argue against each other, face to face and in print, during the years
that followed. One of the main points of contention between the two
parties was representative government. As noted above, Brissot saw
representation as an essential component of republican government.
The Cordeliers regarded representation more warily. Consequently,
they sought to introduce various means that would ensure that the
actions and decisions of 'delegates' – and the fact that they preferred
this term to 'representatives' is itself significant – were kept firmly
under the control of the people who elected them. In particular, they
demanded short terms of office, binding mandates for deputies, and
even a system of popular ratification of the laws.

Desmoulins requested binding mandates: 'it must be admitted that
the powers of our legislative body are only the powers of delegates,
of representatives and that the eternal rules of mandates are in this
question the essence of the matter'.[38] Similarly, Robert justified short
terms of office on the grounds that the decisions of the representatives would be controlled through their knowledge that they would
have to live under the laws that they had made. Desmoulins, La
Vicomterie, and Robert all advocated the popular ratification of laws.
The most extensive exploration of this idea, however, was offered by
René Girardin (1735–1808) in a speech that was delivered to the

Cordeliers Club on 7 June 1791 before being printed on the orders of the club and disseminated among France's patriotic societies.

Responding to the concerns of those who thought that France was too large for anything but representative government, Girardin's model exploited recent developments in printing technology and in the postal service in order to facilitate the popular ratification of laws. Two copies of all the laws decreed by the National Assembly would be sent to each municipality. The citizens would then meet in their respective communes to ratify the laws. The president of each local assembly would introduce the proposed law(s), and each article would then be read out and discussed before being put to the vote. The verdict on each article would be marked in the margin on both copies, and one copy would then remain in the commune while the other would be returned to the National Assembly for counting. Any articles or laws rejected by the majority could be rewritten and sent again for ratification. Girardin concluded:

> It is thus that each citizen without altering their condition, can take part personally in the law, and that it will be ratified by *the people in person*; it is thus that the law will be known by all, that it will be truly sacred, respectable and respected by all, because it will be the work of all.[39]

Girardin's system was strongly endorsed by the club as a whole:

> That it is an eternal truth that a law, when it has only been proposed by a national council composed of delegates of a people, is not yet a law; that is to say that it can be counted only as the object and matter of the law; that it can only become and only really becomes a finished and complete law when, by virtue and by the effect of the ratification of the people, it finds itself converted from a simple proposition of the delegates into its own clear, formal and explicit will.[40]

The Brissotins were particularly keen to challenge this aspect of the Cordeliers' programme. Brissot directly attacked Desmoulins on the issue, accusing him of carrying 'the sovereignty of the people much further, since he wishes to make them ratify all the acts of the legislative power'.[41] He also challenged La Vicomterie's support for the same idea, claiming that, 'if there is a means of having neither law nor liberty, it is by wishing to have all the laws ratified by the six thousand primary assemblies'.[42] La Vicomterie's response pointed to the apparent hypocrisy in Brissot's position, since he had already accepted the necessity of popular ratification of the constitution itself:

I ask you, sir, whether one can ratify [the constitution] without being free to change it? ... I avow that I have not enough shrewdness to conceive how this could be done and why the projected laws that follow, which are necessary links in this constitutional chain, could not as easily be ratified by the people as the constitution itself, which you agree yourself must be done.[43]

Before the Revolution, Girardin had been a friend of Rousseau. It was on Girardin's estate at Ermenonville that Rousseau was living when he died; and after Rousseau's death Girardin set about producing an edition of his friend's works. Consequently, it is perhaps not surprising that Rousseau's ideas exercised an important influence on Girardin's political thought and, indeed, on that of the Cordeliers more generally. Girardin drew the Rousseauian distinction between sovereignty (which he referred to as *constitution essentielle*) and government (which he called *constitution administrative*) and emphasised the need to make national sovereignty a reality. He then discussed Rousseau's critique of representation, quoting directly from the *Social Contract*. It was precisely the Rousseauian hostility to representation that pushed Girardin and other members of the Cordeliers Club to seek more overt means of securing the connection between delegates and those whom they represented. Yet it was not only Rousseauian ideas that provided the foundations for the Cordeliers' republicanism. Members of the club also made explicit and consistent use of the writings of seventeenth-century English republicans in the development of their own republican ideology.[44]

Several members of the Cordeliers Club were responsible for translating key works of the English republican tradition into French. In 1790, Théophile Mandar – a soldier, orator, publicist, and municipal politician – published a translation of Nedham's *The Excellencie of a Free State*, which he enriched with passages from other authors, including Rousseau.[45] Jean-Jacques Rutledge, a journalist and a writer, included an unacknowledged translation of the first six chapters of Harrington's aphoristic work *A System of Politics* in his newspaper *Le Creuset: ouvrage politique et critique*; and in 1792 he submitted to the National Assembly a model constitution produced by him that was closely based on Harrington's *Oceana*.[46] Moreover, various other club members, including Jean-Paul Marat (1744–1793) and Desmoulins,[47] expressed views that echoed English republican ideas, and the club as a whole endorsed such Harringtonian notions as the importance of representatives being forced to live under the laws they had made, or the separation of the proposal of laws from their acceptance or rejection. Yet it is important to note that, rather than simply endorsing earlier ideas, the Cordeliers developed them. Whereas Harrington had called for a bicameral legislature in which the senate would make legislative proposals and the popular assembly would vote to accept or reject them, the Cordeliers combined this idea with an insistence on the popular ratification of laws, and asserted that the National Assembly could propose laws and the whole people, gathered in its primary assemblies, should cast its votes on those propositions.

The Jacobins

Although the Jacobins are the group most closely associated with French republicanism both in academic works and in the popular imagination, they were the most reluctant of the revolutionary groups when it came to espousing republicanism. In part, this reflected the fact that the Jacobin Club emerged from the Breton Club, a meeting place for deputies to the Estates General who were broadly in favour of reform, yet one that, at least early on, retained a relatively conservative character. In the first few years of the Revolution very few members of the Paris Jacobin Club embraced republicanism openly. While some anti-royalist views did circulate and there was much criticism of ministers and of the queen, many Jacobins upheld an attitude of respect for Louis XVI and his position. Michael Kennedy, who published a detailed multivolume study of the various branches of the Jacobin Club, described the typical club member as 'a staunch monarchist [with] a high regard for Louis XVI'.[48] After the king's flight to Varennes, the Montpellier branch circulated a petition calling for an end to monarchy, but only two other clubs responded positively.[49] The Jacobin cautiousness towards republicanism was epitomised by the most famous member in this network, the man who dominated the group at the height of its powers: Maximilian Robespierre. Robespierre was initially impressed by the 'monarchical republic' that Rousseau had proposed for Poland, and urged the Constituent Assembly to adopt it. Moreover, even as late as May 1792, Robespierre seems to have been more comfortable with the broader pluralist definition of republicanism than with its narrow exclusivist understanding:

> I am a republican! Yes, I wish to defend the principles of equality and the exercise of sacred rights that the constitution guarantees to the people against the dangerous systems of schemers who regard it only as the instrument of their ambition. I would rather see a popular

representative assembly and citizens who are free and respected under a king, than a people enslaved and degraded under the stick of an aristocratic senate and a dictator. I like Cromwell no better than Charles I, and I can support the yoke of the Decembirs no more than that of Tarquin. Is it in these words of *republic* or of *monarchy* that the solution to the great social problem rests? Is it these definitions invented by diplomats to class the diverse forms of government which determine the happiness and the misfortune of nations, or the combination of laws and of institutions which constitute real happiness?[50]

Republicanism of an exclusivist variety really took hold among Jacobins only after the popular invasion of the Tuileries on 20 June 1792. This reflects the extent to which it was inspired from below rather than being dictated from above. After this uprising, it was the mayor of Paris, Pétion – a member of the Jacobin Club who, significantly, had been associated with the Brissotins at an earlier time – who petitioned the Legislative Assembly on 3 August, calling for the removal of the king. A week later, a second popular invasion of the Tuileries resulted in the overthrow of the French monarchy.

The Jacobins were not only more reluctant in their republicanism, they also drew on different sources from those of other revolutionaries. In sharp contrast to the Brissotins, the Jacobins placed great emphasis on the works, models, and ideas of the ancients. This ancient inflection is particularly evident in the artistic work of Jacques-Louis David, who became a member of the Jacobin Club in late 1790 and later served as its president. He was elected to the National Convention in September 1792, having been nominated by Marat, and served a term as president there too. He continued to identify with the Jacobins after 1792 and belonged both to the Committee of General Security and to the Committee of Public Instruction during the Jacobin period of rule. He was also a leading figure in the design and enacting of various revolutionary festivals. After Thermidor he suffered arrest and imprisonment on account of his association with Robespierre and the Jacobins. In the pre-revolutionary period David's paintings frequently depicted scenes from ancient history. Both Greek stories (*Death of Socrates*, 1787) and Roman ones (*Oath of the Horatii*, 1784; *Brutus and the Lictors*, 1789) furnished him with subjects. Moreover, the themes and ideas that David depicted were often associated with patriotism and self-sacrifice. The moral world depicted in both the *Oath of the Horatii* and *Brutus and the Lictors* can be seen as prefiguring Jacobinism in its dedication to principle at all costs and the necessity for violent deeds to be sometimes committed in the name of virtue.

Virtue was undoubtedly one of the key concepts for Robespierre and his associates. During the debates surrounding the implementation of national festivals in October–November 1793, Robespierre insisted that there had to be a festival of virtue and that it should take precedence over all the others.[51] While Rousseau is the republican theorist who is often closely associated with the concept of virtue, Robespierre's understanding of this concept owed as much to the ideas of Montesquieu. His account of the place of virtue within popular government echoes Montesquieu's words very closely:

> Now, what is the fundamental principle of democratic or popular government, that is to say, the essential spring which sustains it and which makes it act? It is virtue; I speak of public virtue which made many marvels in Greece and in Rome, and which must produce even more surprising goods in republican France, of this virtue which is nothing but the love of the *patrie* and of its laws.[52]

Of course Jacobin virtue was one side of a coin whose reverse was terror. Terror became the order of the day on 5 September 1793, and in the speeches of Robespierre and of his associate Antoine Saint-Just (1767–94) it was closely related to the concept of virtue:

> If the spring of popular government in peace is virtue, the spring of popular government in times of revolution is at the same time *virtue and terror*: virtue without which terror is disastrous; terror, without which virtue is powerless. Terror is nothing but prompt, severe, inflexible justice – it is therefore a product of virtue. It is not so much a particular principle as a consequence of the general principle of democracy, applied to the most pressing needs of the *patrie*.[53]

Or, as Saint-Just put it more pithily, '[a] republican government has virtue as its principle; or else terror. What do they want who want neither virtue nor terror?'[54]

Keith Baker has argued that the language of terror emerged directly out of Jacobin classical republicanism. He identified three distinct oppositional discourses in pre-revolutionary France. And he argued that one of these, 'the discourse of will' fed most directly into Jacobin thought, whereas the Brissotins were more influenced by 'the discourse of reason'.[55] On this basis Baker went on to explore what he described as 'three mutations of classical republicanism' during the revolutionary period. Associating these three mutations (metastasisation, moralisation, and messianism) respectively with Marat, Robespierre, and Saint-Just, Baker argued that all three served to radicalise the language of classical republicanism and in doing so contributed towards its 'transformation ... into a philosophy of terror'.[56] More recently, this idea has been expressed in slightly different terms by Israel, who has sought to distinguish the democratic republicanism of the Brissotins from the populist authoritarianism of Jacobins like Robespierre and Marat.[57]

While the Jacobins were not early advocates of anti-monarchical republicanism, the regime enacted under their auspices was both built on the foundations of regicide and firmly committed to anti-monarchical rule. The Jacobins sought to avoid not only monarchy, but all forms of single-person rule. Hence their decision to establish a Committee of Public Safety to take on the executive functions of the state. The Jacobins by this stage were also strong supporters of popular sovereignty. The Jacobin constitution of 1793 included the provision of universal manhood suffrage; and, while that constitution was never implemented owing to the threat posed by war and the sense that in consequence normal government had to be suspended in the public interest, universal suffrage was adopted in the elections to the National Convention in September 1792. Finally, the Jacobin position on religion is interesting from a classical republican perspective. Under pressure from below, the Jacobins attacked Christianity and enacted a policy of dechristianisation; but Robespierre was unwilling to eschew religion altogether, as he recognised the valuable function it could perform within society. The Cult of the Supreme Being and associated revolutionary festivals that were proposed and developed during 1793 effectively created a kind of civil religion, similar to that instituted by Numa under the Romans: a religion that would be firmly subordinated to and placed in the service of the state.

The Thermidoreans

The rule of the Jacobins was brought to an abrupt end on 27 July 1794 (9 Thermidor, Year II in the revolutionary calendar), when the Terror and the atmosphere of fear and paranoia that surrounded it reached such lengths that Robespierre, Saint-Just, and various other leading architects of the regime were themselves declared suspects and sentenced to death. Robespierre and Saint-Just were both executed the following day. It has often been assumed that this moment signified the end of, or at least a decisive shift in, the influence of republican ideas in revolutionary France. Baker, for example, presents the Jacobin era as marking the apotheosis of the influence of classical republicanism, and Biancamaria Fontana characterises the 1790s as the years of a decisive shift from classical to modern republicanism.[58]

Yet, despite the change in personnel and a clear move back to the centre ground, the French republic survived; and, as Andrew Jainchill has demonstrated, there was far more ideological continuity than one might think.[59] Indeed, Jainchill argues that it was in fact the period between 1794 and 1804 rather than the Jacobin era that represented the high point of French classical republicanism. Where the rule of the Committee of Public Safety had been characterised by democratic rhetoric and a messianic belief in the possibility of transcending history, '[t]he conceptual matrix through which the post-Terror republican centre understood politics was essentially classical republican in nature'.[60] The republican leaders of this period adopted an historical approach to the understanding of constitutional forms and expressed familiar anxieties about the contingency of the republic, while at the same time adopting typical republican solutions such as the balancing of powers, the importance of cultivating an active citizenry, and an emphasis on the public good. Moreover, this period was also marked by a departure from the democratic tendencies of the Jacobin era that had been reflected in the lionising of the people and an appreciation for the benefits of an elite republic, with a restricted franchise that would secure virtuous legislators, able to enact a stable legislative framework. 'The result', Jainchill explains, 'was a constitution, passed on 22 August 1795, that reflected the early modern classical–republican tradition, both its anxieties and its prescriptions.'[61] Indeed, the commission of eleven tasked with drawing up that constitution not only reflected classical republican ideology in general but also adopted specific mechanisms, not least Harrington's stress on the need for a bicameral legislature on the grounds that it was crucial to separate the proposal of legislation from its acceptance or rejection by assigning these tasks to different bodies. In his report to the Convention on behalf of the commission, François-Antoine de Boissy d'Anglas insisted that it was impossible to establish a 'stable constitution' 'where there exists in the legislative body only one sole and unique assembly'.[62] In Harrington's model it was the upper house, the senate, that would debate and propose legislation and the lower, popular assembly that would vote for or against the proposals. The commission reversed the provision, giving the Council of Five Hundred the task of proposing legislation and allowing the Council of Elders to vote to accept or reject the proposals put forward.

Jainchill shows how these classical republican concerns persisted throughout the period of the directory. The debate over French manners (*moeurs*), for example, was shaped by classical republican concerns. The corruption of French *moeurs* was seen through the lens of Rome's decline and fall, and emphasis was placed on inculcating civic virtue: in the living population, through festivals, through censorship, and even through a civil religion; and in the generations to come, through a system of public instruction.[63] Several attempts were made during this period to establish a civil religion: Lanthenas proposed the establishment of a 'purely civic declaration of faith' to the National Convention in 1795 and Jean-Baptiste Leclerc pursued the issue via legislative means and attempts to establish *théophilanthropie*, a deistic religion that placed emphasis on morality, the virtues of simplicity, and the 'interdependence of domestic and public life'.[64] Details of this cult were set out in the *Manuel des théophilanthropophiles* of 1796. Rather than traditional clergy, there would be a committee of moral direction, and the liturgy would consist of hymns and speeches praising moral philosophy and incorporating maxims from ancient and modern philosophers.

Classical republican echoes can also be found in debates over foreign affairs during this period.[65] The decision to establish sister republics in various conquered territories between 1795 and 1799 instead of simply incorporating that territory into the French republic was partly motivated by the concern that, as in the case of Rome, an expansion of the republic would lead to its downfall. It was believed that, by establishing sister republics, the French could enjoy the benefits of extending their influence without the dangers of expansion.

Conclusion

The French Revolution can be seen as signalling the triumph of the exclusivist understanding of republican government over its pluralist counterpart. Most revolutionaries assumed that republican government was anti-monarchical. This is confirmed by the debate between Sieyès and Paine in 1791, when Sieyès effectively asserts the pluralist position but acknowledges that most of his contemporaries will see him as a monarchist rather than as a republican.

Yet even among self-confessed republicans several distinct positions emerged. This was partly due to the rich legacy of republican ideas on which the French could draw and partly a result of the sense of possibility and innovation that characterised the revolution. The differences largely concerned the role for representation within a republic and the extent to which – as well as the ways in which – popular sovereignty should be exercised.

Sieyès, at one extreme, insisted that representation should determine all aspects of the system and that even the constitution should be ratified by a representative body. At the other extreme, the Cordeliers advocated the popular ratification of all laws. The Jacobins, too, came to celebrate popular power, but they tended to assume that leaders could interpret the popular will from the actions of the people rather than requiring the people to ratify the laws. The Brissotins took a middle position, insisting on the popular ratification of the constitution but accepting that representatives could decide ordinary legislation on behalf of the people.

Republican ideas were not extinguished with Thermidor, but survived to inform the debates of the late 1790s. This period also saw the exportation of French notions of liberty and republicanism abroad, under Napoleon; but those ideas were changed in the process. Contemporaries were shocked by the transformation of patriotism into an economic and military power, which reversed the traditional political logic and produced a large republican empire, driven by reason of state.[66]

While Jainchill insists that the period between 1794 and 1804 reflected continuity with – even a return to – earlier classical republican ideas, he also saw it as a period of development. It was a watershed in the transition from classical to modern republicanism, and was crucial to the emergence of a language of liberalism. While some of the republicans of this period went on to collaborate with Napoleon, others became part of the liberal opposition to the Bonapartist regime. During the 1790s, thinkers such as Charles-Guillaume Théremin and Germaine de Staël (1766–1817) sowed the seeds of a modern form of liberal republicanism that built on the Brissotin foundations.[67] They championed individual rights, representative government, and commercial society, but were more concerned than their predecessors about the effects of commerce on the modern world, fearing that it would lead to war rather than eliminate it. They also placed greater emphasis on the need to cultivate active political participation by the people in order to prevent despotism. Although these writers produced a shift towards liberalism through the priority they accorded individual rights, they continued to believe that the republic was the only form of government appropriate for the modern world.

Thus the seeds of French liberalism can be found in this period. This implies that the distinction between republicanism and liberalism in a French context is by no means as sharp as the Pocockean account of the two would suggest. French liberalism was shaped by classical republican concerns, and the thought of leading nineteenth-century

French liberals, such as Benjamin Constant (1767–1830) and Alexandre de Tocqueville (1805–1859), retains traces of republican ideology. French liberalism might, therefore, be best conceived of as a form of liberal republicanism. This question of the relationship between liberalism and republicanism remained pertinent throughout the nineteenth and twentieth centuries, both in France and beyond.

9

Republicanism in the Nineteenth Century

Introduction

The French Revolution was regarded by many at the time, and has been viewed since, as ushering in a new era. The obvious corollary of this is that the nineteenth century was completely different politically, ideologically, and socially from the seventeenth and eighteenth centuries. Moreover, there was a sense that this trans- formation had affected not just France – and not even just those countries directly affected by the Revolution and its aftermath – but the whole of Europe and beyond. In particular, the Revolution spawned a collection of new ideologies – liberalism, socialism, and conservatism – that have dominated the political landscape ever since. Republicanism, while central to the Revolution, did not map neatly onto any of these new ideologies, and has been viewed in some contexts as having been eclipsed by liberalism. Indeed, as one scholar has argued, '[t]he prevailing historical scholarship gave the strong impression that nothing conceptually meaningful happened in the republican tradition after the American Revolution'.[1]

Yet recent research has shown this to be false. Republicanism took on a new complexion in the nineteenth century. In the United States, practical realities made the relationship between liberty and slavery a thorny and contested issue in the period between the American Revolution and the Civil War, and republican ideas were deployed on both sides and adapted to fit the circumstances. More broadly, the exclusivist sense of a republic as the antonym of monarchy, with one or two exceptions, finally eclipsed the earlier, pluralist understanding. At least as important as the debates between republicans and monarchists, however, were those between republicans and liberals. Yet Pocock's characterisation of republicanism and liberalism as incompatible languages is simply not borne out. In fact, versions of liberal republicanism proved particularly potent during the nineteenth century.

Another development of this period is that the previously strong historical influences on republican thought yielded ground to contemporary influences. The events of 1848 are testimony to this in the ways in which revolutionaries were inspired by and copied one another. British nineteenth-century republicans, too, owed less to the example of the English Commonwealth of 1649–60 and more to the contemporary American, French, and short-lived Roman republics. They felt affinity less with their seventeenth- and eighteenth-century English predecessors than with republican émigrés from Europe who found refuge in London, not least Giuseppe Mazzini. While fragmentary evidence of an international republican network can be found at earlier moments – in the support offered to English republican exiles who fled to Europe in 1660, or in the links between 'sister republics' in the late eighteenth century – it is only in the nineteenth century that we can speak with confidence of republicanism as a transnational movement.

Finally, and perhaps most importantly, republicanism was transformed during this period from a doctrine primarily articulated by political elites to one that appealed to artisans, workers, and, by the 1870s, even women and newly enfranchised former slaves. This was bound to prompt conceptual transformations and meant that the relationship between republicanism and democracy was a further topic of debate during the period. It also prompted the application, to the economic sphere, of what had previously been primarily a political discourse. This transformation can be seen particularly clearly in the North American context, but in Europe, too, there was a convergence of republicanism with labour campaigns and the development of the cooperative movement.

The present chapter will deal first with some of the key republican regimes of the nineteenth century. Attention will be paid to the United States of America, which maintained its republican form throughout the century, and then to France, which has been ruled as a republic continuously since 1870, but which over the first seven decades of the nineteenth century saw more years of monarchical and imperial than of republican rule. The second half of the chapter will consider republicanism as an opposition movement. Attention will be paid to Italy, where the short-lived Roman republic of 1848 was inspired by, and further sustained, an opposition movement. It exercised influence not just in Italy but also in Britain and France, with Felice Orsini's attempted assassination of Napoleon III in 1858. Finally, brief consideration will be given to Britain: while it was never under republican rule during the nineteenth century, and while republicanism was never a dominant ideology, this country provides a case study that contrasts with the others, revealing how and why republican ideas survived even in less than favourable circumstances.

Republican Regimes

The United States of America

The American Republic was by far the most enduring republican model to emerge in the eighteenth century. Indeed, the constitution has remained in place continuously since 1789, fewer than 30 amendments being enacted over a period of more than two hundred years. Yet this should not be taken to mean that the path of American republicanism in the nineteenth century was smooth and uncontested. At the heart of the American Revolution lay a dilemma that would plague the early republic and influence the course of its history during much of the next century. How could a republican system of government, grounded in the concept of freedom, operate effectively in a society that rested on the enslavement of a significant proportion of its population?

The neo-Roman understanding of liberty, which proved so crucial to Renaissance and early modern republicans, was founded on the opposition inherited from Roman law between the freeman and the slave. To be at liberty was, by definition, not to be a slave, and therefore not to be dependent on the will of someone else. This did not mean, however, that ancient republicans had automatically condemned the institution of slavery. On the contrary, the very notion of republican citizenship, with its strenuous requirement for both knowledge and time to engage in political affairs, depended on the idea that citizens had sufficient leisure to educate themselves and to engage in political activities. It was therefore assumed that other groups within the population (in particular women and slaves) would work to provide the basic necessities of food and shelter. Moreover, the rise of independent citizenship in the ancient world actually enhanced the economic importance of slavery, because it became more difficult to compel citizens to work for others, and so slaves were required to work on large plantations as well as in mines and urban workshops.[2]

By the time of the American Revolution chattel slavery had become firmly embedded within colonial society, particularly in the south. Yet it was not so easy for the republicans of the American Revolution, as it had been for the ancients, to reconcile their understanding of liberty as the antonym of slavery with the enslavement of certain groups in society. Alex Gourevitch attributes this problem to the rise in importance of the concept of equality and its requirement that political principles be universal, in other words applicable to all.[3] In part this shift was a consequence of the rise of Christianity. In the ancient world the possession of particular moral qualities was not deemed to be universal. Christianity introduced the notion of universal moral equality, though it took a long time for this aspect of the belief system to be taken sufficiently seriously to require abolition.

Some nineteenth-century American republicans, particularly in the south, simply looked back to the ancient world and revived the idea of republican citizenship as necessarily dependent on slavery. Thus, many southerners, for example John C. Calhoun, presented themselves as the true heirs and guardians of classical republicanism and insisted that the abolition of slavery would be a threat to America's republican political order. 'I fearlessly assert that the existing relation between the two races in the South, against which these blind fanatics are waging war, forms the most solid and durable foundation on which to rear free and stable political institutions.'[4] However, those in the abolitionist movement rejected this justification, accusing its advocates of hypocrisy. In his speech 'What to the Slave is the Fourth of July?', delivered at Corinthian Hall in Rochester, New York on 5 July 1852, Frederick Douglass directly addressed the question set out in his title:

> [A] day that reveals to him, more than all other days in the year, the gross injustice and cruelty to which he is the constant victim. To him, your celebration is a sham; your boasted liberty, an unholy license; your national greatness, swelling vanity; your sounds of rejoicing are empty and heartless; your denunciations of tyrants, brass fronted impudence; your shouts of liberty and equality, hollow mockery ...
>
> You declare, before the world, and are understood by the world to declare, that you 'hold these truths to be self evident, that all men are created equal; and are endowed by their Creator with certain inalienable rights; and that, among these are life, liberty, and the pursuit of happiness'; and yet, you hold securely, in a bondage ... a seventh part of the inhabitants of your country.[5]

The experience and values of the American Revolution and of the republicanism it inaugurated were, then, a powerful stimulus to the abolitionist movement.

It was not only the institution of slav[*sic*]ery that prompted questions regarding the economic underpinnings of American republicanism. The idealisation of America as a republic of citizen farmers, which could be traced back to *Notes on the State of Virginia* by Thomas Jefferson (1743–1826), was given practical expression in the presidencies of Jefferson and James Madison in the first decades of the nineteenth century. They sought to build a republican political economy based on westward expansion and free trade, supported by the idea that an agrarian way of life was necessary to produce the kind of citizens required in a republic.[6] As Jefferson wrote to John Jay from Paris in August 1785, '[c]ultivators of the earth are the most valuable citizens. They are the most vigorous, the most independent, the most virtuous, and they are tied to their country and wedded to it's [*sic*] liberty and interests by the most lasting bands.'[7] Moreover, the abundance of land in America meant that it was possible to open up the prospect of a republic of independent proprietors to a much larger proportion of the population than might have been possible elsewhere. Small citizen farmers and artisans in America could possess sufficient land to guarantee their political and economic independence. Yet realising this ideal was dependent on challenging the monopolisation of land by a few.

Nor was it just the distribution of land that threatened the dream. Ever since Alexander Hamilton in the 1790s, there had been those who argued that republican greatness depended, not on a nostalgic agrarian idyll, but on building an advanced economy, which in turn required the development of commerce, manufacturing, and public finance. By the early 1800s the American economy was already starting to shift away from its agrarian roots, through the development of domestic manufactures. Initially this too could be conceptualised as part of a republican political economy. In Lowell, Massachusetts, an attempt was made to create a model republican community in which the moral character of workers was preserved, and even enhanced, through the imposition of strict moral and religious codes in factories and boarding houses, and the establishment of improvement circles, lectures, and literary magazines.[8]

Yet this view of republicanism soon came to appear outdated as a result of the huge expansion of the urban manufacturing industry. In this context, leaders of the Workingmen's movement such as William Heighton (1801–71) questioned whether the social and economic conditions in America really were conducive to the kind of independence required of republican citizens. The American Revolution, they pointed out, was unfinished, and could be completed only if internal forms of economic servitude were destroyed. It was not only slaves whose freedom and independence was compromised, they argued, but also the growing numbers of industrial workers, who dominated the economy of the north. Thomas Skidmore (1790–1832) spoke in typically republican language of workers as being 'dependent, even for their very existence, upon the pleasure, the caprice, the tyranny' of their employers.[9] Langdon Byllesby (1789–1871) drew the parallel even more directly. 'The very essence of slavery', he pronounced, 'is in being compelled to labour, while the proceeds of that labour is taken and enjoyed by another.'[10]

For some, the existence of wage labour in American society was not a reason to give up the American dream. In a speech addressed to farmers in Wisconsin in 1859, the future president, Abraham Lincoln (1809–65), acknowledged the threat that slavery posed to independence and praised the virtues of free labour. Yet he also suggested that, as long as wage labour was a stage in the life cycle and a stepping stone to a better life, which would allow the poorest in American society to climb to a position of independence through hard work, it need not undermine the notion of an open agrarian republic:

> The prudent, penniless beginner in the world, labors for wages awhile, saves a surplus with which to buy tools or land, for himself; then labors on his own account another while, and at length hires another new beginner to help him. This, say its advocates, is free labor – the just and generous, and prosperous system, which opens the way for all – gives hope to all, and energy, and progress, and improvement of condition to all.[11]

Lincoln, of course, played a key role in the abolition of chattel slavery in America in 1865 through the thirteenth amendment to the constitution. Yet abolition did not mark the end of the debate about liberty and slavery among American republicans, since the condition of former slaves was not always immediately improved by emancipation and the problem of wage labourers remained. Indeed their number was increasing. By 1870 two thirds of the workforce worked for wages and it was by that time more common for such employment to be life-long rather than merely associated with an early period in the life cycle. This situation prompted several responses.

Laissez-faire republicans questioned whether wage labour involved dependency, insisting that it was, in fact, a form of free labour. They argued that wage labourers (unlike slaves) were not tied to a particular employer but could choose whom they worked for, ensuring that contracts were voluntary, so that they remained free and independent. A free labourer was independent, laissez-faire republicans argued, because he controlled his own labour. As William Graham Sumner (1840–1910) argued, 'a society based on contract is a society of *free and independent* men, who form ties without favour or obligation, and *cooperate without cringing or intrigue*'.[12] Frederic J. Stimson (1855–1943) argued, similarly, in *Labor in Its Relation to Law* that 'the recognition of the labourer as a free citizen, free to contract, capable of acquiring contractual rights, has been his great emancipation of the past'.[13] Significantly, as Gourevitch has highlighted, this version of republicanism was closely associated with, and at some points even bled into, liberal arguments, thus constituting one challenge to the idea that republicanism and liberalism were incompatible.

In response to laissez-faire arguments, cooperative republicans presented wage labour in a much less rose-tinted light and developed an analysis of the structural and personal dimensions of economic domination. They continued to stress, as members of the Workingmen's movement of the 1820s and 1830s had done, that wage labourers were dependent on their employers. The Noble and Holy Order of the Knights of Labor was established in 1869; it operated secretly for ten years, but gathered more than 30,000 members by 1880 and 700,000 by 1886.[14] This was the first labour organisation for both white and black workers, and its members were clear that wage labour had no place in a republic and that economic independence needed to be secured for all workers. Its leaders, who included William H. Sylvis (1828–69), Ira Steward (1831–83), George McNeill (1836–1906), and Terence Powderly (1849–1924), were all self-consciously republican in their outlook and used explicitly republican arguments to criticise wage labour. McNeill argued that 'there is an inevitable and irresistible conflict between the wage-system of labor and the republican system of government'.[15] Similarly, Powderly explained that the wage labour system undermined republican liberty by generating economic inequalities that translated into political inequalities. Workers might own their own labour and make a voluntary contract with their employer, but they were not truly free because, if they and their families were to survive, the option of withholding their labour from the market was not genuinely available to them. Moreover, once employed, the worker was subject to the caprice of his employer, and this made him dependent regardless of how benevolently that employer used his power. This was the equivalent of the argument of seventeenth-century republicans like John Milton that subjects were still unfree even under a mild and gentle monarch. There appears to have been some acknowledgement of this link to earlier republican arguments among the Knights of Labor themselves. In an 1882 article from the *Journal of United Labor* slavery was defined in unashamedly neo-Roman terms:

> The weight of chains, number of stripes, hardness of labor, and other effects of a master's cruelty, may make one servitude more miserable than another; but he is a slave who serves the gentlest man in the world, as well as he who serves the worst; and he does serve him if he *must* obey his commands and depend upon his will.

As Gourevitch noticed, this passage was not original to the Knights but was taken from Algernon Sidney's *Discourses Concerning Government*.[16]

While drawing on earlier republican ideas, the Knights adapted them to their own ends. They also went beyond earlier organisations of the Workingmen Party in their insistence that the solution to the problem of wage labour lay in the creation of cooperatives. What they intended by this was not merely consumer cooperatives of the kind that had been established in the English town of Rochdale in the mid-1840s, but '[a]n economy of interdependent producer and consumer cooperatives' in which factories would be collectively owned and managed by the workers themselves.[17] As Powderly explained in his address to the General Assembly of the Knights of Labor in 1880, 'the method by which we hope to regain our independence ... [is] by embarking in a system of COOPERATION WHICH WILL EVENTUALLY MAKE EVERY MAN HIS OWN MASTER – EVERY MAN HIS OWN EMPLOYER.'[18] Several local assemblies of the Knights set up their own small-scale cooperatives, and in Birmingham, Alabama in the 1880s black workers managed and ran their own plantation.

While these developments can be seen as marking the culmination of the radical labour republican tradition, they also served to transform that tradition in fundamental ways. It was now cooperation, rather than just liberty or independence, that was presented as the antithesis of slavery.[19] The notion of republican liberty was fully applied to the economic sphere, and in some ways economic liberty was deemed more important than (and certainly prior to) political liberty. In this way, cooperative republicans challenged any opposition between virtue and commerce. They also adopted an understanding of virtue that depended less on self-sacrifice and more on the pursuit of rational self-interest through the practice of solidarity. By this means, virtue was transformed from a characteristic of independent property owners to one appropriate to workers, and it was to be achieved not via the coercive apparatus of the state but through self-organisation and autodidacticism.

France

The United States of America was not the only country to begin the nineteenth century under republican rule. France, too, was still a republic, at least in name, in 1800. Although the coup of 18 Brumaire (9–10 November 1799) was led by Napoleon Bonaparte (1769–1821) and effectively provided his first step to power, the republic remained in place until he was proclaimed hereditary emperor of the French, on 18 May 1804. The main features of the constitution of Year VIII (1799) were sketched out on the night of 8–9 December by Emmanuel-Joseph Sieyès, Pierre-Louis Roederer (1754–1835), Antoine Boulay de la Meurthe (1761–1840), and Napoleon himself. Agreement was reached on 13 December and the constitution was ratified by popular referendum on 7 February 1800 (though the results were supposedly fixed by Napoleon's brother Lucien).[20] That constitution confirmed the shift from a five-person executive directory to a three-person consulate that had been enacted by *coup d'état*. Thus, despite the coup, the principle of a conciliar executive branch was maintained. In this regard the first French republic was different from the American model and from all subsequent French republics, in that it did not adopt an elected president. Yet, while the principle of shared executive power remained in place, the system was soon corrupted. Even though two of the consuls appointed in the aftermath of the coup, Sieyès and Pierre Roger Ducos (1747–1816), were replaced when the new constitution was implemented, Bonaparte remained as first consul. In that role he had more power than Louis XVI had enjoyed under the constitution of 1791.[21] Moreover, on 2 August 1802 it was decreed that he would hold the position for life.

Andrew Jainchill presents the constitution of Year VIII as marking the triumph of 'liberal authoritarianism' in France. While the form of government was still republican and lip service was paid to the importance of pursuing the public good, it was argued that only a strong central government could achieve this end.[22] Given the centrality of Sieyès to the Brumaire coup and his involvement in drawing up the constitution that emerged from it, it is not surprising that this period saw a brief articulation of the pluralist understanding of republicanism that he had advocated in his debate with Paine in 1791. In private notes, Sieyès referred to France's government as 'a republican monarchy or a monarchical republic'; and this understanding was picked up by others. One pamphleteer declared: 'whenever ... the government renders to each citizen the liberty, safety, protection, and happiness to which he is entitled, the *public good*, the *Republic*, exists in the government, whatever its form'.[23]

Yet Jainchill also suggests that this period witnessed the last gasp of classical republicanism in France, followed by its transformation in the direction of the liberal republicanism of Benjamin Constant and Alexis de Tocqueville. The authoritarianism of Bonaparte's regime was challenged by an opposition group comprising, among others, Constant, Marie-Joseph Chénier, and Pierre-Claude-François Daunou (1761–1840). These figures continued to insist that liberty is best preserved under a republican constitution in which the citizens engage in an active political life. Although it remained unpublished until 1991, Constant's *On the Possibility of a Republican Constitution in a Large Country* articulated the views of this group. Written between 1798 and 1806, the work developed the ideas earlier set out by Charles-Guillaume Théremin, and especially by Germaine de Staël. Constant argued that civil liberty had to be given priority, but that active political participation by the citizens was essential to prevent despotism. He also celebrated the republican form, presenting it as superior to monarchy and, as the title suggested, challenged the idea that republics are suited only to small territories.[24]

Following Napoleon's forced abdication on 4 April 1814, the state reverted not to republican rule, but to monarchy, the count de Provence, brother of Louis XVI, being invited to rule as King Louis XVIII. The charter of 1814, according to which he ruled, was supposedly modelled on the constitution of 1791, but Louis regarded his authority as deriving from divine providence, not from popular sovereignty.[25] Napoleon returned to power briefly the following year, having escaped from exile on the island of Elba and marched with his supporters to Paris. After Louis XVIII was again restored in July 1815, the monarchy became increasingly authoritarian in character. Occasional attempts at insurrection were made, and a secret opposition movement called La Charbonnerie – on the model of Italian Carbonari, 'Charcoal Burners' – gathered as many as 60,000 members.[26] The Charbonnerie was not the preserve of republicans, however, and the group offered no alternative to the restored monarchy. Moreover, the response to any attempted uprisings was harsh. The severity of the repression only increased after September 1824, when Charles X (the former count d'Artois and another of Louis XVI's brothers) acceded to the throne.

In this context, the liberal republicanism of Constant and Daunou offered an alternative to both the authoritarian arguments of royalists and the rationalist liberalism of figures like François Guizot (1787–1874) and the Doctrinaires.[27] Yet, while the liberal republicans continued to emphasise the protection of individual liberties and the importance of citizens pursuing an active political life, the circumstances meant that they tended to call for constitutional monarchy rather than for a republic.[28] Consequently, Constant's lecture at the Athenée Royal in Paris in 1819, which was one in a series on the English constitution, focused not – as his earlier work had done – on the contrast between republics and monarchies, but rather on that between ancient and modern liberty. The former he described as

> exercising collectively, but directly, several parts of the complete sovereignty; in deliberating, in the public square, over war and peace; in forming alliances with foreign governments; in voting laws, in pronouncing judgements; in examining the accounts, the acts, the stewardship of the magistrates; in calling them to appear in front of the assembled people, in accusing, condemning or absolving them.[29]

Modern liberty, by contrast, focused on civil rights, including 'the right to be subjected only to the laws', 'to express their opinion', 'to dispose of property', 'to come and go without permission', and 'to associate with other individuals'.[30] Political rights were reduced to the right 'to exercise some influence on the administration of the government',[31] which could, of course, be achieved under a monarchy as well as under a republic. The modern world, on Constant's account, was distinguished by the invention of representative government and the rise of commercial society (as well as the abolition of slavery, in Europe at least), and these developments reinforced each other. Representation meant that citizens did not need to devote themselves wholeheartedly to politics, so they had time to engage in commerce. At the same time, commerce provided citizens with other interests and sources of happiness than politics and tended to inspire a love of independence. On this basis, Constant argued, the moderns could no longer enjoy the liberty of the ancients. 'Our freedom must consist of peaceful enjoyment and private independence.'[32] True to the liberal republican position, however, he acknowledged the risks of jettisoning the political liberty of the ancients completely, insisting at the end of his lecture that, rather than renouncing either sort of freedom, it was necessary 'to learn to combine the two together'.[33]

The liberal republican compromise was not, however, the only option open to former republicans of this period. The political economist Jean-Baptiste Say continued to think of himself as a republican rather than as a liberal, and maintained his republican beliefs throughout the empire.[34] Having been influenced by Clavière and his Genevan associates during the Revolution, Say sought to develop a form of modern republicanism, and in particular a political economy that was suitable for a large commercial nation such as France. In the context of the empire and then of the restored monarchy, Say advocated a form of republican government that was entirely secular and without hierarchal ranks, but that would nonetheless be held together by virtuous manners.

In 1830 the liberal majority issued a vote of no confidence in the government that led to the dissolution of the Chamber of Deputies and to fresh elections. Angered by this move, Charles X used emergency measures to issue the Four Ordinances of Saint-Cloud. These required liberal newspapers to cease publication, called for the dissolution of the new assembly, and insisted on fresh elections with a significantly reduced franchise. In doing this, Charles ushered in a revolution that saw him replaced by the former duke d'Orléans – now Louis Philippe, king of the French. In bringing a shift from absolute to constitutional monarchy, the Revolution of 1830 – the July Revolution – is sometimes characterised as the French equivalent to England's Glorious Revolution of 1688–9.

France remained a monarchy between 1830 and 1848, but republican sentiments hovered just beneath the surface. Tricolour flags quickly reappeared to replace the white fleur-de-lys of the Bourbons, as reflected in Eugène Delacroix's famous painting *Liberty Leading the People*.[35] Opposition societies, many of a republican character, also reappeared. As their names suggest, groups such as Les Amis du peuple (The Friends of the People) and La Société des droits de l'homme (The Human Rights Society), both of which were established in July 1830, appealed back to the ideas of the 1790s; and, like their forebears, they not only operated in Paris but also commanded a network of provincial clubs. The latter even developed informal relations with similar organisations in Germany, Poland, and Italy.[36] It is also clear from their publications that they sought to engage a wide audience. A pamphlet produced by the Société des droits de l'homme in 1832 reverted to Rousseau's pluralist definition of a republic as 'a state, whatever its form of government, where law is the expression of the general will. All legitimate governments, in which public interest is predominant, are republican.'[37]

At a theoretical level, republican ideas continued to be integrated within liberalism. In *Democracy in America* Tocqueville prioritised modern liberty, while simultaneously insisting on the importance of maintaining a vigorous political life among the citizen body. 'My principal goal in writing this book', he argued, 'has been to combat' the tendency of people in democratic times to immerse themselves in 'private life' and thus to abandon 'public affairs' and 'political life'.[38] Tocqueville's emphasis on politics, his concerns about the corrosive effects of luxury and the size of the American republic, his warnings about the dangers of a powerful executive and the importance of balance, and his sense that freedom and independence were fragile and could only be preserved by popular vigilance, all showed that this leading French liberal still owed much to republicanism. Jainchill describes him as a transitional figure 'whose thinking remained rooted in the early modern classical–republican tradition at the same time as he so eloquently articulated liberal and other more modern sentiments'.[39]

This period also saw the rise of another ideology, which sometimes became integrated with republicanism but also provided a rival to it: socialism. Many leading socialists drew heavily on republican ideas. *Voyage en Icarie*, by Étienne Cabet (1788–1856), presented an ideal of a representative democratic republic and inspired the first large-scale workers' union in France, La Société pour fonder l'Icarie (The Society for the Foundation of Icaria, known as 'the Icarians').[40] Pierre-Joseph Proudhon (1809–65), whose *Qu'est-ce que la propriété?* (*What Is Property?*) was an influential socialist work, declared himself to be a republican as well as an anarchist, although, reflecting the long-standing ambiguity surrounding the precise understanding of republicanism, he wavered as to whether the abolition of monarchy was strictly necessary.[41] Auguste Blanqui (1805–81) was more unequivocal in seeing the republic as the best means of bringing about the social reform he desired. Drawing on Philippe Buonarroti's account of the 1790s radical Gracchus Babeuf, Blanqui called for immediate revolution and the establishment of a republican government. Republican clubs and publications were affected by a major crackdown that followed several attempted uprisings in 1834, but Blanqui campaigned through the Société des familles (Society of Families), which replaced the Société des droits de l'homme, and then through its later incarnation, the Société des saisons (Society of the Seasons). Further uprisings occurred in 1839 and Blanqui was arrested in October, only narrowly escaping the death penalty. With republican societies banned once again, subscription banquets were used as an alternative method of gathering supporters together.

It was one of these subscription banquets that provided the spark for the outbreak of the 1848 Revolution. Discovering that a number of unemployed artisans and students intended to take part in a reform

banquet in the Latin Quarter, the government banned it. The organ-
isers voted 80 to 17 to follow the government injunction and cancel
the event, but demonstrations still went ahead and the situation
quickly escalated, partly fuelled by several years of economic crisis
and harvest failures.[42] Demonstrations were held on 22, 23, and
24 February and barricades were erected on the streets of Paris.
Louis Philippe, realising the seriousness of the situation, abdicated
in favour of his young grandson, but this was not enough for the
crowd, which invaded the National Assembly, making it clear that
only the establishment of a republic would pacify it. As during the
1790s, popular power proved a powerful tool, and on 24 February
the Second French Republic was officially proclaimed. Its declaration
was celebrated with processions, fireworks, and illuminations.[43] The
provisional government embarked immediately on a dramatic reform
programme, which included the introduction of universal male
suffrage, the abolition of slavery in French territories, an end to the
death penalty for political offences, and measures for dealing with
rising unemployment – including the establishment of a scheme of
national workshops and the introduction of a small unemployment
benefit. Republican clubs also sprang up throughout Paris and
beyond, for example the Club des femmes (Club of Women), the
Comité des droits de la femme (Committee for Women's Rights), and
the Club d'émancipation des femmes (Club for the Emancipation of
Women), which demanded rights – including the vote – for women.[44]

Tensions among republicans remained, however, and they failed
to take the whole country with them. Consequently, their policy of
introducing universal suffrage backfired, and at the Easter elections
conservatives gained a majority in the Legislative Assembly. These
conservatives were hostile to the national workshops, which by June
involved 120,000 people. An attempt to enlist those aged 18–25
in the army instead prompted a demonstration and the occupation
of the Assembly on 15 May. Given the numbers involved and the
strength of the general feeling, it is perhaps not surprising that the
Assembly's decision to dissolve the workshops on 20 June sparked
trouble. A protest demonstration began on 22 June, and by the end
of the day 100,000 people gathered in Place du Panthéon. Protests
continued the following day, when barricades were erected in eastern
Paris. The June Days demonstrations were particularly violent. The
official estimate was that over 1,400 were killed, but the actual figure
was probably higher.[45]

The Second Republic struggled on for a short time, a new
constitution being approved on 4 November, but the seeds of its
destruction were sown by the end of the year. In August the freedom

of the press that had been established in February was curtailed. In October it was decided that a president should be elected via universal suffrage. On 10 December, Louis-Napoléon Bonaparte (1808–73), the nephew of Napoleon I, was elected president, having secured 74 per cent of the vote. Aided by continuing divisions among republicans and a second victory for conservatives in the legislative elections of May 1849, Louis-Napoléon gradually curtailed popular powers. He stiffened press censorship, brought in a longer residence requirement for voting, and overturned the rule that stated that a president could not stand for a second term. Finally, on 2 December 1851 he followed in his uncle's footsteps by enacting a *coup d'état*. While he claimed to be acting in defence of the republic, he was made president for life; the republican constitution was soon revised, to give far greater power to the president himself, and on 7 November 1852 France officially became an empire once more.

Republicanism was largely silenced under the empire, which exercised a strict censorship; in this atmosphere republicans chose to abstain from participation in elections.[46] This gradually changed in the late 1850s and 1860s, but the republican ideas that gained traction tended to be associated with moderate figures such as Léon Gambetta (1838–82) and Jules Ferry (1832–1893) rather than with the likes of Blanqui.

Consequently it was the Franco-Prussian War and the lack of alternatives, rather than the strength of republican feeling, that brought the downfall of the Second Empire and finally paved the way for the establishment of enduring republican rule in France.[47] Louis-Napoléon's capture at the Battle of Sedan in early September left little choice but for the establishment of the Third Republic on 4 September 1870. Paris was besieged and the government retreated to Bordeaux. An armistice was finally signed on 28 January 1871, and elections were held to form an assembly that should secure the peace. As previously, this brought victory for conservative voices but dissatisfaction among members of the National Guard; and fears among the left-leaning citizens of Paris that the republic would not meet their desires resulted in the establishment of the Paris Commune, a radical socialist government within the city. The crushing of the Commune in late May 1871 secured the survival of the conservative Third Republic, which went on to become the most durable French government since 1789.

Republican Opposition

Italy

As a result of the French Revolution and the rule of Napoleon I, Italy had briefly enjoyed both republican rule and effective unification. Between 1796 and 1799 six sister republics were established on the Italian peninsula: the Cispadane, the Cisalpine, the Ligurian, the Luccan, the Roman, and the Neapolitan or Parthenopaean republics. The term *democrazia* was preferred to *repubblica* as a description of these political regimes, namely one that distanced them from the aristocratic republics of the *ancien régime*.[48] It is also noteworthy that, although these regimes had been established by the French, the Italians were more sympathetic to the model of representative republican government offered by the Americans – a model that had been conveyed to them via intermediaries such as Gaetano Filangieri (1753–88), a correspondent of Benjamin Franklin, and Fillippo Mazzei (1730–1816), a friend of Jefferson.[49] Republican catechisms of the period often equated republicanism with citizenship and linked it to the natural rights of liberty, equality, security and property, while also insisting that it was compatible with the Catholic religion.[50]

On 17 March 1805 Italy became a kingdom with all its northern and central parts under Napoleon's control. After Napoleon's defeat and the Congress of Vienna, this kingdom was divided once again, but this time the separate states were ruled by unconstitutional, even autocratic governments. While independent in theory, most of them relied on protection from foreign powers, in particular the Austrian Empire, which also had direct rule over Lombardy and the area around Venice.[51] Uprisings against these new regimes in the early 1820s were quickly followed by repression.

Many in Italy favoured the unification of the peninsula, but it was Giuseppe Mazzini (1805–72) who was crucial in tying Italian unification to republicanism and in setting the Italian cause within a wider European campaign for the establishment of free, democratic nation-states. During a spell in prison on a charge of subversive activism against Austrian rule in 1830, Mazzini decided that his life's mission was to unite Italy under a republican government.[52] In exile in Marseille after his release, he established the revolutionary movement La Giovine Italia (Young Italy). In contrast to earlier tendencies, its members explicitly described themselves as republicans rather than democrats.[53] The oath of affiliation to this movement ended with these words: '[c]onvinced that virtue lies in action and in sacrifice

... I swear to dedicate myself wholly and for ever to striving with them to constitute Italy as a Nation, One, Independent, Free and Republican'.[54] Mazzini went on to recruit thousands of members, to establish a periodical entitled *La Giovine Italia* (*Young Italy*), and to encourage insurrections – most of which proved unsuccessful.

Critical of the French Revolution, Mazzini grounded his republicanism in the ideas of Jean-Charles-Léonard Sismondi (1773–1842), a Genevan-born historian who wrote on Italian and French history and on the legacy of the medieval Italian republics that Sismondi described. Citing Sismondi, Mazzini emphasised the commitment to the public good in the Italian city-states of the Renaissance. 'The Italian people pursued the good of all, not the good of the *signori* at the expense of the serfs.'[55] He sought to reimagine that ideal for his own time. 'From the liberty of the nation derive the liberties of the individual citizen, and from the juridical equality of all citizens derives the principle of universal suffrage, which gives the right to participate with the vote in the political life of the nation.'[56] Thus Mazzini called for the establishment of a republic as a crucial partner to reunification, and in the later 1830s and 1840s he embellished this with a reference to 'democracy' and his 'religion of humanity', which undoubtedly owed something to the earlier catechisms. Despite his persistent commitment to democracy, however, Mazzini always derived much of his support from Italy's middle class; and, over time, he became detached from the popular masses, which were drawn instead to socialism and communism.[57] Believing that cultural and ideological change had to precede political change, Mazzini devoted himself during much of the 1830s and 1840s to writing about the cause and publicising it.

The suppression of La Giovine Italia in the early 1830s, together with spending time in exile, led Mazzini to see the Italian struggle in a wider context and to build links with exiles from other countries. He encouraged the establishment of similar movements in Poland, Germany, Switzerland, Greece and even Spain.[58] In 1834, while in exile in Berne, he established Young Europe together with associates from Italy, Poland, and Germany, and in 1847 he and his London friends created the People's International League. These links proved fruitful. One of Mazzini's English associates, William J. Linton (1812–97), used his publication *The English Republic* to clarify and breathe new life into Mazzini's notion of a republicanism infused with democracy and commitment to social welfare.

Just as Mazzini's wider networks and connections were important to the development of his republicanism, so events in Europe in and after 1848 also exerted a profound impact on his life, his ideas, and the wider cause of Italian republicanism. Inspired by events in France, rebellion broke out in Milan in 1848, and the Austrian army was forced into retreat. Further success followed later, in the year when Pope Pius IX was forced to flee after the assassination of his prime minister, Pellegrino Rossi; and leading Italian figures such as Mazzini himself and Giuseppe Garibaldi (1808–82) quickly returned to their homeland. In early 1849 the newly established constituent assembly abolished the temporal power of the papacy and proclaimed the Roman republic. In March 1849 Mazzini was elected triumvir, alongside Carlo Armellini (1777–1863) and Aurelio Saffi (1819–90). This gave him an opportunity for practical action, and there is evidence that he proved adept at administrative and diplomatic tasks.[59] The new regime was particularly progressive, advocating universal male suffrage for all those over the age of twenty-one, freedom of the press and of religion, the introduction of basic social rights, and even a degree of sexual equality.

Success was, however, short-lived. The constitution – the Roman charter – was proclaimed in the city hall on 3 July, but troops were already gathered and soon afterwards the Roman republic was overwhelmed by military force. Crucial to the military campaign was, ironically, the French army of Louis-Napoléon Bonaparte. Mazzini returned to foreign exile in mid-July. Rome was initially governed by a commission of cardinals, but the pope returned in April 1850.

The fall of the Second French Republic and the accession of Napoléon as emperor further damaged the Italian republican cause. These events prompted reappraisal and self-examination; and, while to some extent this resulted in increased solidarity between republicans in different nations, many of Mazzini's former supporters came to believe that progress could best be made and radical politics could best be pursued under non-republican forms of government.[60] Consequently it is not surprising that, after the successful Sicilian revolt in 1859, which made it possible for Garibaldi to capture the whole of southern Italy, unification was carried out under the Piedmontese crown rather than in the name of a popular republic.

Britain

Britain was, of course, not a republic in the strict anti-monarchical sense at any point during the nineteenth century. Yet, despite the dominance of an exclusivist understanding of republicanism by that stage, the tendency to view the British constitution as a republic in the older, pluralist sense did not disappear completely. In 1790 Charles James Fox declared that 'our Constitution was a republic, in the just sense of the word; it was a Monarchy founded on the good of the people'. Similarly, more than one hundred years later, H. G. Wells characterised the British system as a 'Crowned Republic'.[61] Frank Prochaska, in his study of British republicanism in the nineteenth and twentieth centuries, distinguishes three varieties of republican thought that were articulated in Britain during that period.[62] First, there were those who grounded their understanding of the idea of republic in the older, pluralist conception of government in the public good. They were willing to work within the confines of the British monarchy, as long as it operated in the interests of the public – on the grounds, as William Sherwin put it in 1817, that all those 'who promote public welfare', even 'kings, emperors, princes', are 'in the fullest acceptation of the word, decided *Republicans!*'[63] The notion of the royal family working for the public good was encouraged and reinforced by the charitable works that its members increasingly undertook. Prochaska's second group comprises theoretically minded republicans, who favoured the end of monarchy in the abstract but saw little sense in pushing for it under the current circumstances. Finally, Prochaska refers to pure republicans, who called explicitly for the abolition of monarchy. While present in nineteenth-century Britain, this group constituted a very small minority.

The French Revolution and the works inspired by it – such as Paine's *Rights of Man* – were important in igniting popular radicalism and republicanism in Britain. One radical, John Thelwall (1764–1834), is said to have blown the head off a pint of porter, saying 'this is the Way I would serve Kings'.[64] Thelwall was also familiar with English republican ideas, since he chose to name his sons Algernon Sydney Thelwall and John Hampden Thelwall after two seventeenth-century martyrs to liberty. The Society for Constitutional Information continued to demand parliamentary reform; in this it was joined by more plebeian radical groups, such as the London Corresponding Society (LCS), established in November 1792. Reflecting the views of its members, the LCS was uncompromising in its call for annual parliaments and universal suffrage.

After an initial flourish of enthusiasm, events in France after 1793, including the declaration of war with Britain, generally served to silence British republicans and reformers. These events made republicanism less palatable to the British public, and the expression of anti-monarchical views more likely to provoke reaction by the authorities. In May 1794, thirteen members of the LCS were indicted for treason and three subsequently stood trial, though they were acquitted. This episode prompted the passing of the Sedition and Treason Acts, which made it increasingly difficult for organisations like the LCS to operate.

The French Revolution also prompted republican activity – and repression – in Ireland, where the United Irishmen took direct inspiration from, and made alliance with, the French. Frustration with British rule had been on the rise in Ireland since the 1760s and 1770s. A volunteer force was established in 1778, and activists succeeded in establishing Grattan's parliament in 1782; but this body proved a disappointment, as executive power could still be exercised from London and divisions over whether or not to admit Catholics weakened the movement.[65] Familial links to American colonists prompted an interest in events in North America and a sense of connection was encouraged by Benjamin Franklin's description of the Irish as fellow colonial inferiors. But it was the French Revolution that opened a real possibility for action. For one thing, it provided a model of revolution in a Catholic nation, thereby uncoupling the link forged in the English Revolution between republicanism and Protestantism. The leading reformer Wolfe Tone (1763–98) was quick to seize the moment, arguing in *An Argument on Behalf of the Catholics of Ireland* (1791) that the old link between Catholicism and despotism had been rendered obsolete by the French Revolution.[66] On the back of this pamphlet, Tone was invited to Belfast in October 1791 to help found the Society of United Irishmen.[67] Drawing on the American and French examples, this group created the vision of a non-sectarian and inclusive form of democratic politics.

The outbreak of war between Britain and France led to a crackdown on reform groups in Ireland as well as in England and Scotland, and the United Irishmen were banned, but the war also made the French more interested in supporting the Irish rebels. Keen to attack their British enemies in any way they could, and increasingly certain that an invasion of Britain could not be avoided, by the late 1790s the French saw Ireland as a useful base from which to make their attack. General Hoche was particularly keen on this policy, but an expedition led by him to Bantry Bay in the winter of 1796 failed.[68] Hoche's death the following year led to decline in enthusiasm for a British invasion, and in 1798 Bonaparte was heading for Egypt instead. When rebellion broke out in Ireland that same year, the French did respond to Irish requests, but the results were limited. Troops and arms were sent in August and September, but one of the fleets was tracked by the British and captured, and Dutch frigates sent in support of the rebels were also seized.[69] Tone, who was on one of the ships, was taken prisoner and sent to Dublin, where he was tried and convicted on a capital charge; after that he committed suicide.[70] While the Irish Rebellion was primarily a nationalist uprising, the United Irishmen made much of the fact that they were reacting against an occupying power that was monarchical in organisation; and the parallel they drew with America, as well as the inspiration and support they gained from the French, reinforced the republican character of their enterprise.

After the end of the Napoleonic Wars, criticism of the royal family, especially elicited by the cost of the monarchy and the extravagance of figures such as the prince regent, resurfaced in Britain. It was during this period that the Society of Spencean Philanthropists, who presented themselves as followers of the eighteenth-century radical Thomas Spence, became active. At a gathering of supporters at Spa Fields in London in 1816, the Spenceans called for the seizure of the Bank of England and the Tower of London and paraded a tricolour flag of red, white, and green, which was said to symbolise the British republic. Not surprisingly the leaders were quickly arrested and imprisoned. They continued in their campaign, however, and in 1820, after the accession of the prince regent to the throne, in a room on the first floor on Cato Street, they devised a plot to assassinate the entire Cabinet and to make one of their number, Arthur Thistlewood (1774–1820), president of a new republic. The Cato Street conspirators were betrayed to the authorities before they could act and Thistlewood followed his French republican counterparts in being executed.

Marginally more successful than republican attempts at seizing power were the republican publications – particularly the newspapers – that appeared intermittently throughout the nineteenth century. One early example was *Republican*, which was edited by Richard Carlile (1790–1843), initially from his cell in Dorchester Prison, where he had been sent for three years in 1819 for publishing Paine's deistic work *The Age of Reason*. Although he described kings as 'useless' and 'very expensive', Carlile was keen to dissociate republicanism from the French Revolution and placed greater emphasis on popular sovereignty and public welfare than on anti-monarchism. In the preface to his first volume, he declared that 'republican means nothing more when applied to government, than a government which consults the public interest – the interest of the whole people ... It does not argue the necessity of abolishing monarchy to establish a republican government.'[71] By contrast, Carlile emphasised the need for a fair and equal system of representation. After a lull in the 1820s, the 1830s saw the advent of new publications, including James Lorymer's *Republican* and later his *Le Bonnet Rouge* and Hetherington's *Poor Man's Guardian*. In the 1850s Linton's *English Republic*, as well as disseminating Mazzini's ideas, contained 'antiodes' on royal birthdays. Events in France in the 1870s prompted the revival of republican publications. The newspaper *National Reformer*, edited by Charles Bradlaugh (1833–91), had a circulation of 6,000 by 1872 despite its extreme views. In 1873 Bradlaugh also published *The Impeachment of the House of Brunswick*. This book was based on a series of lectures he had given in which he explicitly called for the abolition of the monarchy.

Another key element of nineteenth-century British republicanism was its societies or clubs. Lorymer founded the Republican Association, which met in Theobald's Road in London in the 1830s. Another association that was established around the same time and that drew on older, classical republican demands – for instance for annual parliaments and equal electoral districts – was the London Working Men's Association, founded by William Lovett (1800–77). In 1837 this association was behind the drafting of a six-point petition that became known as 'the People's Charter'. As was the case more generally, support for democracy or socialism did not always coincide with republicanism, and not all Chartists were anti-monarchists. Members of the Chartist movement were not averse to appealing directly to Queen Victoria, asking her to further their cause; and the movement focused on social and political reform rather than on the abolition of the monarchy. But the movement did provide a home and a platform for a number of advocates of the republican cause. George Julian Harney (1817–97), Linton, W. E. Adams (1832–1906), and Joseph Cowen (1829–1900) were among a number of Chartists who expressed exclusivist republican views. Republican associations were also established across the country in the 1850s, in cities as diverse as Cambridge, Cheltenham, Sunderland, and Glasgow. The 1870s witnessed a similar revival, encouraged by anger over several large grants made to Queen Victoria's children. Clubs appeared in Birmingham, Nottingham, Sheffield, Northampton, Jarrow, Middlesborough, and Newcastle in February 1871, and Bradlaugh established a London club in March of that year. Out of these developments two national organisations emerged: the National Republican Brotherhood, established in late 1872 and led by John de Morgan (1848–1926); and a rival organisation, the National Republican League, which was established in Birmingham in 1873.

Transnational links were also important to nineteenth-century British republicans. The Polish dissident Dybowski edited a periodical called the *Republican* during his exile in Britain in the 1830s. The Chartist publication *Northern Star* drew a direct parallel between the 1848 Revolution in France and Chartism when it exclaimed 'let the cry be' 'the Republic for France, and the Charter for England'.[72] French liberty caps and tricolour flags were often displayed at Chartist demonstrations, and on 6 March 1848 a crowd at Buckingham Palace was said to have shouted *Vive la république*. Lajos Kossuth, who had led the 1848 uprising in Hungary, came to England in 1851 and Mazzini spent a significant proportion of his life in Britain. Linton was authorised by Mazzini to act for his Republican Party and he organised small groups to teach republican principles. Mazzini's theories on republicanism proved influential among British radicals not just in London but also, as Marcella Sutcliffe has demonstrated, in Northern England. *Cooper's Journal* promoted the Mazzinian cause, Adams was heavily influenced by Mazzini's *The Duties of Man*, and the Chartist *The People's Paper* drew explicit connections between Italian republicanism or democracy and British Chartism.[73] Sutcliffe argues that the Roman republic was particularly important for keeping the hopes of English republicans alive after the demise of Chartism, though this meant that English Mazzinians were particularly frustrated by the failure of the republican solution in Italy. Orsini's attempted assassination of Napoleon III found particular support in the West Midlands and the North East. The European connection continued well into the 1870s. A mass meeting of an estimated 10,000 people in Trafalgar Square to celebrate the declaration of the Third French Republic in 1870 not only witnessed the donning of red liberty caps by the crowd and the singing of 'La Marseillaise', but also included among its leading figures representatives from Italian and German republican societies.

Conclusion

Republicanism followed distinct paths in the nineteenth century in the different countries in which it took root. In some, such as America and France, it was, at least for a time, an establishment ideology that was used to shore up the government of the day and to justify its actions. But, in those countries and elsewhere, it also became an ideology of opposition that could be used to challenge the establishment and as an incitement to rebellion – and even to revolution. In America the relationship between liberty and slavery was a particular point of contention. As a result, greater emphasis was placed on republican political economy and demands were made for economic as well as political independence. In France, debates centred instead around the distinctions between liberalism, republicanism, and socialism. Republicanism also became more transnational during the nineteenth century, as links between individuals and groups in different nations were deliberately cultivated and provided an important source of strength and inspiration. At the same time, republicanism began to shed its aristocratic and elitist character, which had been reinforced by advocates in America in the 1780s and France in the 1790s. Republican arguments were applied in support of ordinary working people, increasingly numerous demands being made for universal suffrage. Those arguments were also deployed by working people themselves, in whose hands they became a powerful tool for social and political improvement.

Given this situation, it is perhaps not surprising that there are connections to be made between republicanism and the philosophy of Karl Marx. As Bruno Leipold has argued, neither the conventional account of republicanism, which excludes Marx on account of his 'repugnance for the public realm' (Hannah Arendt), nor the orthodox Marxist view, which has him condemn republicans as petty bourgeoisie, is adequate.[74] Not only do Marx's early political writings reflect his commitment to key republican ideas such as popular sovereignty and participation, but his more mature communist thought, too, retained traces of these ideas, which was not the case for all communists. Moreover, like the Knights of Labour in America, Marx extended the objection to arbitrary power from the political to the social sphere, using it to critique the domination of the capitalist and the market over the worker. Ultimately, Leipold argues that Marx's later political thinking constituted a synthesis of republican and communist ideas.

Republicanism continued to operate as an emancipatory tool in the twentieth century, though more for those who had been deprived of their nationhood and oppressed by centuries of colonialism than for those downtrodden by the class system, who tended instead to look to socialism. Yet, by the end of the twentieth century, republicanism was operating much more as an analytical than a practical tool, as advances in republican thought took place in universities and in the pages of academic journals rather than out on the streets and in speeches, proclamations, and pamphlets. It is republicanism's rise to prominence within the academic disciplines of the history of political thought and contemporary political philosophy that will be the subject of the final chapter of this book.

10

Republicanism Today

Introduction

In the twentieth century republican governments continued to operate in countries like America and France, and new republics were established across the globe – from Russia in 1917, through Ireland in 1937, to a whole host of liberated African countries from the 1950s onwards. In some of these places the concepts and ideas that have been explored in this book continued to exercise an influence on actors and events. Irish republicans in the early twentieth century drew inspiration from the example of the United Irishmen, and the Proclamation of the Provisional Government of the Irish Republic, issued in 1916 by Patrick Pearse, echoed earlier republican writings in various respects.[1] Its call for the 'children' of the 'Irish nation' 'to sacrifice themselves for the common good' invoked the republican notion of self-sacrifice in the public interest – a notion that can be traced back at least as far as Cicero. Similarly, both the parallel drawn between the military and the civic aspects of citizenship and the commitment to guarantee 'religious and civil liberty' (a brave promise in a country long divided bitterly on religious lines) had been fundamental to English republicanism in the seventeenth and eighteenth centuries. At the same time, the distinctiveness of the Irish experience is also evident in that document. The whole proclamation is set within a strongly religious framework, in which God is explicitly invoked at the beginning and at the end; particular emphasis is placed on the 'old tradition' of Irish 'nationhood' and on the idea of emancipation; and the language of rights is crucial to the claims made in the document.

As has been argued throughout this book, republicanism has always been a flexible and ambiguous concept, which could be applied to different ends and combined with a variety of other ideas. Yet in the twentieth century it increasingly became detached from its moorings. This is most evident in the context of the United States, where, despite the continuation of the republican form, the early twentieth century saw an increasing shift away from republican political theory and towards liberalism as the dominant ideology. Michael Sandel has traced the rise of what he calls the procedural republic, governed by a form of liberalism that treated the self as unencumbered by particular characteristics and that claimed to be neutral among different conceptions of the good life.[2]

In the context of this growing separation of republican theory from practice, republicanism became a language of contemplation and analysis rather than one of action. During the course of the twentieth century republicanism took its place as an important strand within both the history of political thought and contemporary political philosophy. In the 1940s and 1950s work began to be undertaken on the history of republicanism, particularly on its manifestations in the Renaissance and during the English, American, and French Revolutions. Republicanism became a popular topic for advocates of the Cambridge School approach to the history of political thought, where leading figures such as John Pocock and Quentin Skinner made important interventions in the field. While its investigation has often been presented as the recovery of a forgotten discourse (one that had become overshadowed by liberalism and socialism), the historical research has also fed directly into contemporary political philosophy, which towards the end of the century saw a sudden surge of interest in republicanism as a political theory.[3] Philip Pettit applied the historical research of Skinner and the Cambridge School to contemporary concerns; and he was not the only political philosopher to be inspired by the history of republicanism.[4] The 1980s witnessed a 'republican revival' in American political philosophy that was ignited by a new awareness of the historical legacy of American republicanism and by the desire to deal with contemporary American political and legal problems. Similarly, in 1999 Maurizio Viroli, until then best known for his work on Niccolò Machiavelli, turned his attention from the history of political thought to contemporary Italian politics, attempting to apply the insights of his historical research to understanding Italy's troubled political system.[5]

This chapter will trace the historiography of republicanism in the late twentieth and early twenty-first centuries, examining the different perspectives on it and some of the key historiographical debates. It will end by briefly tracing how this historical rediscovery of republicanism initiated a republican revival in political philosophy in the late twentieth and early twenty-first centuries.

Republicanism and the History of Political Thought

In the mid-twentieth century academics working in several fields began to examine the revival of interest in ancient republican ideas among some later thinkers. In 1955 Hans Baron elaborated on a term he had been using for about thirty years: 'civic humanism', which described a new attitude to politics that took hold in fifteenth-century Florence.[6] In the context of the threat posed by Milanese expansionism, Baron argued, traditional patriotic resistance fused with apolitical Petrarchan humanism and, as a result, the Renaissance interest in ancient letters and wisdom was extended to political matters. At the heart of this new attitude was a rejection of the contemplative life associated with medieval ideals and a celebration instead of worldly values and of the active political life favoured by ancient figures, most notably Cicero. Civic humanism also brought a new understanding of history, which involved a more present-centred approach and particular emphasis on the Roman republic and on Florence's Roman origins. While not necessarily entailing advocacy for a republican government, civic humanism had much in common with republicanism thanks to its celebration of liberty and emphasis on the public good. Moreover, key champions of this vision, such as Salutati and Bruni, played important roles within Florence's republican government.

About ten years before Baron's book appeared, Zera Fink's *The Classical Republicans* uncovered a political counterpart to the revival of classical ideas in the fields of literature, art, and architecture in sixteenth- and seventeenth-century England.[7] At the heart of Fink's interpretation were a handful of English republicans – John Milton, James Harrington, Algernon Sidney, Henry Neville, and Walter Moyle – and the canon of works they produced. Central to Fink's account was the theory of the mixed constitution; and he presented the Venetian republic as a particularly potent model for the English. Subsequent historians developed Fink's account both chronologically and geographically. Caroline Robbins traced three generations of eighteenth-century 'commonwealthmen' who adapted the republican ideas of their seventeenth-century predecessors to new political contexts.[8]

In her conclusion, Robbins noted that, while these commonwealth men had little practical impact in Britain, their ideas exercised

considerable influence on the American founding fathers. This claim
was further developed by Bernard Bailyn in *The Ideological Origins
of the American Revolution* (1967).[9] Bailyn drew on Robbins's work
and on his own reading of American revolutionary pamphlets, to
argue that, while the American revolutionaries were influenced by a
range of languages or discourses, it was the works of the commonwealth men that knitted them together into a 'comprehensive theory
of politics'.[10] This theory offered a particular understanding of the
relationship between power and liberty. It was an understanding that
directly impacted on the way in which the American colonists interpreted the actions of the British government in the 1760s and 1770s,
effectively catapulting them into revolution. In this regard, Bailyn's
book constitutes a compelling case for the influence that political
thought can have on political action. Bailyn's work, alongside that
of Gordon Wood, served to challenge the traditional understanding
of the liberal origins of the American Revolution and constitution. In
doing so it prompted a major historiographical debate, which blazed
for several decades, concerning the relationship between republicanism and liberalism within American thought and the point at
which the former had been superseded by the latter.[11]

With the publication of *The Machiavellian Moment* in 1975, John
Pocock succeeded in connecting these earlier bodies of work, tracing a
broad republican tradition that stretched from the ancient world, via
Renaissance Italy, to revolutionary America.[12] Like Fink before him,
Pocock made much of the theory of the mixed constitution, though
he set it in the context of deeper metaphysical concerns regarding the
mutability, fragility, and mortal nature of human life and politics.
Pocock also stressed the inherent antipathy between virtue and
commerce that was rooted in the idea that commerce and private
wealth were corrupting forces that compromised the independence
of individual citizens and threatened to divert their attention from
the public good.[13] This aspect of Pocock's theory has come under
particular attack. For many years experts on English and American
republicanism have argued that late seventeenth- and eighteenth-
century republicans accommodated and even defended commercial
society.[14] Mark Jurdjevic argues that this is not surprising, given
that, as Baron showed, Florentine civic humanism was itself the
ideology of an ascendant merchant class, and consequently presented
commerce and private wealth not as a threat to the republic but
rather as crucial to its survival.[15] Yet, while suggesting that Pocock
was mistaken in his account of Florentine political thought, Jurdjevic
points out that he was absolutely right with regard to the long-term
continuities within republicanism. 'Pocock was wrong about the

ideal economy of the Renaissance republic, but he now appears right about its continuity with subsequent republican environments.'[16]

Pocock's account was grounded in an essentially Aristotelian understanding of the foundations of republicanism, in which the notion of the active citizen was central, although, more generally, Pocock thought in terms of a composite tradition that incorporated both Greek and Roman elements. Subsequent scholars have foregrounded different foundations. Quentin Skinner's emphasis on liberty as the essential republican concept, and his analysis of a particular form of negative liberty, distinct from the conventional liberal understanding, led him to focus on the Roman origins of republicanism. This concept of liberty, which he initially called 'republican liberty' but later renamed 'neo-Roman liberty', had its origins in the distinction within Roman law between the slave and the freeman and was characterised by lack of dependence on anyone else's will.[17] On this basis, Skinner placed increasing emphasis on the Roman – and especially the Ciceronian – origins of liberty and of republicanism.

Benjamin Straumann has more directly challenged the attempt to lump together Greek and Roman thought under the label 'classical republicanism', arguing that this has obscured a different and distinctive Roman contribution to political thought.[18] That contribution, which was a product of the constitutional crises of the late republic, comprised a view of politics focused on rights and norms achieved and guaranteed by a set of higher-order constitutional rules with a legal character.[19] These higher-order norms, he insists, were more important than virtue and provided material for later thinkers, who recognised that constitutional remedies rather than republican virtue could have prevented the fall of the Roman republic. Moreover, Straumann demonstrates how blurring the boundaries between the Greek and the Roman experience lies at the root of debates over the conflict between republican and liberal ideas not just in the context of the United States of America's founding, but also more broadly.

In part, Straumann's account builds on the work of Eric Nelson, who placed his emphasis on identifying a distinct Greek tradition in republican thought.[20] This form of republicanism took its inspiration from Greek moral and political philosophy and emphasised happiness, justice, and equality over liberty, honour, glory, and virtue. Its advocates therefore did not consider liberty (understood as non-dependence), political participation, and virtue to be of primary importance and instead advocated the corrective redistribution of wealth.

In a subsequent book Nelson presented Israel as another ancient republican model, examining the Hebraic influences on early modern

republicanism.[21] In particular he demonstrated the huge influence
that the Hebrew Bible and rabbinic commentaries and interpretations
exerted on the notion of an exclusivist republic, on arguments in
favour of the redistribution of wealth through measures such as an
agrarian law, and on calls for religious toleration.

Others have challenged the assumption that ancient political ideas
of any description exercised a dominant influence on early modern
republican thought. In *Republics Ancient and Modern* Paul Rahe
challenged the 'classical' character of seventeenth- and eighteenth-
century anglophone republicanism, arguing that it represented a
form of modern republicanism that took its origin less from the
ancients than from their Renaissance reviver and reinterpreter,
Machiavelli.[22] More recently, both Vickie Sullivan and Rahe himself
have elaborated on the significance of this theory for interpretations
of seventeenth-century English republicanism.[23] Crucial here is the
emphasis on the pursuit of interests and on the shaping of behaviour
through constitutional design rather than through reliance on virtue.
Rahe was not, however, the first to downplay ancient in favour of
more modern influences on early modern republicanism. As far back
as 1971, the Italian historian Franco Venturi challenged the conventional view that eighteenth-century republicanism was determined
largely by its ancient legacy.[24] Venturi insisted on the importance of
more recent experiences not just in Italy and England, but also in the
Flemish and German cities and in Holland, Switzerland, and Poland.

Venturi is thus the forefather of another new trajectory within
studies of republicanism: the exploration of it as a European
phenomenon. While the last three decades of the twentieth century
saw deep and detailed research being undertaken on the precise
meaning and use of republican ideas in specific national contexts
and at key moments, it has been Pocock's largely anglophone
account that has dominated broader analyses until recently. Only at
the very end of the twentieth century did the important European
dimension to republicanism, highlighted by Venturi, begin to take
centre stage. In a major project funded by the European Science
Foundation, Skinner and five other scholars established a network
for the study of republicanism as a shared European heritage. After
a series of workshops in cities across Europe from 1996 to 1998 that
explored different facets of European republicanism, two volumes
of articles appeared, edited jointly by Quentin Skinner and Martin
van Gelderen.[25] The essays in this collection explore the role played
by republican ideas during the early modern period in a range of
countries such as Italy, the Netherlands, England, Poland, France,
Germany, and even Spain.

This approach triggered some debate. David Wootton criticised the authors and editors for paying too little attention to the precise use and meaning of the term res publica at different times and in different places.[26] Weighing into the debate on the contrast between the older, pluralist and the more modern, exclusivist understanding of republicanism, Wootton noted that the idea of 'republic' as the antonym of 'monarchy', though it had its origins in Tacitus, only really emerged in fifteenth-century Florence, subsequently being popularised by Machiavelli before it became dominant in the eighteenth century. On this basis Wootton argues that '[r]epublicanism is not a shared European heritage, but a Florentine invention which was disseminated through particular texts, and a language which was adopted and adapted to serve particular purposes'.[27] Notwithstanding Wootton's critique, the Skinner and Van Gelderen volumes have served to open up the idea of republicanism as a transnational movement, to integrate more closely its anglophone and European dimensions, and to prompt research into the exchange of republican ideas between different times and places. Alongside specific work on particularly fruitful exchanges such as the French use of English republican ideas, several overarching surveys have also been published.[28]

Another persistent absence in the historiography of republicanism, which has only recently been addressed, is the role played by religion. This neglect is symptomatic of a wider secularism within the history of political thought.[29] Jonathan Scott sought to fill this gap with regard to seventeenth-century English republicanism, emphasising the role that Protestant ideas, not least resistance theory, had played in its formation.[30] Justin Champion has done something similar for the early eighteenth century in his examination of the influence of heterodox thought on figures such as John Toland and Robert Molesworth.[31] Work on the Hebraic influences on early modern republicanism by Nelson and others has also added to this field.[32] And there is growing interest in re-examining the concept of civil religion, which has long been associated with republican figures such as Machiavelli, Harrington, and Rousseau, and which constitutes one way in which republican and religious ideas were intertwined.[33]

While a great deal of research has already been undertaken into the history of republican thought, there is much that remains to be done. Both the rise of transnational history and the openness of new generations of intellectual historians to the connections between political thought and religious, social, legal, and literary ideas offer fruitful directions for future research. In the midst of turbulent political times there is also the question of what relevance this deep and rich strand of political thought might have for current politics.

The Republican Revival in Contemporary Political Philosophy

The revival of interest in republicanism within historiography in the late twentieth century sparked interest in those ideas among political philosophers. Yet contemporary politics played a role too. The collapse of communism in the late 1980s and 1990s led to the assertion that liberalism had effectively defeated socialism. Yet there was a residual concern that freedom was not properly protected simply by removing all governmental control, not least because not all threats to liberty come from the state itself.[34] Thus the late twentieth and early twenty-first centuries witnessed what has been called the 'republican revival', in which a number of scholars – including Cass R. Sunstein, Michael Sandel, and Philip Pettit – are looking to republican ideas to provide answers to contemporary political issues, to challenge the dominance of liberalism or pluralism within modern western society, and to correct some of the flaws of modern approaches to politics.[35]

Sunstein's article 'Beyond the Republican Revival', which appeared in 1988, was inspired by the wealth of modern historical scholarship that had been undertaken between the 1960s and the 1980s on the role of republican thought in North America during the late eighteenth century.[36] While wary of the simplistic use of history in solving current problems, Sunstein argued that this historical research provided a new lens through which to view late twentieth-century political issues; and he sought to outline the aspects of republican thought that had the strongest claim to contemporary support and to describe the institutional arrangements and 'doctrinal shifts' necessary to implement the best features.[37] He summarised his view of the basic republican commitment as deliberation in government made possible by civic virtue, political equality, universality, and citizenship; and he argued that these principles could be used to guide reform in key areas of public law that were of particular concern at the time he was writing, for example the regulation of campaign finance, the introduction of proportional representation, and the removal of discrimination.

Sandel's book *Democracy's Discontent* (1996) went further than Sunstein's article, using the history of republicanism more explicitly as a basis for questioning the procedural republic of modern liberal America.[38] Sandel argued that key flaws in that system could be rectified by returning to some of the republican ideas and assumptions that lay at the heart of the original constitution, but that had been eroded in the shift towards a procedural republic in the early twentieth century. The book is deeply historical both in its uncovering of the republicanism of the founders and in its tracing of the process by which republicanism lost its dominant position in American political life. Sandel does not shy away from the complexity of that process, yet the message of his book is explicitly present-centred.

Pettit, while sympathetic to Sandel's historical approach, to his aspiration to use history to address present political issues, and to his desire to rekindle enthusiasm for republicanism, criticised *Democracy's Discontent* for lacking substance on the precise nature of the republican ideas that Sandel wanted to revive.[39] As a result, he argued, Sandel advances a negative argument, based on the weaknesses of liberalism rather than focused on the strengths of republicanism. Pettit claimed that such substance could be provided, and Sandel's argument strengthened, by taking seriously Skinner's neo-Roman theory of republican liberty and by placing it at the heart of modern neo-republicanism. This would make explicit the connection between liberty and the need for self-government and offer strong grounds for key institutions, such as the rule of law, restriction on the tenure of public office, public deliberation over important political issues, and participation in their resolution. It would also elucidate the connection between liberty and civic virtue and would support public service and vigilance exercised by the people.

Before reviewing Sandel's book, Pettit had already set out this argument in his own monograph *Republicanism: A Theory of Freedom and Government*, which appeared in 1997.[40] As Pettit explained in that book, he came to republicanism via his interest in political liberty, and so it is perhaps not surprising that the concept of freedom as non-domination should have taken centre-stage in his thought.[41] That concept has the potential, he insisted, to respond to contemporary concerns about being dominated in a way that liberal understandings of freedom cannot, and at the same time offers an appealing vision of how to be free.[42]

Pettit's collaboration with Skinner means that his work, too, is deeply influenced by historical research. He is conscious of the long history of freedom as non-domination that has shaped many of the institutions we associate with modern democracy. Like Sunstein and Sandel, Pettit noted in particular the influence that this concept exercised on the American revolutionaries in their struggle against the British and in their attempts to construct a new republic, though he believed that the concept was subsequently obscured.[43] On this point he again drew on Skinner, who insisted that the modern understanding of liberty, as reflected in the work of John Rawls and Robert Nozick, was Hobbesian or liberal.[44] Pettit's aim, then, was to revive this lost concept, to show its relevance and applicability to the modern world, and to extend its application from a narrow elite to all citizens. He described his book as 'an exploration of what a new republican-politics would involve'.[45]

Pettit is an enthusiastic advocate of the advantages of republican government conceived of in this way. He insists that this kind of government offers a firm rationale for endorsing both egalitarianism and communitarianism,[46] and argues that the republican vision it generates ought to be of wide appeal, addressing key issues raised by environmentalists, feminists, socialists, and multiculturalists.[47] He sees it as encouraging the practice of democratic contestability[48] and emphasises its flexibility, suggesting that it is open to reinterpretation as new interests and ideas arise.[49]

Despite the differences of approach and opinion among these writers, they all underline four components of republican theory: political equality; freedom as self-government; deliberative politics; and civic virtue.[50] The modern republican understanding of equality goes against more traditional republican approaches, which were often built upon the institution of slavery and the exclusion of women from the citizen body. Instead, modern republicans emphasise both moral equality – the equal intrinsic worth of all people – and the political equality of all citizens, the latter comprising equality before the law and equal political rights. While republicans would not generally advocate complete material equality, they do express concerns about the threat that vast inequalities of wealth pose to political equality.[51]

Freedom understood as self-government is central to Skinner's neo-Roman approach to republicanism and lies at the heart of Pettit's version of neo-republicanism. Although originally conceived of in narrowly political terms, this view of liberty was expanded during the nineteenth century by American labour republicans and Karl Marx to embrace the need for workers to be free from domination by employers, and has more recently been used to promote the freedom of women from subjection to men and the freedom of certain racial or ethnic groups from being dominated by others.

Popular deliberation has certainly not been advocated by all those who supported republican government in the past. Harrington and Rousseau both sought to limit this fearing that it would lead to anarchy and disharmony. Nevertheless, political discussion of some kind has often been important to republican thinkers. Harrington, for example, made political debate central to the role of the senate, even though he did not believe that this right should be extended to the popular assembly. Deliberation was fundamental to the modern form of representative government that was developed by the Federalists in America; and it has been particularly important to the brand of neo-republicanism of Americans such as Sunstein.[52] Here the possibility that those involved may revise, or even change, their views as a result of deliberation is set in stark contrast to the pluralist understanding of politics in which individuals bring their existing fixed preferences to the political marketplace and use their bargaining power to strike deals.

Civic virtue has also had a mixed and contested place within republican historiography. The importance of virtue and the prioritising of the public good over private interests have long been emphasised by republican thinkers. Some, however, have remained sceptical as to whether such virtue is possible in practice and, as a result, have tended to prefer dependence on good laws to dependence on good men. Neo-republicans are sensitive to this kind of scepticism, as well as less enthusiastic than their predecessors about using military service to inculcate civic virtue; but many do continue to emphasise the role that education can play in producing good citizens.

Of course, the republican revival has also prompted fresh criticism of republican ideology. Some have questioned the very idea that past republican thought could speak usefully to contemporary concerns. Given the historical background and focus of this thought, there is a danger that it is seen as antiquated. In particular, neo-republicans have sometimes been berated for neglecting the economy – for failing to provide a coherent and comprehensive account of republican economics. Richard Dagger has responded directly to this attack, setting out the main features of a neo-republican civic economy in which the market is preserved, but directed more effectively towards public purposes.[53]

A second criticism that has been levelled, particularly against Sandel and Pettit, is that, following Pocock's original conception, they draw too sharp a distinction between republicanism and liberalism. Indeed, Knud Haakonssen insists that it is now impossible to see a division between the juristic–liberal and the republican traditions as being fundamental to post-Renaissance thought: '[t]he opposition between liberalism and republicanism, while a source of inspiration for the recent revival of the latter, is more an invention of this revival than ascertainable historical fact'.[54] This has prompted some to call, not for republicanism as a complete alternative to liberalism, but rather for some amalgamation of the two. This kind of amalgamation was already being proposed by Sunstein, who deliberately set his conception of republicanism not against liberalism but rather against pluralism, defined as a view of politics as the struggle among interest groups for scarce resources.[55] Sunstein insisted that the distinctive conception of governance that developed during the founding period was an amalgamation of liberal and republican ideas, and he described the founders themselves as liberal republicans. On this basis he sought to defend a form of liberal republicanism in the present.[56] Laborde has taken a different approach, seeking to address head on the liberal responses to neo-republicanism that suggest that it either can be incorporated into liberalism, thereby becoming redundant, or has deeply illiberal tendencies, which make it unappealing.[57] She argues that Pettit's account of a neo-republicanism centred on freedom as non-domination provides a firm and attractive foundation for a republican alternative to modern liberal politics. As she explains, it distances republicanism from both popularism and the exclusive aspects of communitarianism and nationalism. It also offers a distinctive alternative to academic defences of liberal constitutionalism, which, she suggests, has the potential to be more effective against the dangers of arbitrary power, both public and private. As a result, it offers better solutions to the problems of social inequality and can provide the basis for radical democratic reform of public authorities and private institutions and relations. Finally, she argues that Pettit's neo-republicanism is not just valuable as an academic theory but also provides a useful corrective to real-world defences of libertarianism.[58]

A further criticism, which also challenges the way in which the republicanism of the past has been interpreted and on that basis questions the application of republican ideals in the present, has been made by John McCormick. McCormick argues that the republican tradition that is celebrated by the Cambridge School owes more to Guicciardini than to Machiavelli in its focus on the privileges of elites rather than on the participation of the populace. Skinner's concept of neo-Roman liberty, McCormick argues, has focused too much on political domination at the expense of its more subtle and more pervasive social counterpart, failing to recognise that domination may occur among citizens and not just between them and the state. Consequently, McCormick insists that, unless the understanding of republicanism being advocated today is substantially revised, it will end up reinforcing what is worst about modern liberal democracy, namely 'the free hand that socioeconomic and political elites enjoy at the expense of the general populace'.[59] In anticipation of such criticism, Haakonssen suggested that the key issue for modern republican theorists is to find a 'principled replacement' for the notion of citizenship as grounded in private property, one that might prove suitable for an egalitarian republic.[60]

Conclusion

As well as there being further research for historians of political thought interested in republicanism to undertake, it is clear that there are some challenging issues that contemporary political theorists inspired by the history of republicanism must address. The multivalent nature of republican thought that developed over the centuries and has been documented in this book should give those theorists many resources with which to address current political concerns and to create a fruitful political ideology for the future. Republicans have long debated the pros and cons of commerce and luxury, the precise meaning and application of 'liberty' and 'virtue', and the merits of an aristocratic versus a democratic republican political structure, as well as whether a state should aim at conflict or peace and whether genuine virtue is required or merely virtuous behaviour secured by laws and countervailing passions. It may yet be possible, then, to step back from republicanism as an academic tool for analysis and contemplation and move towards republicanism as a practical tool for action.

Notes

Notes to Introduction

1 Cicero, *On the Commonwealth and On the Laws*, ed. and trans. James E. G. Zetzel (Cambridge: Cambridge University Press, 1999), p. 59, translation slightly modified.
2 This passage, and Cicero's more general contribution to republican thought, will be explored in greater detail in Chapter 1.
3 Jean-Jacques Rousseau, *The Social Contract*, in idem, *The Social Contract and Other Late Political Writings*, ed. and trans. Victor Gourevitch (Cambridge: Cambridge University Press, 1997), p. 67. Rousseau's understanding of republican government is examined in detail in Chapter 6.
4 Aristotle's political thought is discussed in greater detail in Chapter 1.
5 Aristotle, *The Politics*, ed. Stephen Everson, trans. Benjamin Jowett, rev. Jonathan Barnes (Cambridge: Cambridge University Press, 1988), p. 61.
6 On this, see Chapter 5.
7 David Wootton, 'The True Origins of Republicanism: The Disciples of Baron and the Counter-Example of Venturi', in Manuela Albertone, ed., *Il repubblicanesimo moderno: L'idea di repubblica nella riflessione storica di Franco Venturi* (Naples: Bibliopolis, 2006), pp. 271–304; James Hankins, 'Exclusivist Republicanism and the Non-Monarchical Republic', *Political Theory* 38.4 (2010): 452–82; Eric Nelson, '"Talmudical Commonwealthsmen" and the Rise of Republican Exclusivism', *Historical Journal* 50.4 (2007): 809–35; Eric Nelson, *The Hebrew Republic: Jewish Sources and the Transformation of European Political Thought* (Cambridge, MA: Harvard University Press, 2010).
8 Hankins, 'Exclusivist Republicanism', p. 453.
9 Marchamont Nedham, *The Case of the Commonwealth of England, Stated*, ed. Philip A. Knachel (Charlottesville: University Press of Virginia, 1969), pp. 127–8.

10 John Milton, *The Readie and Easie Way to Establish a Free Commonwealth*, in idem, *Selected Prose*, ed. C. A. Parties (Harmondsworth: Penguin, 1974), p. 338.

11 Polybius, *The Rise of the Roman Empire* (Harmondsworth: Penguin, 1979), p. 302.

12 Jean Bodin, *On Sovereignty*, ed. and trans. J. H. Franklin (Cambridge: Cambridge University Press, 1992), p. 58.

13 Mark Silk, 'Numa Pompilius and the Idea of Civil Religion in the West', *Journal of the American Academy of Religion* 72.4 (2004): 863–96.

14 Jonathan Scott, *Commonwealth Principles: Republican Writing of the English Revolution* (Cambridge: Cambridge University Press, 2004); Justin Champion, *The Pillars of Priestcraft Shaken: The Church of England and Its Enemies, 1660–1730* (Cambridge: Cambridge University Press, 1992); Justin Champion, *Republican Learning: John Toland and the Crisis of Christian Culture, 1696–1722* (Manchester: Manchester University Press, 2003); Eric Nelson, *The Hebrew Republic*; Mark Goldie, 'The Civil Religion of James Harrington', in Anthony Pagden, ed., *Languages of Political Theory in Early Modern Europe* (Cambridge: Cambridge University Press, 1987), pp. 197–224; Ronald Beiner, *Civil Religion: A Dialogue in the History of Political Philosophy* (Cambridge: Cambridge University Press, 2010).

15 James Harrington, *Political Works*, ed. J. G. A. Pocock (Cambridge: Cambridge University Press, 1977), p. 691.

16 John Adams, *A Defence of the Constitutions of Government of the United States of America* (London, 1787), p. viii.

17 Adams, *Defence*, p. 157. Montesquieu, *The Spirit of the Laws*, ed. Anne Cohler, Basia Miller, and Harold Stone (Cambridge: Cambridge University Press, 1989), p. 159.

18 Adams, *Defence*, p. 157.

19 For more on this, see Chapter 7.

20 Rousseau, *Social Contract*, p. 114. Rousseau's somewhat different solution to the problem of creating a large state republic, as set out in his *Considerations on the Government of Poland*, is explored in Chapter 6.

21 Apart from a few general references such as this one, I have chosen not to offer a detailed account of the historiography of republicanism here. That can be found instead in Chapter 10, since the analysis of the history of republicanism is itself part of the story of republicanism in the twentieth and twenty-first centuries.

22 Isaiah Berlin, 'Two Concepts of Liberty' [1958], in idem, *Four Essays on Liberty* (Oxford: Oxford University Press, 1969).

23 For Skinner's discussion of this concept of liberty, see Quentin Skinner, 'The Idea of Negative Liberty: Philosophical and Historical Perspectives', in Richard Rorty, J. B. Schneewind, and Quentin Skinner, eds, *Philosophy in History* (Cambridge: Cambridge University Press, 1984), pp. 192–221, revised as 'The Idea of Negative Liberty: Machiavellian and Modern Perspectives', in Quentin Skinner, *Visions of Politics*, vol.

2: *Renaissance Virtues* (Cambridge: Cambridge University Press, 2002), pp. 186–212; Quentin Skinner, 'The Paradoxes of Political Liberty', in S. M. McMurrin, ed., *The Tanner Lectures on Human Values*, vol. 7 (Cambridge: Cambridge University Press, 1986), pp. 225–50; and Quentin Skinner, *Liberty before Liberalism* (Cambridge: Cambridge University Press, 1998).

24 Quoted in Skinner, *Liberty before Liberalism*, p. 7.

25 Skinner, *Liberty before Liberalism*, p. 27.

26 Quoted in Skinner, *Liberty before Liberalism*, pp. 86–7.

27 Skinner, *Liberty Before Liberalism*, p. ix.

28 Montesquieu, *The Spirit of the Laws*, p. xli.

29 Frederick the Great, 'Benevolent Despotism', in *The Portable Enlightenment Reader*, ed. Isaac Kramnick (Harmondsworth: Penguin, 1995), p. 458.

30 Rachel Hammersley, 'Rethinking the Political Thought of James Harrington: Royalism, Republicanism and Democracy', *History of European Ideas* 39.3 (2013): 354–370. See also Chapter 4 in this volume.

31 Harrington, *Political Works*, p. 205.

32 Gabriel Bonnet de Mably, *Du Cours et de la marche des passions dans la société*, in *Collection complète des oeuvres de l'abbé de Mably* (Paris: Desbriere, L'An III de la République [1794–5]), vol. 15, p. 170, my translation.

33 Rachel Hammersley, *The English Republican Tradition and Eighteenth-Century France: Between the Ancients and the Moderns* (Manchester: Manchester University Press, 2010), pp. 203–4.

Notes to Chapter 1

1 Elizabeth Rawson, *The Spartan Tradition in European Thought* (Oxford: Clarendon, 1969), p. 5.

2 Rawson, *The Spartan Tradition*, pp. 2–3.

3 Polybius 6.48, in idem, *Histories*, translated by Evelyn S. Shuckburgh (London: Macmillan, 1889). A digital version of this translation can be found at http://perseus.tufts.edu. Translation slightly modified.

4 Plutarch, 'Life of Lycurgus', 1.29 = pp. 293–7 in the Loeb translation of his *Parallel Lives* (Cambridge, MA: Walter Heineman, 1914).

5 Polybius, *Histories*, 6.10.

6 Rawson, *The Spartan Tradition*, pp. 2–3.

7 Polybius, *Histories*, 6.48.

8 On the Athenian system of government, see Simon Hornblower, 'Creation and Development of Democratic Institutions in Ancient Greece', in John Dunn, ed., *Democracy: The Unfinished Journey, 508 BC to AD 1993* (Oxford: Oxford University Press, 1992), pp. 1–16; John Dunn, *Setting the People Free: The Story of Democracy* (London: Atlantic, 2006), esp. the chapter 'Democracy's First Coming', pp.

23–70; Paul Cartledge, *Democracy: A Life* (Oxford: Oxford University Press, 2016).

9 Daniela Cammack, 'The Demos in Demokratia', *Classical Quarterly* 69.1 (2019): 1–20.

10 Daniela Cammack, 'Deliberation in Classical Athens: Not Talking but Thinking', paper presented at the Political Thought and Intellectual History Research Seminar, Cambridge, 21 October 2013. I am grateful to Elly Robson for providing me with a copy of this paper.

11 Daniela Cammack, 'Deliberation in Ancient Greek Assemblies', *Classical Philology* (forthcoming).

12 On the Roman constitution, see Andrew Lintott, *The Constitution of the Roman Republic* (Oxford: Oxford University Press, 1999).

13 Lintott, *Constitution of the Roman Republic*, p. 7.

14 Eric A. Posner, 'The Constitution of the Roman Republic: A Political Economy Perspective', John M. Olin Program in Law and Economics Working Paper No. 540 and Public Law and Legal Theory Working Paper No. 327, pp. 1–35. Chicago, 2010. https://chicagounbound. uchicago.edu/cgi/viewcontent.cgi?article=1496&context=law_and_ economics. See esp. p. 2.

15 Lintott, *Constitution of the Roman Republic*, pp. 33–5.

16 Lintott, *Constitution of the Roman Republic*, p. 32.

17 Posner, 'Constitution of the Roman Republic', p. 15.

18 Posner, 'Constitution of the Roman Republic'; Lintott, *Constitution of the Roman Republic*, pp. 18–19.

19 Polybius, *Histories*, 6.18.

20 Polybius, *Histories*, 6.11.

21 Polybius, *Histories*, 6.18.

22 Polybius, *Histories*, 6.50.

23 Lea Campos Boralevi, 'James Harrington's "Machiavellian" anti-Machiavellism', *History of European Ideas* 37.2 (2011): 113–19, here at p. 115 and Eric Nelson, *The Hebrew Republic: Jewish Sources and the Transformation of European Political Thought* (Cambridge, MA: Harvard University Press, 2010), p. 89.

24 Nelson, *Hebrew Republic*, pp. 3 and 16.

25 Nelson, *Hebrew Republic*, p. 18.

26 Nelson, *Hebrew Republic*, pp. 18–19; Petrus Cunaeus, *Of the Common-Wealth of the Hebrews,* translated by C. B. [Clement Barksdale] (London, 1653).

27 Cunaeus, *Of the Common-Wealth of the Hebrews*, pp. 7–8.

28 Cunaeus, *Of the Common-Wealth of the Hebrews*, pp. 10–15 and 96–99.

29 See Plato, *The Republic*, translated by A. D. Lindsay (London: Everyman, 1992).

30 Plato, *Republic*, p. 101. The 'city' in this sentence is not a real city but Callipolis, the ideal, utopian city that is being hypothesised or 'founded' in this dialogue.

31 Aristotle, *The Politics*, ed. Stephen Everson, trans. Benjamin Jowett,

rev. Jonathan Barnes (Cambridge: Cambridge University Press, 1988), p. 3.

32 Aristotle, *Politics*, pp. 52–3.

33 Aristotle, *Politics*, p. 22.

34 Aristotle, *Politics*, p. 68.

35 Polybius, *Histories*, 6.3.

36 Polybius, *Histories*, 6.10.

37 On the background to and history of this work, see James E. G. Zetzel, 'Introduction', in Cicero, *On the Commonwealth and On the Laws*, ed. James E. G. Zetzel (Cambridge: Cambridge University Press, 1999), pp. vii–xxiv.

38 Miriam T. Griffin and E. Margaret Atkins, 'Introduction', in Cicero, *On Duties*, ed. Miriam T. Griffin and E. Margaret Atkins (Cambridge: Cambridge University Press, 1991), here at pp. xvi–xix.

39 Zetzel, 'Introduction', p. xi.

40 Cicero, *On the Commonwealth and On the Laws*, ed. James E. G. Zetzel (Cambridge: Cambridge University Press, 1999), p. 65.

41 Cicero, *On the Commonwealth*, p. 19.

42 Cicero, *On the Commonwealth*, p. 71.

43 Cicero, *On Duties*, ed. Miriam T. Griffin and E. Margaret Atkins (Cambridge: Cambridge University Press, 1991), pp. 8–9.

44 Cicero, *De re publica; De legibus*, trans. C. W. Keyes (Cambridge, MA: Harvard University Press, 1928), p. 29.

45 Cicero, *On Duties*, p. 28.

46 Cicero, *On Duties*, p. 9.

47 Cicero, *On Duties*, p. 33.

48 Cicero, *On Duties*, p. 23.

49 Jed Atkins, *Cicero on Politics and the Limits of Reason* (Cambridge: Cambridge University Press, 2013), pp. 80–118.

50 Atkins, *Cicero on Politics*, pp. 81–2. A different interpretation of Cicero that places much greater emphasis on the constitutional dimension of his thought has been offered by Benjamin Straumann, *Crisis and Constitutionalism: Roman Political Thought from the Fall of the Republic to the Age of* Revolution (Oxford: Oxford University Press, 2016). His ideas are discussed in Chapter 10.

51 Atkins, *Cicero on Politics*, p. 86.

52 Atkins, *Cicero on Politics*, p. 111.

53 Daniel J. Kapust, *Republicanism, Rhetoric, and Roman Political Thought: Sallust, Livy and Tacitus* (Cambridge: Cambridge University Press, 2011), p. 174.

54 Sallust, *War with Catiline*, 7.1, as quoted in Kapust, *Republicanism*, p. 29.

55 Kapust, *Republicanism*, chs 2 and 3.

56 Benedetto Fontana, 'Sallust and the Politics of Machiavelli', *History of Political Thought* 24.1 (2003): 86–108.

57 Kapust, *Republicanism*, ch. 4.

58 William Walker, 'Sallust and Skinner on Civil Liberty', *European Journal of Political Theory* 5.3 (2006): 237–59.
59 Benedetto Fontana, 'Tacitus on Empire and Republic', *History of Political Thought* 14.1 (1993): 27–40.
60 Kapust, *Republicanism*, p. 171.

Notes to Chapter 2

1 The value of the label 'Renaissance' has been subject to some debate. On this, see Quentin Skinner, 'Introduction: The Reality of the Renaissance', in idem, *Visions of Politics*, vol. 2: *Renaissance Virtues* (Cambridge: Cambridge University Press, 2002), pp. 1–9.
2 Hans Baron, *In Search of Florentine Civic Humanism: Essays on the Transition from Medieval to Modern Thought*, 2 vols (Princeton, NJ: Princeton University Press, 1989); Hans Baron, *The Crisis of the Early Italian Renaissance* (Princeton, NJ: Princeton University Press, 1966).
3 John M. Najemy, 'Civic Humanism and Florentine Politics', in James Hankins, ed., *Renaissance Civic Humanism: Reappraisals and Reflections* (Cambridge: Cambridge University Press, 2000), pp. 75–104.
4 Skinner, *Visions of Politics*, p. 4.
5 Najemy, 'Civic Humanism and Florentine Politics', p. 81.
6 Najemy, 'Civic Humanism and Florentine Politics', p. 92.
7 Baron, *In Search of Florentine Civic Humanism*, vol. 1, p. 11 and vol. 2, p. 187.
8 Francesco Guicciardini, *Dialogue on the Government of Florence*, ed. Alison Brown (Cambridge: Cambridge University Press, 1994).
9 J. G. A. Pocock, *The Machiavellian Moment: Florentine Political Thought and the Atlantic Republican Tradition* (Princeton, NJ: Princeton University Press, 1975), p. 74; Nicolai Rubenstein, 'Political Theories in the Renaissance', in André Chastel et al., *The Renaissance: Essays in Interpretation* (London: Methuen, 1982), pp. 153–200.
10 Skinner, *Visions of Politics*, p. 13.
11 Skinner, *Visions of Politics*, p. 2.
12 On Cicero's importance for civic humanism, see Baron, *In Search of Florentine Civic Humanism*, vol. 1, pp. 94–131.
13 Skinner, *Visions of Politics*, p. 92.
14 William Stenhouse, 'Early Modern Greek Histories and Republican Political Thought', in Wyger Velema and Arthur Weststeijn, eds, *Ancient Models in the Early Modern Republican Imagination* (Leiden: Brill, 2018), pp. 86–108.
15 Eric Nelson, *The Greek Tradition in Republican Thought* (Cambridge: Cambridge University Press, 2004).
16 Guicciardini, *Dialogue on the Government of Florence*, pp. 19, 102.
17 Guicciardini, *Dialogue on the Government of Florence*, p. 134.

18 Jacques Bos, 'Renaissance Historicism and the Model of Rome in Florentine Historiography', in Wyger Velema and Arthur Weststeijn, eds, *Ancient Models in the Early Modern Republican Imagination* (Leiden: Brill, 2018), p. 33.
19 Niccolò Machiavelli, *The Discourses*, ed. Bernard Crick (Harmondsworth: Penguin, 1970), p. 98.
20 Machiavelli, *Discourses*, p. 99.
21 Machiavelli, *Discourses*, pp. 207–8; see also p. 517.
22 Bos, 'Renaissance Historicism', p. 20.
23 Leonardo Bruni, *Panegyric to the City of Florence*, trans. Benjamin G. Kohl, in Benjamin G. Kohl and Ronald G. Witt with Elizabeth B. Welles, eds, *The Earthly Republic: Italian Humanists on Government and Society* (Philadelphia: University of Pennsylvania Press, 1978), esp. pp. 149–54.
24 Baron, *In Search of Florentine Civic Humanism*, vol. 1, pp. 91–2.
25 Baron, *Crisis of the Early Italian Renaissance*; Baron, *In Search of Florentine Civic Humanism*, passim.
26 Bos, 'Renaissance Historicism'.
27 Azo of Bologna, quoted in Skinner, *Visions of Politics*, p. 16.
28 Bruni, *Panegyric to the City of Florence*, p. 151.
29 Bruni, quoted in Baron, *In Search of Florentine Civic Humanism*, vol. 1, p. 31.
30 Bruni, quoted in Baron, *In Search of Florentine Civic Humanism*, vol. 1, p. 33.
31 Skinner, *Visions of Politics*, p. 161.
32 Machiavelli, *Discourses*, p. 115.
33 Machiavelli, *Discourses*, p. 218.
34 Machiavelli, *Discourses*, p. 218; also p. 340.
35 Machiavelli, *Discourses*, p. 433.
36 Machiavelli, *Discourses*, p. 203.
37 Machiavelli, *Discourses*, p. 481.
38 On the distinction between pluralist and exclusivist republicanism, see the Introduction to this volume.
39 Leonardo Bruni, *History of the Florentine People* ed. and trans. James Hankins, 3 vols (Cambridge, MA: Harvard University Press, 2001–7), vol. 2, p. 13.
40 Skinner, *Visions of Politics*, p. 59.
41 Skinner, *Visions of Politics*, p. 28.
42 Quoted in Skinner, *Visions of Politics*, p. 28.
43 Benjamin Straumann, 'The Roman Republic as a Constitutional Order in the Italian Renaissance', in Wyger Velema and Arthur Weststeijn, eds, *Ancient Models in the Early Modern Republican Imagination* (Leiden: Brill, 2018), pp. 53–4.
44 On this matter, contrast Straumann, 'Roman Republic as Constitutional Order', with James Hankins, 'Exclusivist Republicanism and the Non-Monarchical Republic', *Political Theory* 38.4 (2010): 452–82.

45 Skinner, *Visions of Politics*, p. 130.
46 Hankins, 'Exclusivist Republicanism', pp. 453–4.
47 Hankins, 'Exclusivist Republicanism', p. 460.
48 Hankins, 'Exclusivist Republicanism', p. 469.
49 Hankins, 'Exclusivist Republicanism', p. 471.
50 Hankins, 'Exclusivist Republicanism', p. 472.
51 See e.g. Machiavelli, *Discourses*, 19–24.
52 Machiavelli, *Discourses*, pp. 153–4.
53 Machiavelli, *Discourses*, p. 158.
54 Machiavelli, *Discourses*, p. 164.
55 Machiavelli, *Discourses*, p. 246.
56 Machiavelli, *Discourses*, p. 248.
57 Machiavelli, *Discourses*, p. 256; see also p. 275.
58 Machiavelli, *Discourses*, p. 431.
59 Machiavelli, *Discourses*, p. 167.
60 Machiavelli, *Discourses*, p. 168.
61 Machiavelli, *Discourses*, p. 275.
62 Hankins, 'Exclusivist Republicanism', p. 470.
63 Machiavelli, *Discourses*, pp. 392–3.
64 Quoted in Skinner, *Visions of Politics*, p. 47.
65 Quoted in Skinner, *Visions of Politics*, p. 129. See also Baron, *In Search of Florentine Civic Humanism*, vol. 1, p. 134; vol. 2, p. 55.
66 Machiavelli, *Discourses*, p. 275.
67 Skinner, *Visions of Politics*, p. 134.
68 Skinner, *Visions of Politics*, pp. 130–1.
69 Coluccio Salutati, 'Letter to Pellegrino Zambeccari', trans. Ronald G. Witt, in Benjamin G. Kohl and Ronald G. Witt with Elizabeth B. Welles, eds, *The Earthly Republic: Italian Humanists on Government and Society* (Philadelphia: University of Pennsylvania Press, 1978), pp. 111–12.
70 As quoted in Baron, *In Search of Florentine Civic Humanism*, vol. 1, p. 20.
71 Baron, *In Search of Florentine Civic Humanism*, vol. 1, p. 21.
72 Iseult Honohan, 'Freedom as Citizenship: The Republican Tradition in Political Theory', *Republic: A Journal of Contemporary and Historical Debate* 2 (2001): 7–24, here p. 11.
73 Guicciardini's position, by contrast, was more in line with earlier accounts. He believed human beings to be naturally inclined to behave virtuously, but acknowledged that they could be easily corrupted and that laws and honours were required to protect us against this. See Guicciardini, *Dialogue on the Government of Florence*, pp. 53, 132.
74 Machiavelli, *Discourses*, p. 279.
75 Machiavelli, *Discourses*, pp. 513–14.
76 Machiavelli, *Discourses*, pp. 132–3.
77 Machiavelli, *Discourses*, p. 392.
78 Machiavelli, *Discourses*, p. 153.

79 Machiavelli, *Discourses*, p. 311.
80 Machiavelli, *Discourses*, p. 469.
81 Straumann, 'The Roman Republic as a Constitutional Order'.
82 Straumann, 'The Roman Republic as a Constitutional Order', p. 51.
83 Straumann, 'The Roman Republic as a Constitutional Order', p. 55.
84 Machiavelli, *Discourses*, p. 109.
85 Machiavelli, *Discourses*, p. 111.
86 Skinner, *Visions of Politics*, p. 174.
87 Machiavelli, *Discourses*, p. 455.
88 Salutati, 'Letter to Pellegrino Zambeccari', p. 109.
89 Salutati, 'Letter to Pellegrino Zambeccari', p. 110.
90 Machiavelli, *Discourses*, pp. 142–3.
91 Machiavelli, *Discourses*, p. 140.
92 Machiavelli, *Discourses*, pp. 139–41.
93 Machiavelli, *Discourses*, p. 277.
94 Machiavelli, *Discourses*, p. 278.
95 For details of this reputation, see Felix Raab, *The English Face of Machiavelli: A Changing Interpretation, 1500–1700* (London/Toronto: Routledge and Kegan Paul/University of Toronto Press, 1964).
96 Hans Baron makes this point with regard to Petrarch; see Baron, *In Search of Florentine Civic Humanism*, vol. 1. p. 25.
97 Skinner, *Visions of Politics*, p. 68.
98 Machiavelli, *Discourses*, p. 113.
99 Machiavelli, *Discourses*, p. 115; also p. 203.
100 John P. McCormick, 'Machiavelli against Republicanism: On the Cambridge School's "Guicciardinian Moments"', *Political Theory* 31.5 (2003): 615–43.
101 Guicciardini, *Dialogue on the Government of Florence*, pp. 98–100, 66, and 143–5.
102 Ryan Balot and Stephen Trochimchuk, 'The Many and the Few: On Machiavelli's "Democratic Moment"', *Review of Politics* 74 (2012): 559–88.
103 Machiavelli, *Discourses*, p. 117; also p. 282.
104 Machiavelli, *Discourses*, p. 122.

Notes to Chapter 3

1 See in particular Paul Rahe, *Republics: Ancient and Modern* (Chapel Hill: University of North Carolina Press, 1992).
2 On this, see Wyger, Velema and Arthur Weststeijn, eds, *Ancient Models in the Early Modern Republican Imagination* (Leiden: Brill, 2018).
3 Weststeijn, 'Commonwealths for Preservation and Increase: Ancient Rome in Venice and the Dutch Republic', in Velema and Weststeijn, *Ancient Models in the Early Modern Republican Imagination*, pp. 62–85, here 71–2.

4 William Stenhouse, 'Early Modern Greek Histories and Republican Political Thought', and Wessel Krul, 'Painting Plutarch: Images of Sparta in the Dutch Republic and Enlightenment France', both in Velema and Weststeijn, *Ancient Models in the Early Modern Republican Imagination*, pp. 86–108 and 157–88.

5 Jaap Nieuwstraten, 'A Classical Confederacy: The Example of the Achaean League in the Seventeenth-Century Dutch Republic', in Velema and Weststeijn, *Ancient Models in the Early Modern Republican Imagination*, pp. 109–30.

6 Guido Bartolucci, 'The Hebrew Republic in Sixteenth-Century Political Debate: The Struggle for Jurisdiction', in Velema and Weststeijn, *Ancient Models in the Early Modern Republican Imagination*, pp. 214–33. See also Eric Nelson, *The Hebrew Republic: Jewish Sources and the Transformation of European Political Thought* (Cambridge, MA: Harvard University Press, 2010); Mark Somos, 'Irenic Secularization and the Hebrew Republic in Harrington's *Oceana*', in Gaby Mahlberg and Dirk Wiemann, eds, *European Contexts for English Republicanism* (Farnham: Ashgate, 2014), pp. 81–103; and Lea Campos Boralevi, 'Classical Foundational Myths of European Republicanism: The Jewish Commonwealth', in Martin Van Gelderen and Quentin Skinner, eds, *Republicanism*, vol. 1: *A Shared European Heritage* (Cambridge: Cambridge University Press, 2002), pp. 247–61.

7 On the Elzevier republics, see Arthur Weststeijn, *Commercial Republicanism in the Dutch Golden Age: The Political Thought of Johan and Pieter de la Court* (Leiden: Brill, 2012), pp. 40–1 and Velema and Weststeijn, *Ancient Models in the Early Modern Republican Imagination*, p. 12 (= introduction).

8 Gasper Contarini, *The Commonwealth and Government of Venice*, translated by Lewes Lewkenor (London, 1599), p. 15.

9 Quentin Skinner, *Visions of Politics*, vol. 2: *Renaissance Virtues* (Cambridge: Cambridge University Press, 2002), p. 127.

10 Both James Harrington in the seventeenth century and Jean-Jacques Rutledge in the eighteenth noted this.

11 Zera S. Fink, *The Classical Republicans: An Essay in the Recovery of a Pattern of Thought in Seventeenth-Century England* (Evanston, IL: Northwestern University Press, 1945), p. 30.

12 Contarini, *Commonwealth and Government of Venice*, p. 69.

13 Contarini, *Commonwealth and Government of Venice*, pp. 65 and 77–9.

14 Contarini, *Commonwealth and Government of Venice*, p. 42.

15 William Bouwsma, *Venice and the Defence of Republican Liberty* (Berkeley: University of California Press, 1968), p. 58.

16 Weststeijn, 'Commonwealths for Preservation and Increase', pp. 70–1.

17 Bouwsma, *Venice and the Defence of Republican Liberty*, p. 74.

18 Linda Kirk, 'Genevan Republicanism', in David Wootton, ed., *Republicanism, Liberty, and Commercial Society, 1649–1776* (Stanford: Stanford University Press, 1994), pp. 270–309, here pp. 270–1.

19 Richard Whatmore, *Against War and Empire: Geneva, Britain, and France in the Eighteenth Century* (New Haven, CT: Yale University Press, 2012), p. xiii.

20 Quoted in Kirk, 'Genevan Republicanism', p. 273.

21 Whatmore, *Against War and Empire*, p. 21.

22 Eco Haitsma Mulier, 'The Language of Seventeenth-Century Republicanism in the United Provinces: Dutch or European?' in Anthony Pagden, ed., *The Languages of Political Theory in Early-Modern Europe* (Cambridge: Cambridge University Press, 1987), pp. 179–95; Wyger Velema, "That a Republic Is Better than a Monarchy": Anti-Monarchism in Early Modern Dutch Political Thought', in Martin Van Gelderen and Quentin Skinner, eds, *Republicanism: A Shared European Heritage*, vol. 1: *Republicanism and Constitutionalism in Early Modern Europe* (Cambridge: Cambridge University Press, 2002), p. 10.

23 Martin Van Gelderen, 'Introduction', in idem, ed., *The Dutch Revolt* (Cambridge: Cambridge University Press, 1993), pp. ix–xxxiii.

24 Anon., *Political Education*, in Martin Van Gelderen, ed., *The Dutch Revolt* (Cambridge: Cambridge University Press, 1993), p. 182.

25 Anon., *Political Education*, in Martin Van Gelderen, ed., *The Dutch Revolt* (Cambridge: Cambridge University Press, 1993), p. 186.

26 Quoted in Weststeijn, 'Commonwealths for Preservation and Increase', p. 77.

27 Wyger Velema, *Republicans: Essays on Eighteenth-Century Dutch Political Thought* (Leiden: Brill, 2007), p. 6.

28 Weststeijn, 'Commonwealths for Preservation and Increase', pp. 62–85.

29 Thomas Maissen, 'The Helvetians as Ancestors and Brutus as a Model: The Classical Past in the Early Modern Swiss Confederation', in Velema and Weststeijn, eds, *Ancient Models in the Early Modern Republican Imagination*, pp. 259–84.

30 Maissen, 'The Helvetians as Ancestors', p. 261.

31 Maissen, 'The Helvetians as Ancestors', pp. 278–9.

32 Maissen, 'The Helvetians as Ancestors', p. 284.

33 Quoted in Anna Grzeskowiak-Krwawicz, 'Anti-Monarchism in Polish Republicanism in the Seventeenth and Eighteenth Centuries', in Martin Van Gelderen and Quentin Skinner, eds, *Republicanism: A Shared European Heritage*, vol. 1: *Republicanism and Constitutionalism in Early Modern Europe* (Cambridge: Cambridge University Press, 2002), pp. 43–60, here p. 44 n. 1.

34 Grzeskowiak-Krwawicz, 'Anti-Monarchism in Polish Republicanism', p. 43.

35 Tomasz Gromelski, 'Classical Models in Early Modern Poland–Lithuania', in Velema and Weststeijn, eds, *Ancient Models in the Early Modern Republican Imagination*, p. 290, and Grzeskowiak-Krwawicz, 'Anti-Monarchism in Polish Republicanism', p. 45.

36 Grzeskowiak-Krwawicz, 'Anti-Monarchism in Polish Republicanism', pp. 43–45.

37 Grzeskowiak-Krwawicz, 'Anti-Monarchism in Polish Republicanism', p. 44.

38 Quoted in Grzeskowiak-Krwawicz, 'Anti-Monarchism in Polish Republicanism', p. 45.
39 Quoted in Grzeskowiak-Krwawicz, 'Anti-Monarchism in Polish Republicanism', p. 45.
40 Gromelski, 'Classical Models in Early Modern Poland–Lithuania', in Velema and Weststeijn, eds, pp. 300–1; Grzeskowiak-Krwawicz, 'Anti-Monarchism in Polish Republicanism', p. 45.
41 Grzeskowiak-Krwawicz, 'Anti-Monarchism in Polish Republicanism', p. 44.
42 Grzeskowiak-Krwawicz, 'Anti-Monarchism in Polish Republicanism', p. 47.
43 Grzeskowiak-Krwawicz, 'Anti-Monarchism in Polish Republicanism', p. 54.

Notes to Chapter 4

1 See, throughout this chapter, S. R. Gardiner, ed., *The Constitutional Documents of the Puritan Revolution: 1625–60*, 3rd edn (Oxford: Clarendon, 1906); and, concerning the creation of the commonwealth, see 'An Act Declaring England to Be a Commonwealth', in Gardiner's edition, p. 388.
2 For further discussion of the historiography of republicanism, see Chapter 10. Some of the main works on English republicanism are Zera Fink, *The Classical Republicans: An Essay in the Recovery of a Pattern of Thought in Seventeenth-Century England* (Evanston, IL: Northwestern University Press, 1945); J. G. A. Pocock, *The Machiavellian Moment: Florentine Political Thought and the Atlantic Republican Tradition* (Princeton, NJ: Princeton University Press, 1975), esp. pp. 333–422; Blair Worden, 'James Harrington and *The Commonwealth of Oceana*, 1656', 'Harrington's "Oceana": Origins and Aftermath, 1651–1660', and 'Republicanism and the Restoration, 1660–1683', all three in David Wootton, ed., *Republicanism, Liberty, and Commercial Society, 1649–1776* (Stanford, CA: Stanford University Press, 1994), pp. 82–110, 111–38, and 139–93; Quentin Skinner, *Liberty before Liberalism* (Cambridge: Cambridge University Press, 1998); Jonathan Scott, *Commonwealth Principles: Republican Writing of the English Revolution* (Cambridge: Cambridge University Press, 2004); Sean Kelsey, *Inventing a Republic: The Political Culture of the English Commonwealth, 1649–1653* (Manchester: Manchester University Press, 1997); David Norbrook, *Writing the English Republic: Poetry, Rhetoric and Politics, 1627–1660* (Cambridge: Cambridge University Press, 1999).
3 Rachel Hammersley, 'Rethinking the Political Thought of James Harrington: Royalism, Republicanism and Democracy', in *History of European Ideas* 39.3 (2013): 354–70 and Martin Dzelzainis, 'Harrington

and the Oligarchs: Milton, Vane and Stubbe', in Gaby Mahlberg and Dirk Wiemann, eds, *Perspectives on English Revolutionary Republicanism* (Farnham: Ashgate, 2014, pp. 15–33).

4 Sean Kelsey, 'The Death of Charles I', *Historical Journal* 45.4 (2002): 727–54; Sean Kelsey, 'The Trial of Charles I', *English Historical Review* 118 (2003): 583–616.

5 Clive Holmes, 'The Trial and Execution of Charles I', *Historical Journal* 53.2 (2010): 289–316.

6 'The Act Abolishing the Office of King', 17 March 1649, in Gardiner, *Constitutional Documents*, pp. 384–7.

7 However, Blair Worden argues that the ambiguity in this document and the particular form of its wording suggest an attempt to leave open the possibility of a 'mixed monarchical solution' favoured by many MPs. See Blair Worden, *The Rump Parliament, 1648–1653* (Cambridge: Cambridge University Press, 1974), p. 172.

8 'An Act Declaring England to Be a Commonwealth', p. 388.

9 Blair Worden, 'Introduction', in Marchamont Nedham, *The Excellencie of a Free-State Or, The Right Constitution of a Commonwealth*, ed. Blair Worden (Indianapolis: Liberty Fund, 2011), p. xviii.

10 'An Act declaring England to Be a Commonwealth', p. 388.

11 Kelsey, *Inventing a Republic*.

12 John Rogers, *Diapoliteia: A Christian Concertation with Mr. Prin, Mr. Baxter, Mr. Harrington, for the True Cause of the Commonwealth* (London, 1659), Preface.

13 'The Instrument of Government', 16 December 1653, in Gardiner, *Constitutional Documents*, pp. 405–17.

14 'The Humble Petition and Advice', 25 May 1657, in Gardiner, *Constitutional Documents*, pp. 447–59.

15 John Milton, *The Tenure of Kings and Magistrates*, in idem, *Political Writings*, ed. Martin Dzelzainis (Cambridge: Cambridge University Press, 1991), p. 8.

16 Milton, *Tenure*, p. 9.

17 Milton, *Tenure*, p. 11.

18 Milton, *Tenure*, p. 16.

19 Milton, *Tenure*, p. 13.

20 Milton, *Tenure*, p. 32.

21 *Eikōn basilikē: The Pourtraicture of His Sacred Majesty in His Solitudes and Sufferings* (London: Printed by Henry Hills, 1649). For a useful analysis, see Elizabeth Skerpan-Wheeler, 'The First "Royal": Charles I as Celebrity', *Proceedings of the Modern Languages Association* 126.4 (2011): 912–34.

22 John Milton, *Eikonoklastēs: In Answer to a Book Entitled Eikōn basilikē: The Portraiture of His Sacred Majesty in His Solitudes and Sufferings* (London, 1649).

23 John Milton, *A Defence of the People of England*, in idem, *Political*

Writings, ed. Martin Dzelzainis (Cambridge: Cambridge University Press, 1991), p. 251.

24 Milton, *Defence*, pp. 68, 92, 206.
25 Milton, *Defence*, pp. 78 and 216.
26 Milton, *Defence*, p. 80.
27 Eric Nelson, *The Royalist Revolution: Monarchy and the American Founding* (Cambridge, MA: Belknap Press, 2014), p. 114.
28 Milton, *Defence*, pp. 129–30.
29 John Milton, *The Readie and Easie Way to Establish a Free Commonwealth*, 2nd edn (London, 1660), p. 40.
30 Quentin Skinner, 'Conquest and Consent: Thomas Hobbes and the Engagement Controversy', in Gerald E. Aylmer, ed., *The Interregnum: The Quest for a Settlement, 1646–1660* (London: Macmillan, 1972), pp. 79–98.
31 Marchamont Nedham, *The Case of the Commonwealth of England, Stated*, ed. Philip A. Knachel (Charlottesville: University Press of Virginia, 1969), p. 10.
32 Nedham, *The Case of the Commonwealth*, p. 15.
33 Nedham, *The Case of the Commonwealth*, pp. 28–9.
34 Nedham, *The Case of the Commonwealth*, pp. 36–7.
35 Nedham, *The Case of the Commonwealth*, p. 39.
36 Nedham, *The Case of the Commonwealth*, pp. 111–28.
37 Rachel Foxley, *The Levellers: Radical Political Thought in the English Revolution* (Manchester: Manchester University Press, 2013), p. 195.
38 Philip A. Knachel, 'Introduction', in Nedham, *The Case of the Commonwealth of England*, pp. ix–xli, here p. xxxv.
39 Marchamont Nedham, *The Excellencie of a Free State: Or, The Right Constitution of a Common-Wealth. Wherein All Objections are answered, and the best way to secure the Peoples Liberties, discovered: with some errors of Government and Rules of Policy. Published by a Well-wisher to Posterity* (London: Thomas Brewster, 1656), p. 7.
40 Nedham, *The Excellencie of a Free State*, p. 42.
41 Henry Vane, *A Healing Question...* (London: T. Brewster, 1656), pp. 2–3.
42 John Toland, 'The Life of James Harrington', in *The Oceana and Other Works of James Harrington Esq; Collected, Methodiz'd, and Review'd...* (London, 1737), pp. xiii–xliv, here pp. xix–xx.
43 Worden, 'Harrington's "Oceana"', p. 124.
44 Jonathan Scott, 'James Harrington's Prescription for Healing and Settling', in Michael Braddick and David Smith, eds, *The Experience of Revolution in Seventeenth-Century England* (Cambridge: Cambridge University Press, 2011), pp. 190–209.
45 James Harrington, *The Commonwealth of Oceana*, in idem, *The Commonwealth of Oceana and A System of Politics*, ed. J. G. A. Pocock (Cambridge: Cambridge University Press, 1992). On Harrington, see Rachel Hammersley, *James Harrington: An Intellectual Biography* (Oxford: Oxford University Press, 2019).

46 Worden, 'Harrington's "Oceana"', pp. 111–12; Jonathan Scott, 'The Rapture of Motion: James Harrington's Republicanism', in Nicholas Philipson and Quentin Skinner, eds, *Political Discourse in Early Modern Britain* (Cambridge: Cambridge University Press, 1993), here p. 147.

47 *Mercurius Politicus*, 352–6 (5–12 March, 19–26 March, 26 March–2 April, and 2–9 April 1657); J. G. A. Pocock, 'James Harrington and the Good Old Cause: A Study of the Ideological Context of His Writings', *Journal of British Studies* 10.1 (1970): 36–40.

48 Scott, *Commonwealth Principles* and 'The Rapture of Motion'.

49 P. A. Rahe, *Against Throne and Altar: Machiavelli and Political Theory under the English Republic* (Cambridge: Cambridge University Press, 2008), esp. 321–46.

50 For details on these works, see Hammersley, *James Harrington*, esp. pp. 149–66 and 231–48.

51 See e.g. Henry Stubbe, *Essay in Defence of the Good Old Cause...* (London, 1659), esp. Preface and p. 9; Milton, *The Readie and Easie Way*.

52 Milton, *The Readie and Easie Way*, p. 44.

53 James Harrington, *The Commonwealth of Oceana and A System of Politics*, ed. J. G. A. Pocock (Cambridge: Cambridge University Press, 1992), pp. 23–5.

54 Rogers, *Diapoliteia*, p. 77.

55 Henry Stubbe, *A Letter to an Officer of the Army Concerning a Select Senate mentioned by them in their proposals to the late Parliament...* (London, 1660), p. 61.

56 Harrington, *Oceana*, p. 63.

57 Vane, *A Healing Question*, p. 18.

58 Milton, *The Readie and Easie Way*, pp. 49–50.

59 Rogers, *Diapoliteia*, p. 81.

60 James Harrington, *Aphorisms Political*, 2nd edn (London, 1659), p. 2.

61 Harrington, *Oceana*, p. 64.

62 Rogers, *Diapoliteia*, p. 76.

63 Stubbe, *A Letter to an Officer of the Army*, p. 57.

64 Stubbe, *Essay in Defence of the Good Old Cause*, pp. 16–17; see also Henry Stubbe, *The Common-Wealth of Oceana Put into the Balance and Found too Light* (London, 1660), Preface and p. 10.

65 Stubbe, *Essay in Defence of the Good Old Cause*, pp. 16–17.

66 Vane, *A Healing Question*, p. 6.

67 Stubbe, *Essay in Defence of the Good Old Cause*, p. 21.

68 Harrington, *Oceana*, pp. 81–2.

69 Mark Goldie, 'The Civil Religion of James Harrington', in *The Languages of Political Theory in Early Modern Europe*, ed. Anthony Pagden (Cambridge: Cambridge University Press, 1987), pp. 197–222; Ronald Beiner, 'Civil Religion and Anticlericalism in James Harrington', *European Journal of Political Theory* 13.4 (2014): 388–407; Hammersley, *James Harrington*, ch. 11.

70 Vane, *A Healing Question*, p. 18.
71 Harrington, *Oceana*, pp. 244–66. On this, see Hammersley, *James Harrington*, ch. 5.
72 Harrington, *Aphorisms Political*, p. 15.

Notes to Chapter 5

1   On the exile of English republicans to Europe and on the connections they made there, see Gaby Mahlberg, *The English Republican Exiles in Europe During the Restoration* (Cambridge: Cambridge University Press, forthcoming). I am grateful to Dr Mahlberg for providing me with a copy of this book prior to publication. On underground radicalism, see Richard L. Greaves, *Deliver us from Evil: The Radical Underground in Britain, 1660–1663* (Oxford: Oxford University Press, 1986).
2   Caroline A. Robbins, *The Eighteenth-Century Commonwealthman: Studies in the Transmission, Development and Circumstance of English Liberty Thought from the Restoration of Charles II until the War with the Thirteen Colonies* (Indianapolis, IN: Liberty Fund, 2004 [1987, 1959]).
3   Jonathan Scott, *Algernon Sidney and the Restoration Crisis, 1677–1683* (Cambridge: Cambridge University Press, 1991), especially pp. 201–264.
4   Blair Worden, *Literature and Politics in Cromwellian England: John Milton, Andrew Marvell, Marchamont Nedham* (Oxford: Oxford University Press, 2007).
5   John Milton, *A Complete Collection of the Historical, Political and Miscellaneous Works of John Milton*, ed. John Toland (Amsterdam, 1698); Algernon Sidney, *Discourses Concerning Government* (London, 1698); *Memoirs of Lieutenant General Ludlow* (London, 1699); James Harrington, *The Oceana of James Harrington, and His Other Works...*, ed. John Toland (London, 1700). Toland also published works by Denzil Holles and George Monck. However, it is the Milton, Ludlow, Harrington and Sidney volumes that are generally seen as constituting the core of the republican canon.
6   Blair Worden, 'Whig History and Puritan Politics: The Memoirs of Edmund Ludlow, Revisited', *Historical Research* 75 (2002): 209–37.
7   On this point, see the discussion by Justin Champion in idem, *Republican Learning: John Toland and the Crisis of Christian Culture, 1696–1722* (Manchester: Manchester University Press, 2003), p. 100.
8   'The Translator's Preface', in *Franco-Gallia: Or, an Account of the Ancient Free State of France, and Most other Parts of Europe, before the Loss of their Liberties. Written Originally in Latin by the Famous Civilian Francis Hotoman, in the year 1574 and translated into English by the Author of the Account of Denmark*, 2nd edn (London, 1721). See Robert Molesworth, *The Principles of a Real Whig* (London, 1775; cited in full in n. 76 here). A modern edition of *Franco-Gallia*

in Molesworth's translation can be found in Robert Molesworth, *An Account of Denmark with Francogallia and Some Considerations for the Promoting of Agriculture and Employing the Poor*, ed. Justin Champion (Indianapolis, IN: Liberty Fund, 2011), pp. 171–90. See also Justin Champion's 'Introduction' to the volume.

9 John Trenchard and Thomas Gordon, *Cato's Letters* (London, 1733), vol. 1, pp. xvi–xvii.

10 On Bolingbroke, see Rachel Hammersley, *The English Republican Tradition and Eighteenth-Century France: Between the Ancients and the Moderns* (Manchester: Manchester University Press, 2010), pp. 54–63 and Isaac Kramnick, *Bolingbroke and His Circle: The Politics of Nostalgia in the Age of Walpole* (Ithaca, NY: Cornell University Press, 1992 [1968]).

11 Henry St John, Viscount Bolingbroke, *A Dissertation upon Parties*, in idem, *Political Writings*, ed. David Armitage (Cambridge: Cambridge University Press, 1997), pp. 8–9.

12 Thomas Hollis, *Memoirs of Thomas Hollis*, ed. Francis Blackburne (London, 1780), vol. 1, p. 60.

13 On Baron and Hollis, see Robbins, *The Eighteenth-Century Commonwealthman*, esp. pp. 253–64; Caroline A. Robbins, 'The Strenuous Whig, Thomas Hollis of Lincoln's Inn', and 'Library of Liberty: Assembled for Harvard College by Thomas Hollis of Lincoln's Inn', both in B. Taft, ed., *Absolute Liberty: A Selection from the Articles and Papers of Caroline Robbins* (Hamden, CT: Archon Books, 1982), pp. 168–229; P. D. Marshall, 'Thomas Hollis (1720–74): The Bibliophile as Libertarian', *Bulletin of the John Rylands University Library of Manchester*, 266 (1984): 246–63; and B. Worden, 'Introduction', in Marchamont Nedham, *The Excellencie of a Free State* (Indianapolis, IN: Liberty Fund, 2011), pp. xli–lxxxiii.

14 Hollis, *Memoirs*, pp. 58, 118–19, 235–7 and 475.

15 Algernon Sidney, *Discourses Concerning Government* (London: A. Millar, 1763), 'Preface'.

16 Hollis, *Memoirs*, vol. 1, p. 61.

17 John Milton, *The Works of John Milton* (London, 1753), p. v.

18 Milton, *Works*, p. iv.

19 Hollis, *Memoirs*, vol. 1, p. 264.

20 Horace Walpole, *Memoirs of the Reign of King George the Third*, ed. D. Le Marchant (London: Richard Bentley, 1845), vol. 3, p. 331.

21 Hollis, *Memoirs*, vol. 1, p. 59–60.

22 Hollis, *Memoirs*, vol. 1, p. 60.

23 Hollis, *Memoirs*, esp. 1: 82, 87, 126, 180, 197, 217, 222–3, 239, 242–9, 308, 319, 332, and 418.

24 Hollis, *Memoirs*, vol. 1, p. 68.

25 Hollis, *Memoirs*, vol. 1, pp. 68–9.

26 Rémy Duthille, *Le Discours radical en Grande-Bretagne, 1768–1789* (Oxford: Voltaire Foundation, 2017), p. 24.

27 [Walter Moyle and John Trenchard], *An Argument Shewing That a*

Standing Army Is Inconsistent with a Free Government and Absolutely Destructive to the Constitution of the English Monarchy (London, 1697), p. 2; Molesworth, *An Account of Denmark*.

28 Scott, *Algernon Sidney and the Restoration Crisis*, p. 206.

29 Hollis, *Memoirs*, vol. 1, p. 56.

30 Trenchard and Gordon, *Cato's Letters*, vol. 1, p. xxii.

31 John Milton, *Areopagitica* (London, 1644).

32 John Milton, *The Readie and Easie Way to Establish a Free Commonwealth*, 2nd edn (London, 1660), p. 87; James Harrington, '*The Commonwealth of Oceana*' *and* '*A System of Politics*', ed. Pocock (Cambridge: Cambridge University Press, 1992), p. 282.

33 Scott, *Algernon Sidney and the Restoration Crisis*, p. 201.

34 John Toland, *Vindicius Liberius: Or, M. Toland's Defence of himself, Against the late Lower House of Convocation, and Others* (London, 1702), p. 111.

35 Thomas Gordon, *Priestianity: Of a View of the Disparity Between the Apostles and the Modern Inferior Clergy* (London, 1720), p. xiv.

36 John Trenchard and Thomas Gordon, *Independent Whig*, 6th ed. (London, 1732), p. 52.

37 Hollis, *Memoirs*, vol. 1, p. 56.

38 Harrington, '*Commonwealth of Oceana*', p. 81.

39 Molesworth, *An Account of Denmark*, p. 177.

40 Walter Moyle, *An Essay upon the Constitution of the Roman Government*, in idem, *The Works of Walter Moyle Esq* (London, 1726), p. 25.

41 Bolingbroke, *Idea of a Patriot King*, in idem, *Political Writings*, ed. David Armitage (Cambridge: Cambridge University Press, 1997), p. 224.

42 John Toland, *Nazarenus: Or Jewish, Gentile, and Mahometan Christianity*, 2nd edn (London, 1718), p. 17.

43 Henry Neville, *Plato redivivus: Or, A Dialogue Concerning Government...*, 3rd edn, in James Harrington, *The Oceana of James Harrington, Esq; and His Other Works* (Dublin, 1737), p. 583.

44 Moyle, *An Essay upon the Roman Constitution*, p. 13.

45 Toland, *Nazarenus*, p. 40.

46 James Harrington, *Pian piano, or, Intercourse between H. Ferne, Dr. divinity and J. Harrington...* (London, 1656), p. 60.

47 Moyle, *An Essay upon the Roman Constitution*, p. 20.

48 Trenchard and Gordon, *Cato's Letters*, vol. 1 pp. li–liii.

49 See e.g. Neville, *Plato redivivus*, p. 609; Molesworth, *An Account of Denmark*, p. 177.

50 Hollis, *Memoirs*, vol. 1, p. 100.

51 Algernon Sidney, *Discourses Concerning Government*, ed. Thomas G. West (Indianapolis, IN: Liberty Fund, 1990, 1996), pp. 134–5.

52 Sidney, *Discourses* (ed. West), p. 80.

53 Neville, *Plato redivivus*, p. 590.

54 Sidney, *Discourses* (ed. West), p. 234.

55 Trenchard and Gordon, *Cato's Letters*, vol. 1, p. xxxv.
56 Trenchard and Gordon, *Cato's Letters*, vol. 1, p. viii.
57 Trenchard and Gordon, *Cato's Letters*, vol. 1, p. 25.
58 Scott, *Algernon Sidney and the Restoration Crisis*, pp. 227–8.
59 Sidney, *Discourses* (ed. West), p. 186.
60 Henry St John, Viscount Bolingbroke, *Reflections Concerning Innate Moral Principles* (London, 1752), p. 65.
61 Neville, *Plato redivivus*, p. 633.
62 Moyle, *Essay upon the Constitution of the Roman Government*, p. 94. Catharine Macaulay, *Loose Remarks on Certain Positions to be Found in Mr. Hobbes' Philosophical Rudiments of Government and Society with a Short Sketch of a Democraticall Form of Government in a Letter to Signor Paoli*, 2nd edn (London, 1769), p. 24.
63 Neville, *Plato redivivus*, p. 563.
64 Neville, *Plato redivivus*, p. 608.
65 Moyle, *Essay upon the Constitution of the Roman Government*, pp. 72–3.
66 Trenchard and Gordon, *Cato's Letters*, vol. 1, p. 11.
67 Macaulay, *Loose Remarks,* p. 24.
68 Milton, *The Readie and Easie Way*, p. 40.
69 Trenchard and Gordon, *Cato's Letters*, vol. 1, p. lv (= Preface 4).
70 Molesworth, *An Account of Denmark*, p. 173.
71 Molesworth, *An Account of Denmark*, p. 175.
72 Hollis, *Memoirs*, vol. 1, pp. 118–19.
73 Neville, *Plato redivivus*, p. 551; Harrington, *Oceana*, Preface (which was Toland's).
74 Harrington, *Oceana*, Preface, pp. vii–viii.
75 Hollis, *Memoirs*, vol. 1, pp. 93–4.
76 Robert Molesworth, *The Principles of a Real Whig; Contained in A Preface to The Famous Hotoman's Franco-Galia; Written by the late Lord-Viscount Molesworth; And now Reprinted at the Request of the London Association* (London, 1775), p. 12.
77 [John Toland], *Danger of Mercenary Parliaments* (London, 1698), p. 4.
78 [Moyle and Trenchard], *An Argument*, p. 4.
79 John Toland, *The Militia Reform'd...* (London, 1698), p. 22.
80 [Moyle and Trenchard], *An Argument*, p. 4.
81 Toland, *Militia Reform'd*, p. 17.
82 Andrew Fletcher, *A Discourse Concerning Militias and Standing Armies with Relation to the Past and Present Governments of Europe and of England in Particular* (London, 1697); *A Discourse of Government with Relation to Militias* (Edinburgh, 1698).
83 J. G. A. Pocock, *The Machiavellian Moment: Florentine Political Thought and the Atlantic Republican Tradition* (Princeton: Princeton University Press, 1975), esp. pp. 423–505.
84 James Harrington, *The Prerogative of Popular Government* (London, 1658), vol. 1, pp. 10–21 and 83. For further discussion of Harrington's ambivalence over money and of the reasons for it, see Andrew Reeve,

'Harrington's Elusive Balance', *History of European Ideas* 5.4 (1984): 401–25.

85   Trenchard and Gordon, *Cato's Letters*, vol. 1, p. xxi.

86   Mark Jurdjevic, 'Virtue, Commerce, and the Enduring Florentine Republican Moment: Reintegrating Italy into the Atlantic Republican Debate', *Journal of the History of Ideas* 62.4 (2001): 721–43, here 723 and 742.

87   Jurdjevic, 'Virtue, Commerce', p. 727.

88   Steve Pincus, 'Neither Machiavellian Moment nor Possessive Individualism: Commercial Society and the Defenders of the English Commonwealth', *American Historical Review* 103.3 (1998): 705–36.

89   Anon., *The Grand Concernments of England Ensured...* (London, 1659), p. 32.

90   Pincus, 'Neither Machiavellian Moment nor Possessive Individualism', p. 734.

91   Justin Champion, '"Mysterious politicks": Land, Credit and Commonwealth Political Economy, 1656–1722', in Daniel Carey, ed., *Money and Political Economy in the Enlightenment* (Oxford: Voltaire Foundation, 2014), pp. 117–62.

92   Champion, '"Mysterious politicks"', pp. 125 and 133.

93   Harrington, *Oceana*, p. ii (Toland's edn).

94   Harrington, *Oceana*, p. iii (Toland's edn).

95   Champion, '"Mysterious politicks"', pp. 144–5.

96   Champion, '"Mysterious politicks"', pp. 130–1.

97   Champion, '"Mysterious politicks"', pp. 135–9.

98   Champion, '"Mysterious politicks"', p. 129.

99   Champion, '"Mysterious politicks"', p. 137.

100 Trenchard and Gordon, *Cato's Letters*, vol. 4, p. 21.

101 George Bernard Owers, 'Common Law Jurisprudence and Ancient Constitutionalism in the Radical Thought of John Cartwright, Granville Sharp, and Capel Lofft', *Historical Journal* 58.1 (2015): 51–72.

102 John Cartwright, *Take Your Choice! Representation and Respect: Imposition and Contempt: Parliaments and Liberty: Long Parliaments and Slavery* (London, 1776), p. 15.

103 Cartwright, *Take Your Choice!*, p. x.

104 Cartwright, *Take Your Choice!*, pp. 62–77.

105 Cartwright, *Take Your Choice!*, p. 19.

106 Thomas Spence, 'Property in Land Every One's Right', in Alastair Bonnett and Keith Armstrong, eds, *Thomas Spence: The Poor Man's Revolutionary* (London: Breviary Stuff, 2014).

Notes to Chapter 6

1   Richard Whatmore, '"Neither Masters Nor Slaves": Small States and Empire in the Long Eighteenth Century', in Donald Kelly, ed., *Lineages of Empire: The Historical Roots of Imperial British Thought* (Oxford: Oxford University Press, 2009), pp. 53–81.

2 Wyger Velema and Arthur Weststeijn, eds, *Ancient Models in the Early Modern Republican Imagination* (Leiden: Brill, 2018); Dario Castiglione, 'Republicanism and Its Legacy', *European Journal of Political Theory* 4 (2005): 453–65.

3 Wyger Velema, 'Against Democracy: Dutch Eighteenth-Century Critics of Ancient and Modern Popular Government', in Velema and Weststeijn, *Ancient Models*, pp. 190–1.

4 Gaby Mahlberg, *English Republican Exiles in Europe During the Restoration* (Cambridge: Cambridge University Press, forthcoming).

5 The manuscript was discovered by Thérèse-Marie Jallais in the library of the University of Poitiers. Its content is analysed and its context discussed in detail in the articles by Jallais, Gaby Mahlberg and Stefano Villani in Gaby Mahlberg and Dirk Wiemann, eds, *European Contexts for English Republicanism* (Farnham: Ashgate, 2013), pp. 139–93.

6 On this, see Rachel Hammersley, *French Revolutionaries and English Republicans: The Cordeliers Club, 1790–1794* (Woodbridge: Boydell and Brewer, 2005) and Rachel Hammersley, *The English Republican Tradition and Eighteenth-Century France: Between the Ancients and the Moderns* (Manchester: Manchester University Press, 2010).

7 Wyger R. E. Velema, *Republicans: Essays on Eighteenth-Century Dutch Political Thought* (Leiden: Brill, 2007), p. 23.

8 Velema, *Republicans*, p. 24.

9 Velema, *Republicans*, pp. 5 and 53–64.

10 Velema, *Republicans,* p. 2.

11 Velema, *Republicans*, p. 29.

12 Velema, *Republicans*, pp. 51–2.

13 Linda Kirk, 'Genevan Republicanism' in David Wootton (ed.), *Republicanism, Liberty, and Commercial Society* (Stanford, CA: Stanford University Press, 1994), pp. 270–309, here p. 275.

14 Kirk, 'Genevan Republicanism', pp. 276–7.

15 Quoted in Richard Whatmore, *Against War and Empire: Geneva, Britain, and France in the Eighteenth Century* (New Haven, CT: Yale University Press, 2012), p. 49.

16 Kirk, 'Genevan Republicanism', p. 296.

17 Whatmore, *Against War and Empire*, p. 162.

18 Whatmore, *Against War and Empire*, pp. xiv–xv.

19 Kirk, 'Genevan Republicanism', p. 289.

20 Whatmore, *Against War and Empire*, p. 56.

21 Jean-Jacques Rousseau, *The Social Contract and Other Later Political Writings*, ed. Victor Gourevitch (Cambridge: Cambridge University Press, 1997), p. 67.

22 Rousseau, *Social Contract*, p. 92.

23 Rousseau, *Social Contract*, p. 100.

24 Rousseau, *Social Contract*, p. 114.

25 Rousseau, *Considerations on the Government of Poland*, in idem, *The Social Contract and Other Later Political Writings*, ed. Victor Gourevitch, pp. 177–260.

26 Rousseau, *Social Contract*, p. 81.
27 Rousseau, *Social Contract*, p. 68.
28 Rousseau, *Considerations on the Government of Poland*, p. 181.
29 Rousseau, *Social Contract*, p. 78.
30 Rousseau, *Considerations on the Government of Poland*, p. 189, and see also pp. 189–93.
31 Rousseau, *Considerations on the Government of Poland*, p. 185.
32 Rousseau, *Considerations on the Government of Poland*, p. 186.
33 Rousseau, *Social Contract*, p. 71.
34 Rousseau, *Social Contract*, pp. 142–51.
35 Rousseau, *Social Contract*, p. 150.
36 Whatmore, *Against War and Empire*, pp. 69–72.
37 The question of whether Wollstonecraft should be described as a feminist republican remains debatable, but both she and others advocated the application of republican notions of virtue and liberty to women. See Sylvana Tomaselli, review of *Mary Wollstonecraft and Feminist Republicanism: Independence, Rights and the Experience of Unfreedom*, by Lena Halldenius, in *English Historical Review* 131 (2016): 1180–2.
38 Rousseau, *Social Contract*, pp. 72–3.
39 Montesquieu, *The Spirit of the Laws*, ed. and trans. Anne Cohler, Basia Miller, and Harold Stone (Cambridge: Cambridge University Press, 1989), p. 10.
40 Montesquieu, *Spirit of the Laws*, p. 21.
41 Montesquieu, *Spirit of the Laws*, p. 124.
42 Montesquieu, *Spirit of the Laws*, p. 159.
43 Montesquieu, *Spirit of the Laws*, p. 132.
44 Keith Michael Baker, 'A Script for the French Revolution: The Political Consciousness of the Abbé Mably', in idem, *Inventing the French Revolution: Essays on French Political Culture in the Eighteenth Century* (Cambridge: Cambridge University Press, 1990), pp. 86–106; Johnson Kent Wright, *A Classical Republican in Eighteenth-Century France: The Political Thought of Mably* (Stanford: Stanford University Press, 1997).
45 For a fuller discussion of Mably's republicanism, see Rachel Hammersley, 'A French Commonwealth Man: The Abbé Mably', in eadem, *The English Republican Tradition*, pp. 86–98 and Wright, *A Classical Republican*.
46 Gabriel Bonnot de Mably, *Observations sur les grecs* (Geneva, 1749), p. 23, my translation.
47 Gabriel Bonnot de Mably, *Des droits et des devoirs du citoyen*, ed. J. L. Lecercle (Paris: Marcel Didier, 1972), pp. 107–13.
48 Mably, *Des droits et des devoirs du citoyen*, p. 212, my translation.
49 Baker, 'A Script for the French Revolution'.

Notes to Chapter 7

1 John Adams, *A Defence of the Constitutions of the United States of America* (London, 1787), p. 87.
2 Eric Nelson, *The Royalist Revolution: Monarchy and the American Founding* (Cambridge, MA: Belknap Press, 2014).
3 Nelson, *Royalist Revolution*, p. 115.
4 Louis Hartz, *The Liberal Tradition in America: An Interpretation of American Political Thought since the Revolution* (New York: Harcourt, Brace & World, 1955), esp. pp. 3–86.
5 Joyce Appleby, *Liberalism and Republicanism in the Historical Imagination* (Cambridge, MA: Cambridge University Press, 1992); Thomas L. Pangle, *The Spirit of Modern Republicanism: The Moral Vision of the American Founders and the Philosophy of Locke* (Chicago, IL: University of Chicago Press, 1988).
6 Bernard Bailyn, *Pamphlets of the American Revolution, 1750–1776* (Cambridge, MA: Belknap Press, 1965); Bernard Bailyn, *The Ideological Origins of the American Revolution* (Cambridge, MA: Belknap Press, 1967; 2nd enlarged edn 1992). Page references in this chapter are to the 1992 edition.
7 Bailyn, *Ideological Origins*, p. x.
8 Bailyn, *Ideological Origins*, p. 23.
9 Eran Shalev, 'America's Antiquities: The Ancient Past in the Creation of the American Republic', in Wyger Velema and Arthur Weststeijn, eds, *Ancient Models in the Early Modern Republican Imagination* (Leiden: Brill, 2018), pp. 306–28.
10 Bailyn, *Ideological Origins*, p. 32.
11 Nelson, *Royalist Revolution*, p. 58.
12 Nelson, *Royalist Revolution*, p. 63.
13 [Thomas Paine], *Common Sense: Addressed to the Inhabitants of America* (Philadelphia and Boston, 1776), pp. 17–34.
14 [Paine], *Common Sense*, p. 5.
15 Nelson, *Royalist Revolution*, p. 122.
16 Nelson, *Royalist Revolution*, p. 108.
17 [Paine], *Common Sense*, p. 3.
18 [Paine], *Common Sense*, pp. 30–1.
19 [Paine], *Common Sense*, p. 17.
20 Nelson, *Royalist Revolution*, p. 136.
21 Adams, *A Defence*, pp. 33–4.
22 Adams, *A Defence*, p. 67.
23 Adams, *A Defence*, p. 91.
24 Adams, *A Defence*, pp. 52–3.
25 Adams, *A Defence,* p. 93.
26 Adams, *A Defence*, p. 102.
27 Adams, *A Defence*, p. 70.

28 Nelson, *Royalist Revolution*, p. 159.
29 The 'Centinel' can be found at https://oll.libertyfund.org/pages/1787-centinel-letter-i-pamphlet.
30 James Madison, 'Federalist X', in James Madison, Alexander Hamilton, and John Jay, *The Federalist Papers,* ed. Isaac Kramnick (Harmondsworth: Penguin, 1987), pp. 122–8.
31 Madison, 'Federalist X', p. 126.
32 Cited in Richard Tuck, *The Sleeping Sovereign: The Invention of Modern Democracy* (Cambridge: Cambridge University Press, 2015), p. 6.
33 Madison, 'Federalist X', p. 126.
34 Madison, 'Federalist X', p. 127.
35 Madison, 'Federalist X', p. 128.
36 James Madison, 'Judicial Powers of the National Government', 20 June 1788, at https://founders.archives.gov/documents/Madison/01-11-02-0101.
37 Robert G. Parkinson, 'Exclusion at the Founding: The Declaration of Independence', in Rachel Hammersley, ed., *Revolutionary Moments: Reading Revolutionary Texts* (London: Bloomsbury, 2015), pp. 53–60.
38 Nelson, *Royalist Revolution*, p. 7.

Notes to Chapter 8

1 Jonathan Israel, *Revolutionary Ideas: An Intellectual History of the French Revolution from* The Rights of Man *to Robespierre* (Princeton, NJ: Princeton University Press, 2014), p. 87; see also pp. 70–1.
2 Israel, *Revolutionary Ideas*, pp. 103–4.
3 Wessel Krul, 'Painting Plutarch: Images of Sparta in the Dutch Republic and Enlightenment France', in Wyger Velema and Arthur Weststeijn, eds, *Ancient Models in the Early Modern Republican Imagination* (Leiden: Brill 2018), pp. 157–88, here p. 176.
4 See https://revolution.chnm.org/items/show/127. The medal is image 17.
5 Camille Desmoulins, *La France libre* (Paris, 1789), p. 50.
6 Krul, 'Painting Plutarch', pp. 165–6.
7 Rachel Hammersley, *French Revolutionaries and English Republicans: The Cordeliers Club, 1790–1794* (Woodbridge: Boydell & Brewer, 2005); Rachel Hammersley, *The English Republican Tradition and Eighteenth-Century France: Between the Ancients and the Moderns* (Manchester: Manchester University Press, 2010); Andrew Jainchill, *Reimagining Politics after the Terror: The Republican Origins of French Liberalism* (Ithaca, NY: Cornell University Press, 2008).
8 Hammersley, *The English Republican Tradition*, pp. 157–9.
9 Hammersley, *The English Republican Tradition*, p. 160. For the transcript of the debates, see Michael Walzer, ed., *Regicide and*

Revolution: Speeches at the Trial of Louis XVI (Cambridge: Cambridge University Press, 1974). It should be noted that the lessons drawn were not always positive.

10   Simon-Nicolas-Henri Linguet, *La France plus qu'angloise, ou Comparaison entre la procédure entamée à Paris le 25 septembre 1788 contre les ministres du Roi de France, et le procès intenté à Londres en 1640, au Comte de Strafford, principal ministre de Charles premier, roi d'Angleterre* (Brussels, 1788); Jean-Baptiste Salaville, *De la Révolution française, comparée à celle de l'Angleterre, ou Lettre au représentant du peuple Boulay (de la Meurthe), sur la différence de ces deux révolutions: pour servir de suite à l'ouvrage publié par ce représentant sur celle de l'Angleterre* (Paris, 1798).

11   For a comprehensive list of the French translations of English republican works, see Hammersley, *The English Republican Tradition*, pp. 205–7.

12   Louis-Sébastien Mercier, *Jean-Jacques Rousseau considéré comme l'un des premiers auteurs de la Révolution* (Paris, 1791).

13   Israel, *Revolutionary Ideas*, pp. 105, 130, and 151; Joan McDonald, *Rousseau and the French Revolution, 1762–1791* (London: Athlone Press, 1965), p. 156.

14   Israel, *Revolutionary Ideas*, pp. 171–3.

15   Israel, *Revolutionary Ideas*, pp. 24 and 138.

16   Israel, *Revolutionary Ideas*, pp. 151–2.

17   McDonald, *Rousseau and the French Revolution, 1762–1791*.

18   Richard Whatmore, *Against War and Empire: Geneva, Britain, and France in the Eighteenth Century* (New Haven and London: Yale University Press, 2012), p. 172.

19   Whatmore, *Against War and Empire*, p. 242.

20   Whatmore, *Against War and Empire*, p. 225.

21   M. J. Sydenham, *The Girondins* (London: Athlone Press, 1961); Patrice Higonnet, 'The Social and Cultural Antecedents of a Revolutionary Discontinuity: Montagnards and Girondins', *English Historical Review* 100.396 (1985): 513–44; M. S. Lewis-Beck, A. Hildreth, and A. B. Spitzer, 'Was There a Girondist Faction in the National Convention, 1792–1793?', *French Historical Studies* 15 (1987–8): 519–36 (and see pp. 537–48 for commentaries by M. J. Sydenham, A. Patrick, and Gary Kates).

22   Israel, *Revolutionary Ideas*, p. 68.

23   On this organisation, see Gary Kates, *The Cercle Social, the Girondins and the French Revolution* (Princeton, NJ: Princeton University Press, 1985) and Hammersley, *French Revolutionaries and English Republicans*, pp. 20–31.

24   Walzer, *Regicide and Revolution*, p. 157.

25   Jacques-Pierre Brissot de Warville, in *Le Patriote français: Journal libre, impartial et national* (Frankfurt-am-Main, 1989), no. 696, p. 19.

26   Richard Whatmore, 'War, Trade and Empire: The Dilemmas of French Liberal Political Economy, 1780–1816', in Antoon Braeckman,

Raf Feenens, and Helena Rosenblatt, eds, *French Liberalism: From Montesquieu to the Present* (Cambridge: Cambridge University Press, 2012), pp. 169–91, here p. 173.

27 On the political economy of the Brissotins see Richard Whatmore, 'Commerce, Constitutions, and the Manners of a Nation: Étienne Clavière's Revolutionary Political Economy, 1788–93', *History of European Ideas* 22 (1996): 351–68.

28 Emmanuel-Joseph Sieyès, *Political Writings: Including the Debate between Sieyes and Tom Paine in 1791*, ed. Michael Sonenscher (London: Hackett, 2003), p. 172.

29 Richard Tuck, *The Sleeping Sovereign: The Invention of Modern Democracy* (Cambridge: Cambridge University Press, 2015), p. 143.

30 Quoted in Tuck, *The Sleeping Sovereign*, p. 153.

31 Walzer, *Regicide and Revolution*, p. 152.

32 Quoted in Tuck, *The Sleeping Sovereign*, p. 156.

33 Tuck, *The Sleeping Sovereign*, p. 165.

34 For more detail on the Cordeliers, see Hammersley, *French Revolutionaries and English Republicans*.

35 Desmoulins, *La France libre*, p. 38.

36 Desmoulins, *La France libre*, p. 44.

37 Pierre-François-Joseph Robert, *Républicanisme adapté à la France* (Paris, 1790), pp. 1–2.

38 Camille Desmoulins, *Révolutions de France et de Brabant* (Paris, 1789–91), vii, p. 109.

39 René Girardin, *Discours de Réné Girardin sur la nécessité de la ratification de la loi, par la volonté générale* (Paris, [1791]), p. 23.

40 As quoted in Girardin, *Discours de Réné Girardin*, p. 26.

41 Jacques-Pierre Brissot de Warville, in *Le Patriote français: Journal libre, impartial et national* (Frankfurt-am-Main, 1989), no. 586, p. 285.

42 Jacques-Pierre Brissot de Warville, in *Le Patriote français: Journal libre, impartial et national* (Frankfurt-am-Main, 1989), no. 670, p. 639.

43 La Vicomterie, in *Le Patriote français: Journal libre, impartial et national* (Frankfurt-am-Main 1989, no. 683, pp. 695–6 (in answer to Brissot).

44 Hammersley, *French Revolutionaries and English Republicans*.

45 Théophile Mandar, *De la Souveraineté du peuple, et de l'excellence d'un état libre, par Marchamont Needham, traduit de l'anglais, et enrichi de notes de J. J. Rousseau, Manly, Bossuet, Condillac, Montesquieu, Letrosne, Raynal etc.* (Paris, 1790).

46 Jean-Jacques Rutledge, *Le Creuset: Ouvrage politique et critique* (Paris, 1791); [Jean-Jacques Rutledge], *Idées sur l'espèce de gouvernement populaire qui pourrait convenir à un pays de l'étendue et de la population présumée de la France* (Paris, 1792).

47 Marat's initial association was with the Cordeliers, though he later became linked to the Jacobin Club. See Hammersley, *French Revolutionaries and English Republicans*, pp. 19–22.

48 Michael L. Kennedy, *The Jacobin Clubs in the French Revolution: The Middle Years* (Princeton, NJ: Princeton University Press, 1988), p. 239.

49 Kennedy, *The Jacobin Clubs*, p. 239.

50 Maximilien Robespierre, 'Exposition de mes principes', in idem, *Oeuvres*, vols 4–5: *Les Journaux: Lettres à ses commettants*, ed. G. Laurent (Gap: Imprimerie Louis-Jean, 1961), 4: 9.

51 Maximilien Robespierre, 'Pour la consécration du premier jour sans-culottide à la vertu', in idem, *Oeuvres*, vol. 10: *Discours*, ed. Marc Bouloiseau and Albert Soboul (Paris: Presses Universitaires de France, 1967), p. 158. On Robespierre's emphasis on virtue, see M. Linton, 'Robespierre's Political Principles', in C. Haydon and W. Doyle, *Robespierre* (Cambridge: Cambridge University Press, 1999), pp. 37–53.

52 Maximilien Robespierre, 'Sur les principes de morale politique', in idem, *Oeuvres*, vol. 10: *Discours*, ed. Marc Bouloiseau and Albert Soboul (Paris: Presses Universitaires de France, 1967), p. 353. Compare with Montesquieu, *The Spirit of the Laws*, ed. and trans. Anne Cohler, Basia Miller, and Harold Stone (Cambridge: Cambridge University Press, 1989), and see especially the author's foreword at pp. xli–xlii and 22–4.

53 Robespierre, 'Sur les principes de morale politique', p. 357.

54 Antoine Saint-Just, 'Fragments', in idem, *Oeuvres complètes de Saint-Just*, ed. C. Vellay (Paris: Charpentier et Fasquelle, 1908), vol. 2, p. 506.

55 Keith Michael Baker, 'Transformations of Classical Republicanism in Eighteenth-Century France', *Journal of Modern History* 73 (2001): 32–53.

56 Baker, 'Transformations of Classical Republicanism', p. 53.

57 Israel, *Revolutionary Ideas*.

58 Baker, 'Transformations of Classical Republicanism'; Biancamaria Fontana, 'Introduction', in *The Invention of the Modern Republic*, ed. Biancamaria Fontana (Cambridge: Cambridge University Press, 1994).

59 Jainchill, *Reimagining Politics after the Terror*.

60 Jainchill, *Reimagining Politics after the Terror*, p. 10.

61 Jainchill, *Reimagining Politics after the Terror*, pp. 26–7.

62 Cited in Jainchill, *Reimagining Politics after the Terror*, pp. 35–6.

63 Jainchill, *Reimagining Politics after the Terror*, p. 68.

64 Jainchill, *Reimagining Politics after the Terror*, p. 85.

65 Jainchill, *Reimagining Politics after the Terror*, pp. 141–96.

66 Richard Whatmore, '"Neither Masters Nor Slaves": Small States and Empires in the Long Eighteenth Century' in Duncan Kelly, ed., *Lineages of Empire: The Historical Roots of British Imperial Thought* (Oxford: Oxford University Press, 2009), pp. 53–81.

67 Jainchill, *Reimagining Politics after the Terror*, pp. 114–40.

Notes to Chapter 9

1 Alex Gourevitch, *From Slavery to the Cooperative Commonwealth: Labor and Republican Liberty in the Nineteenth Century* (Cambridge: Cambridge University Press, 2015), p. 9.

2 Gourevitch, *From Slavery to the Cooperative Commonwealth*, pp. 21–2.

3 Gourevitch, *From Slavery to the Cooperative Commonwealth*, p. 31.

4 John C. Calhoun, 'Speech on the Reception of Abolition Petitions', delivered on 6 February 1837. Reprinted in Eric L. McKitrick, ed., *Slavery Defended: The Views of the Old South* (Englewood Cliffs, NJ: Prentice Hall, 1963), p. 14.

5 Frederick Douglass, 'What to the Slave Is the Fourth of July?', delivered on 5 July 1852. Reprinted in Frederick Douglass, *Selected Speeches and Writings*, ed. Philip S. Foner (Chicago, IL: Lawrence Hill, 1999), pp. 188–206. The speech can also be found at https://liberalarts.utexas.edu/coretexts/_files/resources/texts/c/1852%20Douglass%20July%204. pdf, which I used here: the quotations are at pp. 10 and 17 in the online version.

6 Michael J. Sandel, *Democracy's Discontent: America in Search of a Public Philosophy* (Cambridge, MA: Belknap Press, 1996), pp. 139–42.

7 Thomas Jefferson to John Jay, 23 August 1785. https://founders. archives.gov/documents/Jefferson/01-08-02-0333.

8 Sandel, *Democracy's Discontent*, pp. 151–2.

9 Quoted in Gourevitch, *From Slavery to the Cooperative Commonwealth*, p. 68.

10 Quoted in Gourevitch, *From Slavery to the Cooperative Commonwealth*, p. 79.

11 'An Address by Abraham Lincoln Before the Wisconsin State Agricultural Society in Milwaukee, Wisconsin, September 30, 1859'. https://www. nal.usda.gov/lincolns-milwaukee-speech.

12 Quoted in Gourevitch, *From Slavery to the Cooperative Commonwealth*, p. 53.

13 Quoted in Gourevitch, *From Slavery to the Cooperative Commonwealth*, p. 59.

14 Gourevitch, *From Slavery to the Cooperative Commonwealth*, p. 99.

15 Quoted in Gourevitch, *From Slavery to the Cooperative Commonwealth*, p. 100.

16 Quoted in Gourevitch, *From Slavery to the Cooperative Commonwealth*, pp. 14–15.

17 Gourevitch, *From Slavery to the Cooperative Commonwealth*, p. 118.

18 Quoted in Gourevitch, *From Slavery to the Cooperative Commonwealth*, p. 121.

19 Gourevitch, *From Slavery to the Cooperative Commonwealth*, p. 167.

20 Andrew Jainchill, *Reimagining Politics after the Terror: The Republican*

Origins of French Liberalism (Ithaca, NY: Cornell University Press, 2008), p. 225.

21 Jainchill, *Reimagining Politics after the Terror*, p. 240.
22 Jainchill, *Reimagining Politics after the Terror*, p. 201.
23 AN 284 AP 2–15. See Jainchill, *Reimagining Politics after the Terror*, pp. 201 and 217.
24 Jainchill, *Reimagining Politics after the Terror*, pp. 275–85.
25 Pamela M. Pilbeam, *Republicanism in Nineteenth-Century France, 1814–1871* (Houndsmills: Macmillan, 1995), p. 62.
26 Pilbeam, *Republicanism in Nineteenth-Century France*, pp. 76–83.
27 Jainchill, *Reimagining Politics after the Terror*, pp. 287–308.
28 Jainchill, *Reimagining Politics after the Terror*, p. 290.
29 Benjamin Constant, 'The Liberty of the Ancients Compared with that of the Moderns', in idem, *Political Writings*, ed. Biancamaria Fontana (Cambridge: Cambridge University Press, 1988), pp. 309–28, here p. 311.
30 Constant, 'The Liberty of the Ancients', pp. 310–11.
31 Constant, 'The Liberty of the Ancients', p. 311.
32 Constant, 'The Liberty of the Ancients', p. 316.
33 Constant, 'The Liberty of the Ancients', pp. 325–7.
34 Richard Whatmore, *Republicanism and the French Revolution: An Intellectual History of Jean-Baptiste Say's Political Economy* (Oxford: Oxford University Press, 2000), p. 12.
35 Pilbeam, *Republicanism in Nineteenth-Century France*, p. 5; Eugène Delacroix, 'Liberty Leading the People'. https://www.louvre.fr/en/oeuvre-notices/july-28-liberty-leading-people.
36 Florencia Peyrou and Juan Luis Simal, 'Exile, Secret Societies, and the Emergence of an International Democratic Culture', in Joanna Innes and Mark Philp, eds, *Re-Imagining Democracy in the Mediterranean, 1780–1860* (Oxford: Oxford University Press, 2018), p. 219.
37 Quoted in Pilbeam, *Republicanism in Nineteenth-Century France*, p. 106.
38 Quoted in Jainchill, *Reimagining Politics after the Terror*, p. 296.
39 Jainchill, *Reimagining Politics after the Terror*, p. 305.
40 Pilbeam, *Republicanism in Nineteenth-Century France*, pp. 166–72.
41 Pilbeam, *Republicanism in Nineteenth-Century France*, pp. 178–81.
42 Pilbeam, *Republicanism in Nineteenth-Century France*, p. 186.
43 Pilbeam, *Republicanism in Nineteenth-Century France*, p. 10.
44 Pilbeam, *Republicanism in Nineteenth-Century France*, p. 193.
45 Pilbeam, *Republicanism in Nineteenth-Century France*, p. 216.
46 Pilbeam, *Republicanism in Nineteenth-Century France*, p. 243.
47 Pilbeam, *Republicanism in Nineteenth-Century France*, p. 264.
48 Gian Luca Fruci, 'Democracy in Italy: From Egalitarian Republicanism to Plebiscitarian Monarchy', in Joanna Innes and Mark Philp, eds, *Re-Imagining Democracy in the Mediterranean, 1780–1860* (Oxford: Oxford University Press, 2018), pp. 27 and 31 and Anna Maria Rao, 'Republicanism in Italy from the Eighteenth Century to the Early Risorgimento', *Journal of Modern Italian Studies* 17.2 (2012): 149–67.

49 Fruci, 'Democracy in Italy', pp. 28–30.
50 Rao, 'Republicanism in Italy', p. 156.
51 Stefano Recchia and Nadia Urbinati, 'Introduction', in idem eademque, *A Cosmopolitanism of Nations: Guiseppe Mazzini's Writings on Democracy, Nation Building, and International Relations* (Princeton, NJ: Princeton University Press, 2009), p. 3.
52 Tim Parks, 'Bloody Glamour', review of C. A. Bayly and Eugenio Biagini, eds, *Guiseppe Mazzini and the Globalisation of Democratic Nationalism 1830–1920* (Oxford: Oxford University Press, 2008), in *London Review of Books* 31.8 (30 April 2009), pp. 28–30.
53 Fruci, 'Democracy in Italy', p. 42.
54 Parks, 'Bloody Glamour'.
55 Quoted in Maurizio Ridolfi, 'Visions of Republicanism in the Writings of Giuseppe Mazzini', *Journal of Modern Italian Studies* 13.4 (2008): 468–79, here p. 469.
56 Quoted in Ridolfi, 'Visions of republicanism', p. 471.
57 Recchia and Urbinati, 'Introduction', p. 6.
58 Peyrou and Simal, 'Exile, Secret Societies', p. 219.
59 Recchia and Urbinati, 'Introduction', p. 5.
60 Ridolfi, 'Visions of republicanism'.
61 Charles James Fox and H. G. Wells, as quoted in Frank Prochaska, *The Republic of Britain, 1760 To 2000* (London: Allen Lane, 2000), p. xvi.
62 Prochaska, *Republic of Britain*, pp. xvi–xviii.
63 Quoted in Prochaska, *Republic of Britain*, p. 43.
64 Quoted in Prochaska, *Republic of Britain*, p. 26.
65 Kevin Whelan, 'Three Revolutions and a Failure', in Cathal Póirtéir, ed., *The Great Irish Rebellion of 1798* (Boulder, CO: Mercier, 1998), pp. 26–36, here pp. 29–30.
66 Whelan, 'Three Revolutions and a Failure', p. 32.
67 Marianne Elliott, 'Wolfe Tone and the Republican Ideal', in Cathal Póirtéir, ed., *The Great Irish Rebellion of 1798* (Boulder, CO: Mercier, 1998), pp. 49–57, here p. 51.
68 Hugh Gough, 'France and the 1798 Rebellion', in Cathal Póirtéir, ed., *The Great Irish Rebellion of 1798* (Boulder, CO: Mercier, 1998), pp. 37–47, here p. 40.
69 Gough, 'France and the 1798 Rebellion', p. 45.
70 Elliott, 'Wolfe Tone and the Republican Ideal', pp. 55–7.
71 Quoted in Prochaska, *Republic of Britain*, p. 44.
72 Quoted in Prochaska, *Republic of Britain*, p. 81.
73 Marcella Pellegrino Sutcliffe, *Victorian Radicals and Italian Democrats* (Woodbridge: Boydell & Brewer, 2014).
74 Bruno Leipold, *Citizen Marx: The Relationship between Karl Marx and Republicanism* (DPhil thesis, Oxford, 2017), p. 226.

Notes to Chapter 10

1   'The Provisional Government of the Irish Republic to the People of Ireland'. https://cain.ulster.ac.uk/issues/politics/docs/pir24416.htm.

2   Michael J. Sandel, *Democracy's Discontent: America in Search of a Public Philosophy* (Cambridge MA: Belknap Press, 1996), p. 116.

3   Knud Haakonssen, 'Republicanism', in Robert E. Goodin and Philip Pettit, eds, *A Companion to Contemporary Political Philosophy* (Oxford: Blackwell, 1993), p. 568.

4   See in particular Philip Pettit, *Republicanism: A Theory of Freedom and Government* (Oxford: Oxford University Press, 1997) and Frank Lovett and Philip Pettit, 'Neorepublicanism: A Normative and Institutional Research Program', *Annual Review of Political Science* 12 (2009): 11–29.

5   Maurizio Viroli, *Republicanism*, translated by Antony Shugaar (New York: Hill & Wang, 2002).

6   Hans Baron, *The Crisis of the Early Italian Renaissance: Civic Humanism and Republican Liberty in an Age of Classicism and Tyranny*, 2nd rev. edn (Princeton, NJ: Princeton University Press, 1966 [1955]). See also Hans Baron, *In Search of Florentine Civic Humanism*, 2 vols (Princeton, NJ: Princeton University Press, 1988). A similar view to that of Baron was put forward in books published in Italian in 1952 and 1954 by Eugenio Garin. For some of the debates emerging from Baron's work, see James Hankins, ed., *Renaissance Civic Humanism: Reappraisals and Reflections* (Cambridge: Cambridge University Press, 2000).

7   Zera Fink, *The Classical Republicans: An Essay in the Recovery of a Pattern of Thought in Seventeenth-Century England* (Evanston: Northwestern University Press, 1945).

8   Caroline Robbins, *The Eighteenth-Century Commonwealthman: Studies in the Transmission, Development, and Circumstance of English Liberal Thought from the Restoration of Charles II until the War with the Thirteen Colonies* (Indianapolis, IN: Liberty Fund, 2004 [1959]).

9   Bernard Bailyn, *The Ideological Origins of the American Revolution* (Cambridge MA: Belknap Press, 1992 [1967]).

10 Bailyn, *Ideological Origins*, p. 54.

11 Gordon S. Wood, *The Creation of the American Republic, 1776–1787* (Chapel Hill: University of North Carolina Press, 1969); Robert E. Shalhope, 'Republicanism and Early American Historiography', *William and Mary Quarterly* (1982): 334–56; Daniel T. Rodgers, 'Republicanism: The Career of a Concept', *Journal of American History* 79 (1992): 11–38; Joyce O. Appleby, *Liberalism and Republicanism in the Historical Imagination* (Cambridge MA: Harvard University Press, 1992); Alan Gibson, 'Ancients, Moderns, and Americans: The Republicanism–Liberalism Debate Revisited', *History of Political Thought* 21 (2000): 261–307.

12 J. G. A. Pocock, *The Machiavellian Moment: Florentine Political Thought and the Atlantic Republican Tradition* (Princeton, NJ: Princeton University Press, 1975).

13 Pocock, *The Machiavellian Moment*; J. G. A. Pocock, 'Virtues, Rights, and Manners: A Model for Historians of Political Thought', in idem, *Virtue, Commerce, and History: Essays On Political Thought and History, Chiefly in the Eighteenth Century* (Cambridge: Cambridge University Press, 1985), pp. 37–50.

14 Appleby, *Liberalism and Republicanism*; Steve Pincus, 'Neither Machiavellian Moment nor Possessive Individualism: Commercial Society and the Defenders of the English Commonwealth', *American Historical Review* 103.3 (1998): 705–36.

15 Mark Jurdjevic, 'Virtue, Commerce, and the Enduring Florentine Republican Moment: Reintegrating Italy into the Atlantic Republican Debate', *Journal of the History of Ideas* 62.4 (2001): 721–43.

16 Jurdjevic, 'Virtue, Commerce, and the Enduring Florentine Republican Moment', p. 743.

17 As noted in the Introduction, Skinner was building here on Isaiah Berlin's famous essay 'Two Concepts of Liberty', in idem, *Four Essays on Liberty* (Oxford: Oxford University Press, 1969). Skinner developed his ideas in Quentin Skinner, 'The Idea of Negative Liberty: Philosophical and Historical Perspectives', in Richard Rorty, J. B. Schneewind, and Quentin Skinner, eds, *Philosophy in History* (Cambridge: Cambridge University Press, 1984), pp. 193–221, revised as 'The Idea of Negative Liberty: Machiavellian and Modern Perspectives', in Quentin Skinner, *Visions of Politics*, vol. 2: *Renaissance Virtues* (Cambridge: Cambridge University Press, 2002) pp. 186–212; Quentin Skinner, 'The Paradoxes of Political Liberty', in S. M. McMurrin, ed., *The Tanner Lectures on Human Values*, vol. 7, (Cambridge: Cambridge University Press, 1986), pp. 225–50; Quentin Skinner, 'Machiavelli's *Discoursi* and the Pre-Humanist Origins of Republican Ideas' and 'The Republican Ideal of Political Liberty', in Gisela Bock, Quentin Skinner, and Maurizio Viroli, eds, *Machiavelli and Republicanism* (Cambridge: Cambridge University Press, 1990), pp. 121–41 and 293–309; and Quentin Skinner, *Liberty before Liberalism* (Cambridge: Cambridge University Press, 1998).

18 Benjamin Straumann, *Crisis and Constitutionalism: Roman Political Thought from the Fall of the Republic to the Age of Revolution* (Oxford: Oxford University Press, 2016), especially pp. 1–22.

19 Straumann, *Crisis and Constitutionalism*, p. 11.

20 Eric Nelson, *The Greek Tradition in Republican Thought* (Cambridge: Cambridge University Press, 2004).

21 Eric Nelson, *The Hebrew Republic: Jewish Sources and the Transformation of European Political Thought* (Cambridge, MA: Harvard University Press, 2010).

22 Paul A. Rahe, *Republics Ancient and Modern: Classical Republicanism and the American Revolution* (Chapel Hill: North Carolina University Press, 1992).

23   Vickie B. Sullivan, *Machiavelli, Hobbes, and the Formation of a Liberal Republicanism in England* (Cambridge: Cambridge University Press, 2004); Paul A. Rahe, *Against Throne and Altar: Machiavelli and Political Theory under the English Republic* (Cambridge: Cambridge University Press, 2008).

24   Franco Venturi, *Utopia and Reform in the Enlightenment* (Cambridge: Cambridge University Press, 1971).

25   Quentin Skinner and Martin van Gelderen, eds, *Republicanism: A Shared European Heritage*, 2 vols (Cambridge: Cambridge University Press, 2002). At least two further volumes also came out of this project.

26   David Wootton, 'Review of Republicanism: A Shared European Heritage', *English Historical Review* 120 (2005): 135–9.

27   David Wootton, 'The True Origins of Republicanism: The Disciples of Baron and the Counter-Example of Venturi', in Manuela Albertone, ed., *Il repubblicanismo moderno: L'idea di republicca nella riflessione storica di Franco Venturi* (Naples: Bibliopolis, 2006), pp. 271–304, here pp. 271–2. For further discussion of the debate surrounding the rise of republican exclusivism, see Chapter 1.

28   Johnson Kent Wright, *A Classical Republican in Eighteenth-Century France: The Political Thought of Mably* (Stanford CA: Stanford University Press, 1997); Rachel Hammersley, *French Revolutionaries and English Republicans: The Cordeliers Club, 1790–1794* (Woodbridge: Boydell & Brewer, 2005); Raymonde Monnier, *Républicanisme, patriotisme et Révolution française* (Paris: L'Harmattan, 2005); Rachel Hammersley, *The English Republican Tradition and Eighteenth-Century France: Between the Ancients and the Moderns* (Manchester: Manchester University Press, 2010); Marchamont Needham, *De la souveraineté du people et de l'excellence d'un état libre, traduit de l'anglais par Théophine Mandar*, ed. Raymonde Monnier (Paris: CTHS, 2011); Raymonde Monnier, 'Les Enjeux de la traduction sous la Révolution française: La transmission des textes du républicanisme anglais', *Historical Review/Revue Historique* 12 (2015): 13–45; Rachel Hammersley, ed., *The Historiography of Republicanism and Republican Exchanges*, special issue of *History of European Ideas*, 38.3 (2012); Gaby Mahlberg and Dirk Wiemann, eds, *European Contexts for English Republicanism* (Farnham: Ashgate, 2013).

29   Alistair Chapman, John Coffey, and Brad S. Gregory, eds, *Seeing Things Their Way: Intellectual History and the Return of Religion* (Notre Dame, IN: University of Notre Dame Press, 2009), esp. pp. 44–74. It should be noted that some of Skinner's work, such as volume 2 of the *Foundations*, does engage with religious texts and ideas; see Quentin Skinner, *The Foundations of Modern Political Thought*, vol. 2: *The Age of Reformation* (Cambridge: Cambridge University Press, 1978).

30   Jonathan Scott, *Commonwealth Principles: Republican Writing of the English Revolution* (Cambridge: Cambridge University Press, 2004).

31   Justin Champion, *The Pillars of Priestcraft Shaken: The Church*

of England and its Enemies, 1660–1730 (Cambridge: Cambridge University Press, 1992); Justin Champion, *Republican Learning: John Toland and the Crisis of Christian Culture, 1696–1722* (Manchester: Manchester University Press, 2003).

32 Nelson, *The Hebrew Republic*; Lea Campos Boralevi, 'James Harrington's "Machiavellian" Anti-Machiavellism', *History of European Ideas* 37.2 (2011): 113–119; Ronald Beiner, 'James Harrington on the Hebrew Commonwealth', *Review of Politics* 76 (2014): 169–93; Mark Somos, 'Irenic Secularization and the Hebrew Republic in Harrington's Oceana', in Gaby Mahlberg and Dirk Wiemann, eds, *European Contexts for English Republicanism* (Farnham: Ashgate, 2013), pp. 81–103.

33 Mark Goldie, 'The Civil Religion of James Harrington', in Anthony Pagden, ed., *The Languages of Political Theory in Early Modern Europe* (Cambridge: Cambridge University Press, 1987), pp. 197–222; Ronald Beiner, *Civil Religion: A Dialogue in the History of Political Philosophy* (Cambridge: Cambridge University Press, 2010); Ronald Beiner, 'Civil Religion and Anticlericalism in James Harrington', *European Journal of Political Theory*, 13.4 (2014): 388–407. Also visit https://newcastlecivilreligion.wordpress.com (which has a reading list).

34 Iseult Honohan, 'Freedom as Citizenship: The Republican Tradition in Political Theory', *Republic: A Journal of Contemporary and Historical Debate* 2 (2001): 7–24, here p. 16.

35 For a more detailed account of this revival, Cécile Laborde's survey is a good starting point: Cécile Laborde, 'Republicanism', in Michael Freeden, Lyman Tower Sargent, and Marc Stears, eds, *The Oxford Handbook of Political Ideology* (Oxford: Oxford University Press, 2013), pp. 513–35.

36 Cass R. Sunstein, 'Beyond the Republican Revival', *Yale Law Journal*, 97.8 (1988): 1539–90.

37 Sunstein, 'Beyond the Republican Revival', 1539–41.

38 Sandel, *Democracy's Discontent*.

39 Philip Pettit, 'Reworking Sandel's Republicanism: A Review of Michael Sandel, *Democracy's Discontent: America in Search of a Public Philosophy*'. *Journal of Philosophy* 95.2 (1998): 73–96.

40 Pettit, *Republicanism*.

41 Pettit, *Republicanism*, pp. vii–ix.

42 Pettit, *Republicanism*, p. 4.

43 Pettit, *Republicanism*, p. 299.

44 Skinner, *Visions of Politics*, p. 161.

45 Pettit, *Republicanism*, p. 51.

46 Pettit, *Republicanism*, pp. 110–126.

47 Pettit, *Republicanism*, pp. 132–47.

48 Pettit, *Republicanism*, pp. 171–205.

49 Fresh discussions of the history of republicanism and how it can inform contemporary debates have emerged not only in the anglophone world, but also in places such as France and Italy. See Laborde, 'Republicanism', pp. 513, 517–8 and 520 and Viroli, *Republicanism*.

50 Richard Dagger, 'Neo-Republicanism and the Civic Economy', *Politics, Philosophy & Economics* 5.2 (2006): 151–73, here p. 154; Honohan, 'Freedom as Citizenship'.
51 Dagger, 'Neo-Republicanism and the Civic Economy', 154. Sunstein, 'Beyond the Republican Revival', pp. 1552–3 and 1576–7.
52 Sunstein, 'Beyond the Republican Revival', pp. 1548–51.
53 Dagger, 'Neo-Republicanism and the Civic Economy'.
54 Haakonssen, 'Republicanism', pp. 570–1.
55 Sunstein, 'Beyond the Republican Revival', p. 1546.
56 Sunstein, 'Beyond the Republican Revival', p. 1589.
57 Laborde, 'Republicanism', pp. 514, 518.
58 Laborde, 'Republicanism', pp. 518–31.
59 John P. McCormick, 'Machiavelli against Republicanism: On the Cambridge School's "Guicciardinian Moments"', *Political Theory* 31.5 (2003): 615–43, here p. 616.
60 Haakonssen, 'Republicanism', p. 574.

Index